THE SOCIAL WORLD OF JESUS AND THE GOSPELS

In order to interpret historical writings, readers must not employ their modern understanding of the world, but must strive to grasp the perceptions and social contexts of the original audience. To assist the twentieth-century New Testament reader in understanding the meaning of the New Testament is the goal of this collection of essays. *The Social World of Jesus and the Gospels* provides the reader with a set of workable scenarios for reading the New Testament: How did first-century persons think about themselves and others? Did they think Jesus was a charismatic leader? Why did they call God "Father"? Were they concerned with their gender roles?

The eight essays in this collection were previously published in books and journals generally not available to many readers. Carefully selected and edited, this collection will be both an introduction and an invaluable source of reference to Bruce Malina's thought.

Bruce J. Malina is Professor of Theology at Creighton University, Nebraska. He has pioneered social scientific criticism of the New Testament for the past quarter of a century, and published widely in the field. His most recent book is *On the Genre and Message of Revelation: Star Visions and Sky Journeys* (1995).

THE SOCIAL
WORLD OF JESUS AND
THE GOSPELS

Bruce J. Malina

London and New York

First published 1996
by Routledge
11 New Fetter Lane, London EC4P 4EE

Simultaneously published in the USA and Canada
by Routledge
29 West 35th Street, New York, NY 10001

© 1996 Bruce J. Malina

Typeset in Garamond by
Florencetype Ltd, Stoodleigh, Devon

Printed and bound in Great Britain by
Redwood Books, Trowbridge, Wiltshire

British Library Cataloguing in Publication Data
A catalogue record for this book is available from the British Library

Library of Congress Cataloguing in Publication Data
Malina, Bruce J.
The social world of Jesus and the Gospels / Bruce J. Malina.
p. cm.
Includes bibliographical references and index.
1. Bible N.T. Gospels–Social scientific criticism.
2. Sociology, Biblical. 3. Jews–Social life and customs–To
70 A.D. 4. Palestine–Social life and customs–To 70 A.D.
I. Title. BS2555.6.S55M35 1996
226'.067–dc20
96-12602 CIP

ISBN 0–415–14628–3(hbk)
ISBN 0–415–14629–1(pbk)

To
Dr. K. C. Hanson
friend, colleague, scholar
with gratitude
for suggesting this book
and for practical advice and editing skills

CONTENTS

CONTENTS

ILLUSTRATIONS

FIGURES

TABLES

ACKNOWLEDGMENTS

Ch. 1, first published as "Reading Theory Perspective: Reading Luke–Acts," originally appeared in *The Social World of Luke–Acts: Models for Interpretation*, ed. Jerome H. Neyrey, © 1991 Hendrickson publishers, and is used with permission.

Ch. 2 was originally published as "Dealing with Biblical (Mediterranean) Characters: A Guide for US Consumers," *Biblical Theology Bulletin* 19 (1989), 127–41; Ch. 3 was originally published as "Let Him Deny Himself" (Mark 8:34//): A Social Psychological Model of Self-Denial," *Biblical Theology Bulletin* 24 (1994), 106–19; Ch. 4 was originally published as "Mary – Woman of the Mediterranean: Mother and Son," *Biblical Theology Bulletin* 20 (1990), 54–64; and Ch. 5 was originally published as "Jesus as Charismatic Leader?," *Biblical Theology Bulletin* 14 (1984), 55–62, and all appear with the permission of the editors of *Biblical Theology Bulletin*.

Ch. 6, first published as "Patron and Client: The Analogy Behind Synoptic Theology," originally appeared in *Forum*, a journal of the foundations and facets of Western culture, issue 4/1. Copyright ©1988 by Polebridge Press, PO Box 6144, Santa Rosa, CA 95406. Used with permission. All rights reserved.

Ch. 7 was originally published as "Christ and Time: Swiss or Mediterranean," *Catholic Biblical Quarterly* 51 (1989), 1–31 and appears with permission of the publisher, the Catholic Biblical Association of America.

Ch. 8 was originally published as "The Received View and What it Cannot Do: III John and Hospitality." pp. 171–94 in John H. Elliott (ed.) *Semeia*, Vol. 35: *Social-scientific Criticism of the New Testament and its Social World*. Decatur, GA: Scholars, 1986, and appears here with permission of the publisher, the Society of Biblical Literature.

INTRODUCTION

Over the past decade or so, I have published these essays, among others, in response to a range of problems in the field of New Testament interpretation. The problems in question had surfaced in the course of my attempting to make the craft of New Testament exegesis understandable to US undergraduate students. I take the goal of New Testament interpretation to be to discover what some original group of first-century eastern Mediterraneans understood when the documents now contained in the New Testament were read to them. Hence my task is to find out what the documents had to say and what they meant to their original recipients. I presume that meaning, then as well as now, ultimately resides in the social system shared by persons who regularly interact with each other. The problems bound up with understanding another group's social system so as to interact meaningfully with members of that group are at the root of the problems that surround New Testament interpretation. The way I have come to resolve these problems has been possible largely due to my interaction with colleagues from a range of disciplines, colleagues willing to explain how their presuppositions and question-sets might be brought to bear upon my problem. The result, of course, is a perspective that some like to call multidisciplinary, as though it were some novel venture, fraught with difficulty and deviating from common practice.

The interpretation of documents from alien times and cultures, however, has always been multidisciplinary. Since the advent of the sense of history in the eighteenth century, historically oriented biblical scholars have assumed mastery of a range of disciplines as fundamental to the toolkit of their craft. Consider the "disciplines" that are generally brought to bear in the task of historical biblical interpretation: history (ancient, medieval and modern), proficiency in ancient languages (at least Hebrew, Greek, Aramaic and Latin) and modern languages (at least German – though most Catholic interpreters handle Italian, Spanish and French as well), literary theory (ancient, medieval and modern) theology (ancient, medieval and modern) and philosophy (ancient, medieval and modern). The overall purpose of historically oriented biblical interpretation is to discover what some ancient biblical document meant to its original audience.

While the social dimensions of human behavior have been a focused center of concern early on in this century in departments of philosophy, history and/or ethics, it was largely around mid-century that disciplines such as sociology, cultural/social anthropology and social psychology reached a level of sophistication that allowed for and required academic independence from other university departments. Since philosophy, history and ethics were already part and parcel of that discipline called biblical interpretation, it was only a matter of time before the "social sciences" joined the toolkit. From the 1950s on, the proliferation of field studies and of cross-cultural data in the social sciences made it all the more obvious that biblical interpretation was, indeed, a form of cross-cultural study. Furthermore, it has become equally obvious that the distinctive systems of meaning of various human societies derive from and maintain their distinctive social systems. Meanings derive from the social systems into which human beings have been singly enculturated and socialized.

The advent of sociolinguistics (another offshoot of the tools in the interpreter's toolkit) made it more than clear that language is a tri-level affair. At its most concrete, language comprises soundings and markings that consist of somewhat abstract patterns called wording (for example, words, sentences, short pieces of language called paragraphs, syntactical patterns and the like). So meaning is expressed in rather abstract patterns of language realized concretely in patterns of soundings (speaking) and markings (writing). Sociolinguists insist that the meanings realized in the patterns realized in the soundings and markings derive from the social system of the speaker. When a prospective hearer shares the same social system as the speaker, they readily understand each other. If each has a different social system, they would either misunderstand or not understand each other.

Obviously the task of the historically oriented biblical interpreter must be to discover the social system of those to whom some given biblical document was directed so as to eavesdrop on a conversation that took place several thousand years ago. How might one listen in on such ancient communications while being considerate of ancient hearers and readers of biblical writings? The first chapter in this book addresses this question. The question is fundamentally one of reading. Access to biblical writings is through reading (or having another read to us). How in fact do people read?

Ever since Francis Bacon's *Novum Organum* or Giambattista Vico's *Scienza nuova,* modern scholars have warned that one ought not to make generalizations on the basis of a single instance. Ancients were not averse to this (*ab uno disce omnes,* "learn everything from a sampling of one," Vergil suggests). After all, for the ancients, human beings were unalterable since people of the past were no different from those of the present; hence one ought to study history in order to learn how to live today (*historia magistra vitae,* "history teaches how to live"). Yet even the ancients suggested that one ought not to base one's judgment of reality solely on the basis of one's own preferences (*nemo judex in causa sua,* "no one involved in a case can be an impartial judge"). In any event, in spite of all such warnings, most literate readers base their understanding of what they do as they read on their own introspection. Now enter the experimental psychologists with a battery of tests to investigate the nature of the reading process. The outcome in general is that what one brings to one's reading is far more significant than what one presumably reads out of some document. To be a considerate reader of ancient documents, one must bring to one's reading a range of scenarios rooted in the social system of the author/audience of the document to be read.

Social systems consist of social institutions, values clustered around value objects and types of typical persons. Value objects include the self, others, nature, time, place and God(s). The set of questions addressed by the first series of chapters (2–4) look to the type of self typical of those who people the pages of the New Testament. These were collectivist selves whose focal social institution was the family (not modern individualists whose focal social institution is economics). The following two chapters deal with central roles in the scenarios suggested by gospel authors. Thus the problem in Chapter 5 is that of using a label such as "charismatic" of a first-century Mediterranean such as Jesus. The model of "charismatic" does not fit the ancient Mediterranean. Hence how might Jesus be duly described if not as charismatic? Further, the problem in Chapter 6 is that of God as "Father" and Jesus' role in that relationship. Ancient Mediterraneans sought to "kinify" relations, especially in that dimension called patron–client. God was the Patron in the sky ("Father who art in heaven"), while Jesus brokered or mediated God's patronage. What does such patronage entail?

The problem raised in the chapter on time (Chapter 7) is that of the value object called time. Most people would agree that the first-century Mediterranean world was a peasant society characterized by an advanced agrarian economy rooted in kinship and politics. In the perception of people in those days there was a domestic economy and a political economy, but no free-standing economy. The rules and roles of kinship and/or politics were those that controlled the economic institution. Similarly, there was a domestic religion and a political religion, but no free-standing religion. The rules and roles of kinship and/or politics were those that described and prescribed religious behavior. Now, in peasant societies around the world today, the time orientation of peasants is always the present. More specifically, the preferred value orientation of dealing with significant dimensions of life is to adopt what is at hand, what is present (for example, better a weak old horse today than the promise of a wonderful strong horse in the distant future). If the world of Jesus were such a present-oriented society that looked to the past (for example, the updated Scripture of Israel) for direction, then why all the emphasis in modern interpretation on "eschatology," on future, on the tension between the "now" and the "not yet?" Does such emphasis actually emerge in the New Testament documents, or is it something modern which future-oriented theologians and their followers read into those documents?

The question of how often theological cues or church beliefs unwittingly direct the attention of modern readers is further illustrated in Chapter 8, on the problems raised by the "Received View." The term "Received View" comes from the history of science and refers to the prevailing way of doing science, controlled by prestigious schools, scholars and editors. The Received View in biblical interpretation is more concerned with contemporary relevance and theological pay-off than with the concerns of the first-century Mediterraneans depicted in those documents. This perspective, of course, leaves large lacunae in our understanding of first-century Mediterranean Christians. And it leaves the considerate reader with the problem of how to shake off the Received View. In the final chapter, then, I consider the difficulties raised by the Received View while using first-century Mediterranean hospitality as the point of departure. While hospitality features prominently in all of the gospels, it is the focus of that brief document called the third letter of John. Hence it is in dialogue with gospel scenarios of hospitality and the third letter of John that I spin out the dimensions of the Received View as a problem, and in the process explain the meaning of first-century Mediterranean hospitality.

I would hope that this sampling of essays will whet the reader's appetite for more information about first-century Mediterranean society and its culture(s). As an interpreter of the New Testament, I have as my goal to be a considerate, historically sensitive reader of those documents. I would like to know what the original witnesses to the event of Jesus had to say and what they meant to say in their own societal setting. To this end, I believe that one must have in one's exegetical toolkit a set of scenarios that might enable one to read as a fair and considerate reader of a document from another time, another place, another culture and another social system. To by-pass explicit consideration of the social system of the ancient Mediterranean means to bootleg or smuggle in social-system scenarios from another time and place. While the resulting meanings might provide warrants for contemporary behavior (for example, liberation, ordination of women, revolution, equal rights and the like), the warrants cannot be said to derive from the biblical witness. In fact, when added to the existing toolkit of historical interpretation, concern for the social setting of those who have produced the New Testament documents can only yield a better understanding of the persons whom one meets on the pages of the New Testament. I would hope that this selection of essays might prove beneficial in the task of historical reading.

Bruce J. Malina

Part I

THE QUESTION OF READING

1

READING THEORY
PERSPECTIVES

INTRODUCTION

Suppose for a moment that you are an American visitor to Jerusalem
in the Roman Palestine of the mid-first-century AD. It is morning
during the dry season. The Mediterranean sun shines brightly. You
decide that it is a good day to go to Gaza to see what is new by
way of caravan imports from Egypt. So early in the morning, with
sea breezes still cool in the hills, you begin the seaward walk down
from Jerusalem on the Gaza–Jerusalem road. Not too far in front
of you, you see a person walking, going in the same direction as
you are. Suddenly you hear a man's voice coming from over a rise
in the road. That voice says something that sounds as follows:

כַּשֶּׂה לַטֶּבַח יוּבָל וּכְרָחֵל לִפְנֵי גֹזְזֶיהָ
נֶאֱלָמָה וְלֹא יִפְתַּח פִּיו:
מֵעֹצֶר וּמִמִּשְׁפָּט לֻקָּח וְאֶת דּוֹרוֹ
מִיְשׂוֹחֵחַ כִּי נִגְזַר מֵאֶרֶץ חַיִּים:

Obviously what you have just heard are not the squiggles you see
written here. Rather what you have heard were sounds, strange
sounds, sounds as strange as the above squiggles. You notice now
that the man in front of you also stops. You go up to him and ask:
"What did that mean?" He shrugs his shoulders in response.
Obviously he does not understand English. So you open your arms,
shrug your shoulders and throw your head back slightly in that
Mediterranean gesture that means: "What is going on, then?" Light
dawns in his eyes and he proceeds to tell you:

Ὡς πρόβατον ἐπί σφαγὴν ἤχθη,
καὶ ὡς ἀμνὸς ἐναντίον τοῦ

3

κείραντος αὐτὸν ἄφωνος, οὕτως οὐκ
ἀνοίγει τὸ στόμα αὐτοῦ.
Ἐν τῇ ταπεινώσει ἡ κρίσις αὐτοῦ
ἤρθη· τὴν γενεὰν αὐτοῦ τίς
διηγήσεται; ὅτι αἴρεται ἀπὸ τῆς
γῆς ἡ ζωὴ αὐτοῦ.

Again, you get a downpour of strange sounds, indicated here by the strange squiggles used to write down those sounds. By now, you figure out that what the man is telling you in his strange sounds is his version of the sounds you both heard.

It should occur to you by now that you are a foreigner in a foreign land where a familiar thing such as conversing with someone in English is equally alien. Now, what would you need to understand your friendly fellow traveler? How would you get to understand his strange sounds? I suggest that the way to come to understand your first-century acquaintance is not unlike the way you would get to understand a contemporary foreigner who does not know English, yet with whom you wish to communicate. Furthermore, I suggest that trying to understand a writing such as Luke–Acts involves the same procedure as attempting to understand foreigners speaking to you in their own language. Only in the case of Luke–Acts, as with the example above, you are the foreigner. For, any historically sensitive reading of New Testament writings necessarily puts the reader in the role of a stranger in that extremely strange and curious land of the first-century eastern Mediterranean.

The authors of the biblical writings as well as the persons they portrayed all came from this region. They wrote their books in those strange squiggles we call the Hebrew and Greek alphabets. And these strange squiggles all stand for extremely strange patterns of sounds quite alien to most US ears. How would one get to understand such strange sounds and read the alphabets that stand for those sounds? Would it be sufficient to transcribe your informant's sounds into our own alphabet? If you did so, it would look as follows:

Hos probaton epi sphagen echthe, kai hos amnos enantion tou keirantos auton aphonos, houtos ouk anoigei to stoma autou. En te tapeinosei he krisis autou erthe. Ten genean autou tis diegesetai? hoti airetai apo tes ges he zoe autou.

Even in our own alphabet, there is not much that looks familiar. Does the statement sound any more familiar if you try to read it?

Moreover, would a translation of the Greek give you the meaning of what your fellow traveler intended to tell you? The Greek translates out as follows:

> As a sheep led to the slaughter or a lamb before its shearer is dumb, so he opens not his mouth. In his humiliation justice was denied him. Who can describe his generation? For his life is taken up from the earth.

Does this translation tell you what the statement means? If you looked in a biblical concordance, you would find that this passage is from Acts 8:32–3 and quotes Isa. 53:7–8 in a Greek translation such as the one your travelling companion gave you. Does that help you understand what is going on now? If you read the passage in Acts 8, you will find out that the one whose voice you initially heard was a black man, probably a proselyte of the house of Israel on pilgrimage to Jerusalem. He is described as a eunuch from the court of Queen Candace in Ethiopia. You will likewise find out that the person from whom you inquired about what was being said was a follower of Jesus of Nazareth named Philip. His Greek name might tell you why he preferred to talk to you in Greek. In Acts, Philip is described as a "deacon." Now that you have a name, social role, some minimal information about the words you heard and basic geographical and chronological orientation, can you interpret the passage translated above?

If other people knew only your name, social role, some of your statements and some geographical and chronological information about you, would you say that they can now really understand you? If they had some minimal information about an esoteric book you might be reading, would that suffice to help them understand that book and why you are reading it? What more would they have to know? Would a story of your family history suffice now? Would a story of your life help?

Notice that these questions cover the who, what, when, where and how of the situation. They have not raised the why question, the question of meaning. Why read a passage from Isaiah on the road? Why the need for a Greek translation? Why the social role of an Ethiopian official, why the subsequent behavior of Philip? And if we stick to the passage itself, why the mention of lamb and sheep? Why humiliation? And in a Christian writing such as Acts, why this passage from the Israelite religious tradition in Isaiah? The answers to all these questions require historical information of the who, what,

5

when and where sort. But to find out the why, the meaning of it all in the lives of people, requires information from the social system of the time and place of the original audience of this work.

To read Luke–Acts as we propose to do in this book requires familiarity with the social system presupposed by and conveyed through the language patterns that are presented in the Greek squiggles of the Greek texts. As we shall have occasion to indicate, the meanings people share are rooted in and derive from a social system. "Social system" refers to the general ways in which a society provides its members with a socially meaningful way of living. The social system includes (1) culture, i.e. the accepted ways of interpreting the world and everything in it; (2) social structures, i.e. the accepted ways of doing things such as marrying, having children, working, governing, worshiping and understanding God; and (3) accepted individual self-understanding, accepted ways of being a person. People use language to have some effect on each other in terms of the meanings that constitute the social system. And people learn those meanings along with the language of their society in the process of growing up in that society.

Incidentally, why do we presume that the strange alphabet of the Greek New Testament can be understood at all? It seems that as a rule human beings continually find patterns everywhere they look, and they invariably find some meaning in those patterns. In the above example, the voice you heard clearly sounded as though it followed some pattern of cadence and articulation. It was not a scream, shriek, moan, groan or any other sort of unpatterned sound. If it sounded patterned it must have been communicating meaning of some sort. Or so one would logically conclude. The response to your quizzical gesture produced another shower of sound that surely sounded patterned with cadence and articulation. Again, it seemed clear that the man was saying something intelligible. His utterance sounded like it should be conveying meaning of some sort because it was clearly patterned (Johnson 1978:3–7).

The case with *squiggles* on a page is quite similar. Look at the Hebrew and Greek passages printed above. While they are not English, they are surely not the chaotic doodlings of a 2-year-old claiming to write something. They seem to be patterned and to follow a definite sequencing. The presumption which most humans share about patterned soundings and squiggles is that they convey meaning in some way. They are intended to communicate something to another human being. How? Reading is learning how to see patterns in the squiggles. Such patterns are called *wordings*. The wordings, in turn, reveal *meanings*, but only on condition that we share the same social system as the persons who initially wrote the squiggles. A translation of Luke that simply says his words in terms of our words hardly mediates the meaning of the Greek text, the meaning of Luke and his audience. The reason for this is that meaning is not in the wordings. Rather meaning is in the social system consisting of individual persons and their individual psychological and physical being, which is held together by a shared culture, shared values and shared meanings along with social institutions and social roles to realize those values and meanings. For example, take a basic New Testament Aramaic word such as *'abba* (translated into Greek as *patēr*, and into English as "father"). Would the English, "father," fill you with the meanings which a first-century Palestinian, Israelite native speaker thought and felt with this word? Frankly, no! Again, I suggest that for a native English speaker who has never lived in an Israelite, Aramaic-speaking community, the word *'abba* always means the very same thing as the English "father," since it invariably refers to the roles, behaviors, and meanings ascribed to US fathers. The only way to get "father" to really mean what an Israelite, Aramaic speaker such as Jesus might have meant by *'abba* is to get to know the social system within which the role of *'abba* worked (see Elliott 1990:174–80; Malina 1988; Barr 1988). The reason for this is that *what people say or write conveys and imparts meanings rooted in some social system.* The purpose of this chapter is to explain why this is the case and what that might mean for our understanding of that human skill called reading.

For literate people, the process of reading is often taken for granted, much like seeing or hearing. Few people reflect upon that set of behavioral skills picked up most often in elementary school. Yet access to the Bible in general, and to the books called Luke–Acts in particular, is totally dependent upon reading. Not a few readers innocent of what the reading process entails share a variant of what the computer-literate would call the "WYRIWYG" viewpoint (What You Read Is What You Get). We call this the fallacy of the "immaculate perception." Such naivety can be found among both professional and non-professional students of the Bible, just as it can among those whose access to primary sources of information requires reading (for example, historians and literary critics of all stripes). The presumption that what one reads derives directly from the writing that one confronts is a presumption founded on the belief that

7

writings are objective objects, simply "out there," and are to be handled like any other objects such as rocks or sticks. Such a presumption disregards the developing psychological uniqueness of the reader (called subjectivity). And it also disregards the reality that makes communication with language possible at all, that is, the social system shared by readers and their social groups as well as writers and their social groups.

To immerse the subjective and social dimensions of human being within some all-encompassing objectivity is to condemn a person to perpetual ethnocentrism and anachronism. For the simple fact is that the squiggles on the page (regardless of alphabet) have to be deciphered somehow into articulate and distinct patterns by a reader to give access to the meanings communicated through the squiggles by the author. If reader and writer share the same social system, communication is highly probable. But if reader and writer come from mutually alien social systems, then as a rule, non-understanding prevails, as is the case above where you, the reader, are the stranger in a strange land. Should a translation of the wording (words and sentences) be offered, apart from a comparative explanation of the social systems involved, misunderstanding inevitably follows. In other words, should there be a person available to turn the squiggles into sounds, these sounds too need to be decoded by a hearer to gain access to the sender's meanings – again, provided both share the same social system.

This description of hearing and reading a text might sound rather involved. However, it is truly necessary both to dispel the naive objectivism of the "Take up and read!" variety and to facilitate considered analysis. Reading is not simply sounding out the squiggles written or printed on a surface. I am acquainted with persons who can sound out what I know to be Polish or Hebrew or Greek or Latin without understanding much or anything of what they so readily perform. Reading is not simply turning markings into soundings. Rather, reading always involves decoding the markings and/or soundings into the wordings and, finally, having the wordings yield the meanings they convey from some author or speaker in a specific social system.

This may all sound like another Teutonic belaboring of the obvious, yet it bears emphasizing since nearly all interpreters of the Bible, professional and non-professional, take the reading process for granted. Further, one often gets the impression that these interpreters all too innocently assume that the categories of their elementary school grammar, generally learned at the concrete stage of human cognitive development, are categories that refer to concrete realities. Thus the letters, words and sentences of spoken language are presumed to be concrete, meaning-bearing, linguistic entities. After all, when we write down what we say, do we not put down concrete letters, words and sentences? And these concrete words and sentences are presumed to have meanings that are directly accessible to people by the simple process of learning to look at them. The process is not unlike collecting concrete, individual stamps, coins and butter-flies.

But is this in fact the case with language? Is not language a flow of patterned soundings articulating wordings and expressing meanings? Are not words and sentences deriving from the level of word-ings arbitrarily set apart into discrete entities? Are not words and sentences in fact abstractions and ideas treated as concrete things? Are they not then "thingified" concepts created by ancient and mod-ern grammarians and lexicographers to facilitate their logical analyses of human thinking, a dubious enterprise at best (Fishman 1971: 91–105)? People in fact do not utter words. Rather they utter a whole tissue of patterned, articulate and cadenced sounds which the literate grammarian breaks into smaller repeatable pieces. The full segments of sound are wordings. The smaller repeatable pieces of sound are set apart like cells in a culture dish and called words. Illiterate persons are not aware that they speak words. When asked to repeat a word, illiterates invariably begin at a point which they consider the beginning of their previous utterance (Lord 1960: 99–138; Ong 1982:31–77).

If words are not the locus of meaning, neither are language systems as such. In spite of the fact that modern Greek and Hebrew speakers can express the world of contemporary society and science quite well, there is still the suspicion that "biblical thought" is different from our own, because of the nature of the languages of the Bible. This is the much-quoted Whorfian hypothesis applied to the Bible. In the 1940s, B. L. Whorf advanced the hypothesis that cultural differences including ways of reasoning, perceiving, learning, distin-guishing, remembering and the like are directly relatable to the structured differences between languages themselves (see Whorf 1956). For example, the tenses of the Hebrew verb would make ancient Israelites perceive the reality of time in a distinctive way. The sociolinguist Fishman notes (1971:92): "Intriguing though this claim may be it is necessary to admit that many years of intensive research have not succeeded in demonstrating it to be tenable." As reading theory indicates, it is not to the structured differences between languages that we have to look, but to the social systems of different peoples.

READING

Every theory of reading presupposes a set of assumptions concerning the nature of language and the nature of text. How does language work? How does text work? And how does reading work? It is quite apparent that written language does not live in scrolls or books. The markings on a page stand for wordings that represent meanings that can come alive only through the agency of the minds of readers. Before setting out a model of describing what happens when a person reads, I shall begin by setting out some assumptions about language and text.

On language

There is an explanation of the nature of language that is rooted in the presupposition that human beings are essentially social beings. Everything anybody does has some social motivation and some social meaning. From the point of view of this approach, the chief purpose of language is to mean to another, and the purpose of this meaning is to have some effect on another. This perspective is often called sociolinguistics.

The approach to sociolinguistics adopted here derives from Michael A. K. Halliday (Halliday 1978; see also Cicourel 1985). In this perspective, language is a three-tiered affair consisting of (a) soundings/spellings that (b) realize wordings that (c) realize meanings. And where do the meanings realized in language come from? Given the experience of human beings as essentially social beings, those meanings come from and in fact constitute the social system. This three-tiered model of language would have the Bible reader ask: What social system or social meaning is being expressed in the wordings realized in the spellings of biblical "texts"? Everyone who can read the Bible surely has a rather full understanding of how "the world" works. "The world," however, that we understand so well is the particular world into which we have been socialized and enculturated. This is our twentieth-century, Euro-American understanding of how the world and everything and everybody in it works. Without

10

further suspicion and awareness, the untutored reader will necessarily perceive "the world" of Luke (i.e. the social system expressed in the wordings realized through the spellings of biblical "texts") as if it were his or her own social system. We call this misreading ethnocentrism, that is, imagining that all people everywhere and at all times think just like me.

The point is all the more obvious at the level of "words." As noted previously, words are artificial, arbitrary creations of grammarians cut out of wordings that realize meanings. These words are then said to convey meaning and this they do as labels, marking off objects of social interest. Yet even in this case, the meanings attached to the labels derive from a social system. Consider the following Greek words written in our equivalent alphabet: Christ, baptism, charism, apocalypse, blasphemy and chrism. Does writing those words in our alphabet make them any more understandable or meaningful? Take note that for us "Christ" is Jesus of Nazareth's last name; "baptism" is an initiation rite in Christian churches; "charism" is what popstars and politicians have when we really like them; "apocalypse" is a story or vision of the end of the world; "blasphemy" is filthy words directed to God; and "chrism" is holy oil used by the Orthodox Church and by Anglo- and Roman Catholics. None of these meanings were attached to these words as early Christians used them.

Rather, for early Christians "Christ" is a Greek translation of the Israelite social role termed "Messiah" in Hebrew. The word simply cannot be translated adequately since that social role and its job description are typical solely of ancient Israelite society. Similarly, "baptism" refers to dipping in a liquid, much as John the Dipper did to people who came to him at the Jordan in the first century; the dipping symbolized a change of one's way of thinking and feeling about life in general and people in particular. "Charism" is the outcome of patronage, what one receives from a patron in the patron–client relationships typical of the Mediterranean. "Apocalypse" means revelation, making known something that was previously not known; "blasphemy" means dishonoring a person by words; and "chrism" means olive oil used for rub-downs of varying sorts.

Without some awareness of other social forms, of other cultures and of other times and places, a person cannot but presume that everyone is human in the same way he or she has been taught to be human. So when readers find their gospel translation telling them what Jesus says of marriage and divorce, the reader will obviously,

11

clearly and surely refer those statements to marriage and divorce as the reader experiences them. The same with Jesus' statements on taxes, forgiveness, God as Father, the family, one's "brothers" and enemies and the like. What all this means is that to be fair to the biblical authors and the persons they refer to, one must make some effort to learn about their culture and the social forms realized through their language in order to get some grasp of the meanings they impart.

What is a Text?

Furthermore, if what the biblical reader does is read a biblical text, what in fact is a "text"? What does it mean to interpret a text? Once again, we have the elementary school, literate but untutored intuition that a text is anything written down. More often than not, a biblical text is a sentence printed in the Bible and cited from it. Some people even call such a piece of written wording a "scripture" or a "scriptural text." How such a piece of written wording quoted apart from the rest of the text to which it belongs (its co-text, i.e. its accompanying text) is to convey meaning at all is a question most often not considered. And this is a crucial consideration since from the perspective of the way people communicate, *a sentence is not a text*. A sentence is simply a sentence. As we have all memorized in elementary school, a sentence is a group of words that expresses a complete thought. In sociolinguistics, however, a text is a "meaningful configuration of language intended to communicate" (De Beaugrande 1980:1).

Just as a sentence is the unit of wording that expresses thought in language, so a "text" is the unit of articulating meaning in language. And since humans use language to mean, "text" is the normal mode of imparting meaning with language. If interpretation is the process of discerning meaning, then "text" will be the unit of interpretation.

On the other hand, texts are formed for the most part by pasting together complete thoughts set forth in those wordings marked off by grammarians as sentences. It often takes a lengthy set of sentences, of complete thoughts, to realize a simple meaning. As an extreme case, take a philosophical work in several volumes dealing with the meaning of "being" or "time," or any other foundational metaphysical idea. To express such meaning may take thousands of sentences.

From the sociolinguistic point of view, each biblical document is a "text," since each document is the unit of meaning to be interpreted. At times we quote sentences by way of putting down thoughts or ideas. But such sentences are not "texts." Sentences are distinctive in that they can be understood. But texts are distinctive in that they can be interpreted. Very often sentences are well understood, but simply cannot be interpreted. For example, "He does so and continues to do so." For such a sentence to make sense, it must be restored to its textual setting. Yet texts always need interpretation since all dimensions of a social system cannot be expressed at once in a text. *Some information necessary for a full understanding of a text is always lacking.* The interpreter provides this information so that the person or thing being interpreted can be readily and rather fully understood. For adequate communication to take place, then, text needs "context" (literally: *with + text*) consisting of the social system within which the linguistic communication originally took place.

Elements of reading

Admittedly the foregoing material might seem obscure and esoteric. So it is useful here to summarize the three basic points made above concerning language, reading and texts.

(a) Language = *squiggles – wordings – meanings.*
   Obviously, our focus must be on *meaning*, which derives from the social system.
(b) Reading = understanding *squiggles* (*wordings + meanings*). Again, we attend to the meaning aspect of language, which can only be known when the social system of the communicator is known.
(c) Text = *unit of meaning*, which needs *interpretation*. Unlike sentences, which are units of wordings, texts refer to the larger unit, such as Luke–Acts; whereas sentences can be understood at some level, texts can be interpreted.

In sum, meanings realized in texts inevitably derive from some social system. Thus to interpret the originally intended meanings set out in the text called Luke–Acts, the contemporary reader must have access to the social system(s) available to the original audience of those texts. To recover those social systems, we believe it essential to employ adequate, explicit social science models (for classical antiquity, see Carney 1975; Malina 1993). What is lacking for an historical interpretation of the meaning imparted through the ancient texts

13

that we read is information which might facilitate that reading in terms of the meanings familiar to the original audience of those texts. But what sort of information? In what form? To clarify this contention, we now turn to reading theory.

INTRAPERSONAL AND INTERPERSONAL DIMENSIONS OF READING

It is a truism in our society that human beings are simultaneously both individual and social beings. This means that any piece of human activity as well as human living as a whole will have individual as well as social features. People, therefore, reveal both intrapersonal (individual) and interpersonal (social) dimensions in all of their activities. Reading is no exception. It is quite possible that the range of various meanings which derive from the reading of some common text derive from individual differences in the reader's knowledge and skills. Readers, however, rarely, if ever, read alone even when they alone read. For example, Harste, Burke and Woodward (1982) argue that reading is a "socio-psycholinguistic process." The psycholinguistic dimension of the process is the individual, psychological aspect rooted in the way individuals, given their individual, psychological stage of development, perform the activity of reading. The sociolinguistic dimension looks to the group and to the social system that holds it, that is, the social aspect invariably connected with any form of human interaction, including linguistic ones. They offer the following explanation of these dimensions (italics in the original):

> In considering a given text, the *language setting* which includes where the language is found (home, school, store), in what culture (United States, Israel, Saudi Arabia), and for and by whom it was produced (peer, superior, subordinate) modifies the *mental setting* in terms of what schema the reader accesses. The accessed schemata direct strategy utilization and, hence, sampling of language setting.
> (Harste, Burke and Woodward 1982:108)

The language setting and the available strategies of utilization are typically social and best analyzed by *socio*linguistics. On the other hand, an individual person's mental setting is psychological and best analyzed by *psycho*linguistics. But both dimensions are involved in the process of reading. Hence the interpersonal and intrapersonal

14

aspects to reading. For the language setting is interpersonal context, while the mental setting is intrapersonal context. Bloome and Green (1984:413–14), for example, suggest that the individual's background knowledge, skills and general approach to reading can be viewed as the *intra*personal context of reading. The intrapersonal context involves an individual's available collection of scenarios or schemes of how the world works, the level of abstraction the individual can master, his or her usual cognitive style and the like. Thus intrapersonal context describes the mental setting: the internalized schemes, scenarios and models that the individual reader has available for rearrangement in the course of a reading. The intrapersonal is best studied by the methods of experimental psychology and best described in terms of psychological models. However, psychological development is always rooted in some primary group, hence in the social dimensions of human being. And this is where the interpersonal context enters the discussion.

The *inter*personal dimensions of reading would involve the language setting within a social system as well as how reading events are organized within a society: how participants interact, what motivates them to read, what influence they bring to bear on the reading process and the way the reading process influences their interactions. We shall consider the interpersonal dimensions of reading later.

We can summarize the preceding material conveniently in Table 1.

Table 1 Dimensions of reading

Aspects of reading	Human dimensions	
	Individual	Social
Reading dimension	*Intra*personal	*Inter*personal
Reading strategy	*Psycho*linguistic	*Socio*linguistic
Reading setting	Mental setting	Language setting

Intrapersonal dimension: models of reading

I think it bears repeating that biblical scholarship, professional and non-professional, is ultimately rooted in the reading of ancient written texts. In fact, biblical interpretation is the interpretation of written language. Since biblical study consists in studying texts and entails reading and interpreting written language, it is important to

15

have some verifiable theory of how reading takes place. This point has been entirely overlooked in handbooks of exegetical method. How does a reader get to understand the meanings through the wordings in the writings? The professional study of the Bible often involves learning about ancient writing systems (orthography) and the mastery of equally ancient wording systems (lexico-grammar). The outcome of such study set down in dictionaries and grammars has produced many interesting data. It is one thing, however, to collect data, and quite another to interpret those data. Are dictionary definitions and grammatical generalizations generally trustworthy? How can one verify them? Again, we come back to the reading process. Here I shall focus upon the meanings that get imparted in the process of reading. While contemporary experimental psychology affords us a number of models for understanding the activity of reading, there are at bottom two major models of reading comprehension currently in vogue (after Sanford and Garrod 1981).

Model one: reading and ideas

I call the first model the *propositional model*. This model considers the text to be read as a sort of supersentence. Perhaps this perspective derives from the way we have been taught languages, with the classroom focus on wording, that is, on the sentence and word level. In this view, what happens when a person reads is that the text being read evokes mental representations in the mind of the reader; these representations consist of a chain or series of propositions which derive directly from the sentences that constitute the text. The text is made up of sentences, which in turn are made up of words. A sort of initial proof of this fact is that one can and often does outline what is read as one studies a text. This outline, when adequate, brings out the chain of propositions latent in the text.

Readers then basically perform two tasks. They parse the text into propositional units and then connect the resulting propositions in some way. This connection takes place by means of some superstructure that emerges from the process of outlining. Scholars who adopt this model often call this superstructure a deep structure, story grammar, narrative grammar or something of the sort. As many will recognize from their "lit." courses, this sort of model undergirds contemporary structural, semiotic, deconstructionist, "Marxist" and aesthetic literary criticism. Such criticism forms the foundation of the biblical exegesis based on these types of criticism (see for example,

Detweiler 1985; Malina 1986; Moore 1988). They are generally rooted in a propositional model of reading. However, the experimental research available indicates that the propositional model is considerably off target since its description of reading is not what goes on in the mind of a reader at all (see Sanford and Garrod 1981, on whom this discussion rests).

This does not mean, however, that texts cannot be parsed in terms of their overall structures or text grammars (for a full survey of such techniques, see Meyer and Rice 1984:319–51). Indeed, structural exegesis has been done on a number of texts. The question, however, is whether such analysis gets to the *meanings* encoded in the *wordings* expressed in the *squiggles* which one learns to sound out in reading. If the structures mediating meaning are rooted in and derive from the social system in which communication (originally) takes place, propositional models miss the mark. They are rooted in the wording aspect of the text, not its meaning. As such they allow for judgments of aesthetics, of niceness or prettiness in speech. They can also serve as a springboard for ideas derived from a sort of associational flow of ideas. Such propositional models of reading comprehension imply a conceptual approach to texts.

Among non-linguists, the obvious validity of such propositional models seems to derive from the fact that literate people can and do take notes on what they read. They can outline paragraphs and chapters. Obviously, since the notes are presumed to derive directly from the texts, the fact must be that the text consists of concepts in propositional form which I, the literate reader, extract as I read. Among linguists, however, such models seem to be rooted in presuppositions about the nature and function of language that derive from treating highly abstract entities such as words and sentences as though they were objective things.

But words and sentences are not the end-products of language. On the contrary, the end-products of language are spoken and/or written texts, that is, meaningful configurations of language intended to communicate. And what texts invariably communicate is meaning from a social system within specific contexts. On the other hand, for not a few biblical interpreters, such models seem to be rooted in some religiously based enterprise, often articulated in terms of propositions that go to form a theological system, a set of truths. In fact such theological propositions are abstracts or summaries of larger, engrossing stories that form the basic stuff of religion (Barr 1987). And what religious texts, as a rule, set forth are

17

those larger, comprehensive stories. If, then, a text does not present a chain or series of propositions, what does it evoke in the mind of a reader?

Model two: reading and scenarios

A second model of reading comprehension might be called a *scenario model*. By way of contrast, if the *propositional model* attended to the *wordings*, then the *scenario model* focuses on *meaning*. Some synonyms for the term "scenario" here include schema, frames, scenes, scripts, gestalts, active structural networks and memory organization packets (Casson 1983:429). This model considers the text as setting forth a succession of explicit and implicit mental representations consisting of scenes or schemes. These, in turn, evoke corresponding scenes or schemes in the mind of the reader. Such scenes or schemes are composed of a series of settings, episodes or models. These latter derive directly from the mind of the reader, who carries out appropriate alterations to the settings, episodes or models as directed by the text.

As in the previous explanation, here too the reader must perform two tasks: (a) call to mind some appropriate scene, scheme or model as suggested by the text; and (b) use the identified scene, scheme or model as the larger frame within which to situate the meanings proposed in the text as far as this is possible. In other words, the reader uses the text to identify an appropriate domain or frame of reference and then rearranges that domain according to the arrangements suggested in the text being read.

Unlike the propositional model, the scenario model of reading does have some validation from contemporary experimental psychology. Meyer and Rice (1984:327) remark that even the structural linguist van Dijk

> suggests appealing to the content of the topic of discourse, as organized in a "frame," to describe certain macrostructural attributes. For example, a text about a war will derive some of its organization from a war "frame," in which is represented component states and the necessary or probable conditions and consequences of wars in general."

Such frames are the scenarios, scenes, schemata and the like which the writer evokes in the writing and which the reader brings to the reading.

This model of reading *squiggles* which encode *wordings* which realize *meaning* from a social system is not too different from the social psychology model of how human beings "read" situations. All human beings carry on an interpretative enterprise. As a rule, people carry in their heads one or more models of "society" and "human being" which greatly influence what they look for in their experiences, what they actually see, and what they eventually do with their observations by way of fitting them into a larger scheme of explanation along with other facts. In this respect, every human being, tutored or not, is no different from any trained observer in our society (Garfinkel 1967:262–83). For example, every scientist, like every other human being, holds some general conception of the realm in which he or she is working, that is, some mental picture of how it is put together, how it works and how one ought to feel about it. Of course, the same is true of the biblical interpreter, professional or non-professional.

The scenario model of reading begins with the fact that nearly every adult reader has an adequate and socially verifiable grasp of how the experienced world works. As readers, people bring this awareness to a text. In the linguistic interchange that is reading, an author is allowed to present some distinctive sets of scenarios of the working world that in effect suggest and motivate the reader to rearrange the scenarios which he or she brings to the reading. Effective communication depends upon the considerateness of the writer or speaker. Considerate authors attempt to understand their readers. As a result of such understanding, considerate authors will take up and elaborate the scenarios shared by their readers. And more than this, considerate authors will always make the effort to develop the scenarios actually employed by beginning with what the reader knows and coupling to what is known the new, unknown features that they wish to impart to readers and hearers. Meyer and Rice note:

> Haviland and Clark (1974) have suggested that both the writer and the reader participate in a "given–new contract." Under the contract, the writer is constrained to be relevant (i.e. not confuse the reader with extraneous information), to cooperate, and to consider what the reader knows or doesn't know. Thus the writer constructs his/her sentences so that the "given" or antecedent information (what the reader is expected to know) and the "new" information (what the author is adding to this

knowledge) are clearly differentiated. .... Research has shown that readers' comprehension is impaired when this contract is violated by putting "new" information into the topic or "given" position in a sentence.

(1984:326)

Of course, by such standards the authors of the New Testament documents "violate the contract" and are all inconsiderate. For they neither begin with what we know about the world nor make any attempt to explain their ancient world in terms of scenarios which we might understand from contemporary, Euro-American experience. The authors of the New Testament documents presume that we who read those documents are first-century eastern Mediterraneans, sharing a social system poised on honor and shame, fully aware of what it means to live a city and/or village life, totally immersed in a sick-care system concerned with the well being of unfortunates, believing in limited good assuaged by patrons and brokers, and the like. Given the fact that the New Testament documents are first-century works rooted in a specific time and place, it would be rather silly to expect the authors of those documents to envision readers two thousand years removed. Hence it would seem that if we seek to be fair to biblical authors, we shall have to make the effort to be considerate readers. The considerate reader of documents from the past will obviously make the effort to bring to his or her reading a set of scenarios proper to the time, place and culture of the biblical author.

Granted the need to be a considerate reader, the contemporary student of Luke–Acts will have to learn a set of scenarios comprising scenes, schemes or models of varying abstraction and typical of the first-century eastern Mediterranean. In our own society, the scholarly articulation of such scenes, schemes and models has generally been the métier of social scientists. For this reason, it would seem that the social science approach to biblical interpretation is best suited to the task of reading the biblical books with a view to understanding the meanings communicated by their authors. Such a scenario model of reading might be called the social context approach.

In summary, of the two models of reading discussed, only the scenario model has any empirical evidence to support it. It attends to meanings, not just wordings. And so, only the scenario model can avoid problems of ethnocentric or inconsiderate reading of texts. Only it fully takes into account the social dimensions of reading:

the interpersonal dimension, whose strategy is explained by socio-linguistics.

Reading and the interpreter

If the scenario model sketched out above is indeed the way readers comprehend, it would seem that the best which contemporary biblical scholars can offer their clientele is a set of scenarios, scenes, models, frames and domains of reference deriving from and appropriate to the first-century eastern Mediterranean world from which the text called Luke–Acts derives. This would seem to be the primary way to facilitate adequate understanding of biblical authors and the persons they present. For the understanding and interpretation of any sort of text is ultimately rooted in a society where persons share common institutions and a common culture, i.e. shared scenarios of how "the world" works in terms of the persons, groups, objects and attitudes that constitute it. All interpretation, it would seem, requires such models and ultimately rests on such models (see Malina 1982:229–31).

INTERPERSONAL DIMENSIONS

The foregoing explanation of reading theory is based on psychology, the psychology of the reader (hearer); hence it represents the *intra*-personal dimension. As we have noted, psychological perspectives of reading are primarily concerned with the individual reader and how that reader establishes a meaning for a text. Of primary concern for considerate reading in this regard are the background knowledge and skills that a reader brings to the task of interpreting a text. The range of various meanings deriving from the reading of some common text clearly derives from individual differences in the readers' knowledge and skills. Yet as pointed out above, readers rarely, if ever, read alone. The scenario model of reading described above, with its focus on the reader's mental setting, is largely such a psychological model. Yet as previously noted, it requires the accessing of social settings deriving from some primary group; thus it is anchored in the social or *inter*-personal dimension of reading. A consideration of reading and social setting will underscore this point.

Reading and social setting

The interpersonal dimension of reading looks to how reading events are organized within a society. This dimension entails some understanding of the general social system along with a consideration of some specific aspects of reading events such as how participants interact, their influence on the reading process and the way the reading process influences their interactions. How do people use reading to establish a social context? How does the social context then influence reading practice and the communication of meaning (Bloome and Green 1984:396)?

In Luke–Acts, for example, one of the most prominent reading events describes a synagogue-reading of Isaiah. "Jesus stood up to read; and there was given to him the book of the prophet Isaiah. He opened the book and found the place where it was written: 'The Spirit of the Lord is upon me'" (Luke 4:16–18). What interpersonal dimensions are involved in this reading event? What information would an interpreter need to understand it? How does such biblical reading establish a social context in the synagogue? And how does the context, the gathering of Galilean Israelites in this case, influence reading practice and the meanings communicated? Did it matter that many of the people there were illiterate? that they did not understand Hebrew?

Clearly one must know the general cultural and historical features of the author's world. This includes (a) the values and structures of the first-century eastern Mediterranean and the Palestinian Israelite context, (b) the lack of historical sense common to people of the period, (c) the roles of various professional Bible interpreters, that is, the scribes, (d) their modes of interaction and (e) the methods of interpreting the texts of the Bible based upon their contemporary needs. In sum, one needs to know the range of scenarios for social interaction actually available in the first-century eastern Mediterranean in general and in the area of Bible reading in Israelite Palestine in particular. This is the interpersonal context of reading, and it is a primary concern in sociolinguistic perspectives of reading.

Relative to biblical interpretation, the question here is:

> *Who* says *what* to *whom* about *what*,
> in *what* setting and for *what* purpose?

Setting and purpose as well as the persons who interact there are determined largely by institutional arrangements, for example, synagogue, public challenge based on citing the Bible, temple, public teaching, private teaching and the like. How reading takes place in these various environments is determined by the environmental settings which replicate institutional pressures. In synagogue preaching, for example, the biblical passage will be explained in terms of some contemporary occurrence, while in debate the passage will be used to dishonor opponents, and in temple discussions the readings might look to legal precedent.

The situation of biblical interpretation in the modern world is quite similar in terms of questions to be asked, yet quite different in terms of presuppositions to be posited. For Euro-American Bible reading, the interpersonal involves such general cultural and historical features as the societal values and social structures of the country of the reader, the historical sense shared by secondary school graduates in their society, the groups of various professional Bible interpreters in the specific Euro-American countries and their modes of interaction, the methods of interpreting the texts of the Bible based upon previous questions about what to look for, in sum the range of scenarios for social interaction actually available in the contemporary West in general and in the area of Bible reading in particular. Relative to biblical interpretation, the question here is who says what to whom about what in what setting for what purpose. Setting and purpose as well as the persons who interact in a given setting are determined largely by available institutional arrangements: learned society, university, seminary, church, Sunday school, non-professional Bible study, charismatic prayer group, etc.

The types of readings taking place in these various environments are determined by their environmental settings, which replicate institutional pressures. For example, the Bible may be read within the framework of some Euro-American educational institution. Thus at a learned society or university, biblical books are viewed in terms of various educational concerns determined by the prevailing educational institution in the society. On the other hand, we can envision Bible reading within a setting distinctive of the religious institution. Seminary, church, Sunday school and the like pressure readers to understand what they read in terms of the prevailing religious institution of their socialization. Then, the Bible may be read for political purposes, for gaining or applying power: it may be cited by politicians, feminists or other activist interpreters with a view to changing institutions. Finally, the Bible may equally be used, not read, within the economic institution. Thus it would be highly appropriate for a Chinese soldier who never heard of "religions of the book" to perceive this book as a sheaf of paper and use the fine paper of a Bible to roll a cigarette. He sees the book in terms of utilitarian concerns determined by the prevailing economic institution. Often Bible salespersons and publishers share a similar perception determined by norms of the economic institution. In such an institutional perspective, reading is not at issue.

Thus we are acutely aware of two social settings for reading, that of the author and that of the reader. In the case of Luke–Acts, typical modern readers may be acutely aware of their own social setting, but totally oblivious of Luke's world and his social setting. It is the purpose of the chapters which follow to apprise the considerate reader precisely of Luke's social setting by offering adequate scenarios of the way his world worked.

Reading and societal context

While environmental settings do indeed determine types of reading and non-reading, by far the most significant initial cue to the inter-personal dimension of reading derives from what Hall has called the prevailing language "context" generally in vogue in a society (1976:91–101 and 1983:59–77). Hall refers to *low-context* and *high-context* societies.

Low- and high-context societies

Low-context societies produce detailed texts, spelling out as much as conceivably possible, leaving little to the imagination. The general norm is that most things must be clearly set out, and hence information must be continually added if meaning is to be constant. Such societies are fine-print societies, societies "of law" where every dimension of life must be described by legislators to make things "lawful," even including, for example, detailed legal directions about how much fat is allowed in commercially sold sausage. The *Congressional Record*, a document produced by the US government, offers hours of low-context reading for whoever might wish to be entertained in this way. Hall considers the US and northern European countries as typically low-context societies.

High-context societies produce sketchy and impressionistic texts, leaving much to the reader's or hearer's imagination. Since people believe that few things have to be spelled out, few things are in fact

24

spelled out. This is so because people have been socialized into shared ways of perceiving and acting. Hence, much can be assumed. People presume, for example, that helping out a person in dire need makes that person obligated for the rest of his or her life to the helper. There simply is no need to spell out all these obligations, as we would when we sign for a car loan. In high-context societies, little new information is necessary for meaning to be constant. Hall lists the Mediterranean, among other areas, as populated with high-context societies. Clearly the Bible along with other writings from ancient Mediterranean peoples fit this high-context profile.

How different, then, it is for low-context, US and northern European readers to read some high-context text. Attuned to detail, they simply do not know what is assumed in a low-context society. It is the purpose of historical biblical interpretation to fill in the assumptions of the low-context documents that form the New Testament, assumptions which the authors of those documents shared with low-context readers of their Mediterranean world.

It will help us understand Hall's observations about high- and low-context societies if we attend to their respective communication problems. The typical communication problem in low-context societies such as the US, for example, is giving people information they do not need, hence "talking down" to them by spelling out absolutely everything. Consider the endless amount of information printed by the US Government Printing Office alone. In contrast, the typical communication problem in high-context societies is not giving people enough information, hence "mystifying" them. Consider the broad range of mystifications and hidden meanings derived from the Mediterranean, high-context Bible in the hands of sincere and honest low-context US and northern European readers.

Biblical mystifications and hidden meanings are contrived in a number of ways and for various reasons in our low-context societies. In the 1950s, I have been told, a Presbyterian preacher in Scotland proved that God did not want teenage girls to put their hair in a top knot since Jesus said that top knots must come down, as follows: "Let him who is on the house-*top not go down*" (Mark 13:15). Compared to all the non-Mediterranean, anachronistic and ethnocentric information dredged from the Bible over the past two millennia, the demystified top knot seems slightly innocuous. For given the lack of information in the high-context documents that the biblical documents are, not a few Bible "readers" lose interest in meanings at all.

25

Empathy, not interpretation

At times, the social context in which the Bible is "read" directly develops empathy among members of the gathering, with almost no attempt at meaning and understanding. The context then is more of an encounter session than a worship service requiring a homily or sermon. This is not unlike a number of TV talk shows where ideas and experiences do not have to be presented at all in order to excite a viewer/ hearer's interest. The excitement is due to empathy, not to interpretation.

> The talk show wants very much to let us know how people feel about things. Part of the time it succeeds. But even when it succeeds there is a certain distortion: All we find out in the end is how they feel, not what things mean. . . . The talk show, which has certain formal resemblances to the town meeting, does not have to do anything but express feelings. Because the talk show imitates democratic political institutions while playing only to the expression of feeling, it really does diminish democratic character. Imagine a Parliament or Congress in which the members had nothing to do but say how they felt – there would be no persuasion, no tally, no legislative accomplishment. The form of the town meeting goes badly with the feeling of an encounter session.
>
> (Berman 1987:52–3)

So too the form of public proclamation of a text intended to communicate meaning goes badly with the encounter session catharsis sought after by not a few individualistic American Bible readers.

Contextualized – decontextualized reading

Some analysts distinguish between contextualized and decontextualized reading. *Contextualized* literacy is writing or print which gets meanings from context, (for example, stop sign, envelope, newspaper advertisement or article). Thus by being in a "New Testament," the single early Christian documents are "Scripture" and get their religious meaning from where they are found. And by being bundled along with another collection of earlier eastern Mediterranean writings, Israel's "Scripture," the New Testament draws further cultural and social meaning from the time and place of its having been collected into a Bible.

Decontextualized literacy is writing or print which gets its meanings from the print itself, without support from the contextual surround. Thus a written work takes on meaning solely due to the reader! Most modern Euro-Americans reading the *Rig Veda* (Hindu writing) or *Tripitaka* (Buddhist writing) would find those works sufficiently decontextualized so as to focus on their aesthetic impact alone (Bloome and Green 1984:406). Similarly, the effort to read the Bible as literature, for its aesthetic majesty and universal ideas, involves an attempt at decontextualizing since any aesthetic-literary, ahistorical framework is decontextualized. Much of the reader-response approach to literature is equally decontextualized, totally dismissing the social dimensions of author, original audience and the text in question (for example, Iser 1972; Moore 1988). But as far as the Bible is concerned, since nearly all Euro-Americans have heard of the Bible and have some inkling that it deals with "religion," it would seem that the reading of even snippets of the Bible in the West is always socially contextualized in the realm of "religion." The question for professional interpretation is what context is most appropriate for a fair and just reading of the Bible. Are all of the contexts listed previously amenable to supporting the considerate reader described above?

Keeping the intrapersonal and interpersonal together

Various analysts of the reading process warn against separating the intrapersonal context from the interpersonal context. While the two contexts can be theoretically segregated, difficulties arise in specifying relationships between them (Bloome and Green 1984:414). Part of those difficulties relates to the nature of the phenomena themselves. That is, in order to explore the intrapersonal context, the interpersonal context must be "frozen" or stopped. In "freezing" the interpersonal context, however, the nature of the interpersonal context is distorted since the interpersonal context is an evolving, continuing, dynamic process.

For biblical studies, the question of contexts might be put as follows: What relationship can historical biblical interpretation have for churches? If the scenarios required for a considerate reading of the gospels are first-century eastern Mediterranean ones, of what relevance can the gospels be to twentieth-century Americans? One way in which researchers have attempted to capture both the intrapersonal and interpersonal contexts without distorting either has been through

27

juxtaposing research perspectives. For biblical studies, this would require a reflexive awareness of our late-twentieth-century US society and the scenarios it requires for making sense of contemporary writings, as well as a reflexive awareness of first-century eastern Mediterranean society and the scenarios it required for making sense of writings from that time and place. Juxtaposing the two perspectives would yield the insights of comparative distancing. The people described in biblical writings can be seen in their attempt to make meaning in terms of their own experience, much as we must in terms of our own experience. What ties us and them together is that for believers, they are ancestors in faith being looked at through comparative lenses that are some two thousand or more years thick. Their experiences with the God of Israel, the Father of Jesus of Nazareth, can still resonate for us and allow for appreciative understanding. Yet while the God of Israel might abide forever, the experience of our ancestors will ever remain foreign and alien regardless of how spuriously familiar we might be with it.

CONCLUSION

Given the nature of reading, one of the primary goals of biblical scholarship should be to offer a range of scenarios with which the twentieth-century reader might interact with those first-century Mediterranean documents and get to understand what the author said and meant to say to his original first-century eastern Mediterranean audience. The New Testament writings are high-context documents. Much if not most of what is needed for adequate interpretation is simply left unsaid and presumed known from the cultural experience of the first-century eastern Mediterranean reader. This is another reason for scholarship to provide first-century Mediterranean scenarios quite naturally taken for granted by writers from the period.

Providing such scenarios, and so filling in the context, facilitates a modern reader's task of interpreting the text. A fair reading of any document has its intrapersonal and interpersonal dimensions. The intrapersonal is psychologically oriented, requiring an adult reader with a sense of history to be a considerate reader by building the most adequate scenarios possible. In order to be a fair and impartial listener, the considerate reader must be willing to switch levels of abstraction within the scenarios as need arises.

The interpersonal dimension looks to the reading process as a social event. Thus modern Euro-American readers of the New Testament are presumably contextualized readers with a sense of history. They read and/or hear these documents in social settings such as church or school, in public or in private. US fairness, therefore, requires that the reader's first step be *to strive to understand what the author says and means to say to his Mediterranean hearers in terms of their culture and within their social setting*. Theirs was a high-context society, with much of what they intended to communicate totally absent from the text, yet rather firmly in place in the common social system into which they were socialized. The considerate reader needs to fill in the social system in order not to be mystified.

In the US and northern Europe, the reading of New Testament documents takes place in two interpersonal contexts: the educational institution and the religious institution. In the educational institution we are presumably motivated by the value of *knowing the truth*: What did the author in fact say and mean? How does this relate to the early Christian movement and its subsequent development? In the religious institution, the value that motivates us is, among others, "to *know the basis for the faith* that is in us": What did the author in fact say and mean? How does this relate to Christian faith?

Reading theory indicates that the primary task of the interpreter is adequate scenario building. Whether our context is education or religion or both, we are still obliged to build adequate scenarios. Otherwise, we can only insert our own words and meanings into the mouths of biblical authors, behavior that manifests the intellectual sins of anachronism and ethnocentrism. Thanks to the common "religious" quality ascribed to biblical books, when we do manage to stick our words into the mouth of biblical authors, we clothe our words with the infallibility and inerrancy ascribed to the Bible. Now, this might do for fundamentalist preachers since their own infallibility and inerrancy are crucial to a successful preaching career, for example, in TV show business.

But for most readers the requirement of adequate scenario building is simply a question of being fair to biblical authors and the people described in their texts. Such adequate scenario building involves the same steps as getting to understand a group of foreigners with whom we are inevitably and necessarily thrown together, for better or worse. We can choose to ignore the foreigners; this would be simply to ignore the Bible. In that way we can never find out what those authors said and meant to say. On the other hand, if we choose to accept and use the Bible as text, we can force those presented in the biblical books to comply with our idea of them much as the Israeli or former South African governments have done with their subjected populations. As we all know, this involves brutal beatings, concentration camps, unconscionable reprisals and a foreseeable bloody future to get those people to comply with the preconvictions of their conquerors. We can treat and have treated our biblical witnesses in much the same way. Two thousand years of European and American history simply point up how original biblical meanings have been bloodied and perverted, how the experiences of biblical people have been used to herd people in directions opposed to their own experience, how in response to their having been mishandled in terms of the Bible, so many of our contemporaries dismiss biblical experience as totally irrelevant. On the other hand, we can come to understand our strange and alien biblical ancestors in faith. We can learn to appreciate them and learn to live with their witness even as we must find God in our own contemporary experience. And it is the reading process that both enables and facilitates this task.

REFERENCES

Barr, David L. (1987) *New Testament Story: An Introduction*. Belmont, CA: Wadsworth.

Barr, James (1988) "'Abba Isn't 'Daddy.'" *Journal of Theological Studies* 39:28–47.

Berman, Ronald (1987) *How Television Sees its Audience: A Look at the Looking Glass*. Newbury Park, CA: Sage.

Bloome, David and Judith Green (1984) "Directions in the Sociolinguistic Study of Reading." pp. 395–421 in P. David Pearson (ed.) *Handbook of Reading Research*. New York: Longman.

Carney, Thomas F. (1975) *The Shape of the Past: Models and Antiquity*. Lawrence, KS: Coronado.

Casson, Ronald W. (1983) "Schemata in Cognitive Anthropology." *Annual Review of Anthropology* 12:429–62.

Cicourel, Aaron V. (1985) "Text and Discourse." *Annual Review of Anthropology* 14:159–85.

De Beaugrande, Robert (1980) *Text, Discourse and Process: Toward a Multidisciplinary Science of Texts*. Advances in Discourse Processes 4. Norwood, NJ: Ablex.

Detweiler, Robert (ed.) (1985) *Semeia* vol. 31: *Reader Response Approaches to Biblical and Secular Texts*. Decatur, GA: Scholars.

Elliott, John H. (1990) *A Home for the Homeless: A Sociological Exegesis of I Peter, Its Situation and Strategy*. 2nd ed. Minneapolis: Fortress Press.

Fishman, Joshua A. (1971) *Sociolinguistics: A Brief Introduction*. Rowley, MA: Newbury House.

Garfinkel, Harold (1967) *Studies in Ethnomethodology*. Englewood Cliffs: Prentice-Hall.

Hall, Edward T. (1976) *Beyond Culture*. Garden City: Doubleday.
—— (1983) *The Dance of Life: The Other Dimensions of Time*. Garden City: Doubleday.
Halliday, Michael A. K. (1978) *Language as Social Semiotic: The Social Interpretation of Language and Meaning*. Baltimore: University Park.
Harste, J., C. Burke and V. Woodward (1982) "Children's Language and World: Initial Encounters With Print." pp. 105–31 in J. Langer and M. Smith-Burke (eds) *Reader Meets Author: Bridging the Gap – A Psycholinguistic and Sociolinguistic Perspective*. Newark, DE: International Reading Association.
Haviland, S. E. and H. H. Clark (1974) "What's New? Acquiring New Information as a Process in Comprehension." *Journal of Verbal Learning and Verbal Behavior* 13:512–21.
Iser, Wolfgang (1972) "The Reading Process: A Phenomenological Approach." *New Literary History* 3:279–89.
Johnson, Allen W. (1978) *Quantification in Cultural Anthropology: An Introduction to Research Design*. Palo Alto: Stanford University Press.
Lord, Albert R. (1960) *The Singer of Tales*. New York: Atheneum.
Malina, Bruce J. (1982) "The Social Sciences and Biblical Interpretation." *Interpretation* 37:229–42; reprinted pp. 11–25 in Norman K. Gottwald (ed.) *The Bible and Liberation*. Maryknoll, NY: Orbis Press.
—— (1983) "Why Interpret the Bible with the Social Sciences?" *American Baptist Quarterly* 2:119–33.
—— (1986) "Reader Response Theory: Discovery or Redundancy." *Creighton University Faculty Journal* 5:55–66.
—— (1988) "Patron and Client: The Analogy Behind Synoptic Theology." *Forum* 4/1:2–32.
—— (1993) *The New Testament World: Insights from Cultural Anthropology*. Rev. ed. Louisville: Westminster/John Knox.
Meyer, Bonnie J. F. and G. Elizabeth Rice (1984) "The Structure of Text." pp. 319–51 in P. David Pearson (ed.) *Handbook of Reading Research*. New York: Longman.
Moore, Stephen D. (1988) "Stories of Reading: Doing Gospel Criticism As/With a 'Reader.'" pp. 141–59 in David J. Lull (ed.) *Society of Biblical Literature 1988 Seminar Papers*. Atlanta: Scholars.
Ong, Walter J. (1982) *Orality and Literacy: Technologizing of the Word*. New York: Methuen.
Rostagno, Sergio (1976) "The Bible: Is an Interclass Reading Legitimate?" pp. 19–25 in *The Bible and Liberation – Political and Social Hermeneutics*. Berkeley, CA: Community for Religious Research and Education.
Sanford, A. J. and S. C. Garrod (1981) *Understanding Written Language: Explorations of Comprehension Beyond the Sentence*. New York: John Wiley and Sons.
Whorf, Benjamin L. (1956) *Language, Thought and Reality: Selected Writings of Benjamin Lee Whorf*. Ed. John B. Carroll. Cambridge, MA: MIT.

31

Part II

THE QUESTION
OF FIRST-CENTURY
MEDITERRANEAN
PERSONS

2

FIRST-CENTURY MEDITERRANEAN PERSONS

A preliminary view

INTRODUCTION

It is curious, to say the least, that many Americans read the Bible and claim to understand what its authors mean. For early Christian authors and their audiences were radically different from contemporary US Bible readers in the way they thought of persons. Americans inevitably consider persons individualistically, as psychologically unique beings. This feature is apparent from our television programming from the nightly news through soaps to talk shows. If these shows are any indication, they demonstrate that Americans are totally bent on understanding the self, on solving individual problems individualistically, on realizing individual potential. The stories we share and which rivet our attention invariably point to the individual self pursuing its self-fulfillment in an unfriendly, often hostile social world (Berman 1987:100–102). When Americans take up their Bible, they inevitably bring the same set of expectations to their scriptural reading as they bring to their TV viewing. In both persons are always understood individualistically and psychologically. The purpose of this chapter is to suggest an alternative scenario for imagining the Mediterranean persons who appear on the pages of the Bible, specifically on the pages of the gospels and letters. In this alternative scenario, persons are not considered individualistically; in fact, first-century Mediterranean persons never thought psychologically in the way we do. Even speaking of those human beings as "persons" is somewhat of an anachronism since there is no word for "person" in Hebrew, Greek or Latin. Hence when I use the word "person" of biblical personages and their contemporaries, I mean only "individual human being."

First-century Mediterraneans knew other people "socially," in terms of gender-based roles, in terms of the groups in which a person was ever embedded, and with constant concern for public awards of respect and honor. I should like to call this way of understanding persons a scenario of the strongly group-bound individual, or strong group collectivistic person for short. This sort of individual contrasts with the mainstream US person who is weakly group-bound and most often feels himself or herself not bound to any group at all. This is the weak group individual, the individualistic person, for short.

I therefore suggest that perhaps biblical authors and their original audiences perceived human beings and human activity quite differently from people in the US. Perhaps they thought rather differently about who a person might be and what might be the expected range of human behavior. Such a suggestion is not terribly surprising. The fact is that for some time now, historically minded critics of the Bible have called attention to the deviant personality types described in biblical books. Among more recent authors, Heikki Räisänen, for example, has argued that in his letters, St Paul shows himself to be a less coherent and less convincing thinker than is commonly assumed; Paul's conception of the law is inconsistent, unintelligible and unarguable (1986:3–24). Räisänen's arguments are quite persuasive. Yet granted that Paul developed the type of argument that he did, why would first-century eastern Mediterranean people respect and give allegiance to a person who was incoherent, unconvincing, inconsistent, unintelligible and opaque? Given their mode of attachment to Paul, were the apostle's Greek-speaking audiences derived from a first-century Mediterranean in which "a strong individualism prevails in most segments of Greek society alongside of a search for community" (Doohan 1989:49), or is such a description simply a retrojection of contemporary US experience into the world of early Christianity?

What sort of scenarios for understanding human beings both as persons and as groups must contemporary readers bring to their gospel and epistle reading so that their authors might be understood in a fair and equitable manner? Recent attempts at understanding Mediterranean persons include Stendahl's hypothetical intuitions about Paul deriving from his history of ideas approach (Stendahl 1963), quite similar to Rappaport's approach to Josephus' personality (Rappaport 1976). Such intuitive approaches offer little by way of testable explanation. On the other hand, Theissen's psychobiology (1987) and Callan's rather straightforward psychological assessment (1987, with an excellent overview of previous psychological studies) overlook the difficulties involved in psychological analysis. Psychologically oriented historians as a rule give little attention to the problem of selecting some adequate analytic framework from the many that exist (Prochaska 1979). Moreover, they often ignore the obstacles to an adequate psychological assessment of absent, idiosyncratic subjects which have been well articulated by Stannard (1980). Stannard's arguments have not been shaken by the insistence, for example, of Doohan (1984) or Vanhoye (1986) that it is necessary and legitimate to study Paul's unique personality in terms of modern psychology. The question is how to carry off the task in some intellectually responsible manner.

Given the various constraints involved in dealing with individual, unique personalities in cross-temporal and cross-cultural perspective, it seems that at present the best we can attempt is a type of regional character study, patterned after the national character studies of the 1940s and 1950s. These studies have been picked up once again, now under the label of social psychology (see Seelye 1985:35–6). In our case the goal will be a social psychology built upon a circum-Mediterranean modal personality, along with the idiosyncrasies of the culture and distinctiveness of social structure in the given time and place. On the basis of such a configuration, we might discuss cultural groups and the types of personalities such groups might allow for.

To begin with, then, I submit that early Christian authors and their audiences did not at all comprehend the idea of an individual person in his or her uniqueness. To underscore this aspect of Mediterranean perception I open with a consideration of the strong group individual.

MEDITERRANEAN PERSONS

As a cultural orientation, US individualism is still a totally alien way of being a person in the Mediterranean region. If this is true today, it certainly was true of the past. Geertz has tried to develop a somewhat precise and specific definition of the "individual" as founded in current, mainstream US behavior. He tells us that the individual here is "a bounded, unique, more or less integrated motivational and cognitive universe, a dynamic center of awareness, emotion, judgment and action organized into a distinctive whole and set contrastively both against other such wholes and against its social and natural background." And he goes on to note that this way of being human is, "however incorrigible it may seem to us, a rather peculiar idea within the context of the world's cultures" (Geertz 1976:225). To understand the persons who populate the pages of the canonical Christian writings, then, it is important not to consider them as individualistic. No first-century person would see Jesus or anyone else as *personal* Lord and Savior. First-century Mediterraneans were simply unaware of the personal, individualistic, self-concerned focus typical of contemporary American experience. Given Mediterranean social experience, such self-concerned individualism would appear deviant and detrimental to other group members. For group survival it would be dysfunctional, and hence dangerous. Behavior that indicates self-concerned individualism is noticed, but it is disdained and variously sanctioned. If those people were not individualistic, what or how were they?

For people of that time and place, the basic, most elementary unit of social analysis was not the individual person considered alone and apart from others as a unique being, but the dyadic person, a person always in relation with and connected to at least one other social unit, usually a group. Contrast, for example, an American and somebody like Paul attempting to explain why they might regard someone as abnormal. The American will look to psychology, to childhood experiences, personality type, to some significant event in the past that affects an adult's dealing with the world. Biography in the US is a description of psychological development in terms of singular events of an individualistic, unique person passing through the psychological stages of life. An abnormal person is assessed as one who is psychologically "retarded," or one who is deviant, because "neurotic" or "psychotic" through "having been an abused child," and the like (see Malina and Neyrey 1996).

The ordinary Mediterranean person, in the past and present, is not psychologically minded. In fact Mediterraneans, as a rule, are anti-introspective. For elite ancients, basic personality derives largely from ethnic characteristics which are rooted in the water, soil and air native to the ethnic group. Aristotle, for example, has noted:

> Let us now speak of what ought to be the citizens' natural character. Now this one might almost discern by looking at the famous cities of Greece and by observing how the whole inhabited world is divided up among the nations. The nations inhabiting the cold places and those of Europe are full of spirit but somewhat deficient in intelligence and skill, so that they

continue comparatively free, but lacking in political organization and capacity to rule their neighbors. The peoples of Asia
on the other hand are intelligent and skilful in temperament,
but lack spirit, so that they are in continuous subjection and
slavery. But the Greek race participates in both characters, just
as it occupies the middle position geographically, for it is both
spirited and intelligent; hence it continues to be free and to
have very good political institutions, and to be capable of ruling
all mankind if it attains constitutional unity. The same diver-
sity also exists among the Greek races compared with one
another: some have a one-sided nature, others are happily
blended in regard to both these capacities.

(*Politics* 1327b1–2 Loeb)

Fuller explanation of how the characteristics of various ethnic groups
derive from the places they inhabit, the air they breathe and the
water they drink is clearly set forth in the Hippocratic corpus,
becoming common knowledge among elites, and points of honor
among non-elites as well (see *Airs, Waters, Places*; Strabo, *Geography*).
And just as ethnic groups have their own geographical location,
they likewise evidence geographically rooted ethnic stereotypes by
which other groups might assess them. For example, Tiberians have
"a passion for war" (Josephus, *Life* §352 Loeb); Scythians "delight
in murdering people and are little better than wild beasts" (Josephus,
Against Apion §269 Loeb); "Cretans are always liars, evil beasts, lazy
gluttons" (Titus 1:12); in "the seamanship of its people . . . the
Phoenicians in general have been superior to all peoples of all times"
(Strabo, *Geography* 16.2.23 Loeb); "this is a trait common to all the
Arabian kings" that they do "not care much about public affairs and
particularly military affairs" (Strabo, *Geography* 16.4.24 Loeb).

Furthermore, with their unsurprising ethnocentrism, ancient
Mediterraneans divided the peoples of the world in terms of their
own broad ethnic reference group and the rest of the world. Thus
while Greek writers in general spoke of "Greek and Barbarian" (for
example, Strabo, *Geography* 1.4.9 Loeb; also Paul at Rom. 1:14),
Paul of Tarsus would speak of "Judean and Greek" (Rom. 1:16 and
passim; 1 Cor. 1:24 and *passim*; Gal. 3:28; Col. 3:11), a perspective
evidenced in the narrative of Acts (Acts 14:1; 18:4; 19:10.17; 20:21).

Ancient biography is a description of a person's having fulfilled
stereotypical roles that cluster to form a sort of typical prominent
or deviant status, with no particular attention paid to psychological

developmental stages apart from raw physiological growth periods (i.e. childhood and adulthood). What is distinctive about a person's life is not psychological or personal development but the events that a person had to confront (read, for example, any of Plutarch's *Lives*). For the abnormal, a Mediterranean such as Paul, for example, would say "Satan prevented us," "hand him over to Satan," "they are sinners," "he was possessed." Plutarch explains the demise of those responsible for the death of Julius Caesar as follows:

> However the great guardian genius (*megas daimon*) of the man, whose help he had enjoyed through life, followed upon him even after death as an avenger of his murder, driving and tracking down his slayers over every land and sea until not one of them was left, but even those who in any way soever either put hand to the deed or took part in the plot were punished.
> (*Lives: Caesar* 59.2 Loeb)

And Josephus tells us that in a battle with Sulla and royalist troops outside of Bethsaida Julias, his horse, stumbled in a marshy spot, and he broke his wrist; "and my success on that day would have been complete had I not been thwarted by some demon" (*Life* §402 Loeb). Such designations of abnormality indicate that "the person is in an abnormal position because the matrix of relationships in which he is embedded is abnormal" (Selby 1974:15). The problem is not within a person but outside a person, in faulty interpersonal relations. There really is nothing psychologically unique, personal and idiosyncratic going on within a person at all. All people in a family, neighborhood or town situated in a distinctive region are presumed to have the same experiences. If any distinctions hold, they are regional and gender-based.

This does not mean that strong group people have weak egos. Once egos are formed in such cultures, individuals are strong enough not to alter in the slightest, even in an alien environment with hostile and competing values. The strong group person has an ego embedded in the group. As a matter of fact, all members of the group share a mutuality of perspective, a virtual identity with the group as a whole and with its individual members. There is no polarity or binary opposition between the individual and the group in which he or she is embedded. Such an embedded ego carries within values and voices which echo years after one might be transplanted to some new location. The formation and thorough embeddedness of the ego in the social reality of the group is much like the formation and embeddedness of the embryo in the womb. Thus the embedded, strong group ego is a mode of social psychological being, just as the embryo emergent from the womb is a mode of biological and psychological being.

In other words, to paraphrase Geertz,

> our first-century person would perceive himself as a distinctive whole *set in relation* to other such wholes and *set within* a given social and natural background; every individual is perceived as embedded in some other, in a sequence of embeddedness, so to say.
>
> (Malina 1993:68)

Such persons define themselves rather exclusively in terms of the groups in which they are embedded; their total self-awareness emphatically depends upon such group embeddedness. To paraphrase M. Bowen (1978), one might say that such persons are immersed in and share "an undifferentiated ethnic ego mass." And they believe that other persons are part of such an undifferentiated mass as well. For example, since in Mediterranean perspective all Americans form an undifferentiated ethnic ego mass, it would be impossible for a Middle Easterner to view the kidnaping of a single American as a random act. There is nothing random about kidnaping a person belonging to an opposing group since any group member equally well represents the whole group.

Strong group persons do not seem to go through the stages of ego formation typical of Western individualistic persons. Although they are single beings, individual persons, presumably unique in their individual being as Americans are, their psychological ego reference is primarily to some group, not primarily to some unique self. It is groups that are unique, not individual persons. If it is true to say that ego always mediates between group needs (the collective) and individual needs (the unique), then weak group individualists suppress consciousness of group needs and keep individual needs in constant focus. On the other hand, strong group individuals suppress consciousness of individual needs and keep group needs at the forefront of their attention. The strong group problem is that it is usually the immediate group's (family, faction, village, neighborhood of a city) needs that are the focus of interest, not that of the total ethnic group. Josephus, for example, notes that for the Israelite priesthood, it is this larger society that is of concern: "At these sacrifices prayers for the welfare of the community must take precedence of those for ourselves; for we are born for fellowship, and he who sets its claims above his private interests is specially acceptable to God" (*Against Apion* §196 Loeb); here "private interest" means private group-interest, not private individual-interest as it would mean in the US. For such strong group persons, "I" always connotes some "we" (inclusive of the "I"). While the "I" is a single individual, one can presume that any communication from such an "I" is invariably a communication from a "we." And all strong group persons know what "we's" are involved in their singular interactions.

We might say, with good reason, that a type of social as opposed to psychological awareness pervades strong group persons. They are not psychologically minded at all. They are simply not introspective. For example, consider the institution of keeping females away from males. Philo tells us:

> Market-places and councils-halls and law-courts and gatherings and meetings where a large number of people are assembled, and open-air life with full scope for discussion and action – all these are suitable to men both in war and peace. The women are best suited to the indoor life which never strays from the house, within which the middle door is taken by the maidens as their boundary, and the outer door by those who have reached full womanhood.
>
> (*Special Laws* 3.169 Loeb)

This is a gender division of space, male and female space, men's and women's quarters. Such separation is replicated by other gender-based space prohibitions (at the common outdoor oven or common water supply) as well as by the presence of persons whose task it is to maintain such separation, for example, chaperons.

For an understanding of biblical morality, it is important to realize that such techniques for gender separation indicate that behavioral controls exist in the social situation, not in the individual conscience. Behavioral controls are social, deriving from a set of social structures in which all persons are expected to participate and to which they are to adhere. Quite definitely, behavioral controls are not within the person. Hence behavioral controls are definitely not "psychological," inwardly assimilated and under the control of the choice of "conscience." It is situations that are controlled and that control, not individual persons following internalized norms. Group members invest the controlling and controlled situation with the full force of custom. Consequently, people do not expect others

42

to control their behavior by following internalized norms; the individual conscience is simply not an ethical norm, sacred or otherwise (Hall 1959:114).

On the other hand, a person is expected to lose control in certain social situations, while persons in the vicinity are required to furnish the restraining force. For example, close women relations are to attempt to jump into the grave of the deceased but also to be held back by others; individuals ready to square off in a fight expect those around them to hold them back; feuds go on escalating, yet mediators are to intervene to restrain the feuding parties (see Boehm 1984). Similarly, Mediterraneans have traditionally believed that a male could not possibly suppress the strong urges that surely take possession of him every time he is alone with a pre-menopausal woman. And women are considered even more unable to resist males. Persons of both sexes, then, do not expect personal inhibition to suffice to control their behavior; rather "will power" is expected to be furnished by other people (Hall 1959:66–7). Consequently, being strongly embedded in a group entails strong social inhibition along with a general lack of personal inhibition.

The stories and ethical systems of Israelite Yahwism, Mediterranean Christianity, Rabbinic Jewish religion and Islam have duly codified these social, anti-introspective and non-individualistic beliefs. The values and lines of behavior which tend to strengthen group cohesion are considered positive values, virtues. On the other hand, those values and lines of behavior which can in any way be detrimental to group cohesion are considered negative values, vices or sins. Notice that all biblical ethical inventories, whether the traditional Ten Commandments (Exod. 20:2–17), or the directives of the Sermon on the Mount (Matt. 5–7), or the listing of "the evil things that come from within and defile a man" (Mark 7:21), or Paul's catalogue of the "works of the flesh" (Gal. 5:19–21; see also 1 Cor. 6:9–10) – all these are essentially and fundamentally concerned with the maintenance and strengthening of group cohesion. These inventories highlight dysfunctional behaviors that directly lead to inner-group antagonisms and group dissolution. As such they are directed to members of the group, whether it be Israel (Ten Commandments), the revitalized house of Israel of Matthew (which is not to be "like the Gentiles who salute only their brethren" Matt. 5:47), or the community using Mark's gospel, or Paul's Corinthian and Galatian Christians.

In other words, these ethical lists are not universalizing. They are not even remotely concerned with individual spiritual development, growth in holiness, paths of perfection, personal relationship with God and the like. They are not lists of vices to be avoided by the individual soul in its journey back to God. They all presume the presence of other people, either other group members or outsiders, since they are aimed at maintaining good relations especially with fellow group members. Such codification points to the strong group quality of such ethical systems. Sanctions against their transgression would be sought in community control rather than individual responsibility (for example, Deut. 21:18 or 1 Cor. 5:3). To understand how Mediterranean persons are socialized in strong group fashion, one must begin, it would seem, with the main social institution of the region, kinship.

SEEING THE WORLD
THROUGH KINSHIP LENSES

While all human societies presumably are witness to kinship institutions, the Mediterranean world treats this institution as primary and focal. E. T. Hall (1959:144) has noted relative to some male who wishes to invite a female out for a date:

> The choice as to whether he acts or not is his. What is not his to decide fully is the language he will use, the presents he can give her, the hours he can call, the clothes he can wear, and the fact that in the United States the woman has the ultimate say in the matter.

Now Hall continues, quite apropos our discussion here:

> An American these days will not normally consider the revenge of the brothers as a price for seeing a woman without her family's permission, nor will it cross his mind that she might lose her life if she chooses to be intimate with him. These are not "alternatives" which occur to him as he is weighing the choice of patterns available to him. Death of the woman and revenge on the man are within the expected range of behavior in the less Europeanized parts of the Arab world. This sort of example is rather obvious and is the type of point which has been made many times and dismissed just as many times. Our rationalization is that it is "uncivilized" to kill one's sister just because she was intimate with a man. What we often don't know and have difficulty accepting is that such patterns fit into

44

larger overall patterns and that what is being guarded is not the sister's life (though she may be deeply loved) but a centrally located institution without which the society would perish or be radically altered. This institution is the family. In the Middle East the family is important because families are tied together in a functional interlocking complex. The accompanying network (and obligations) satisfies many of the same functions that our government satisfies. The sister is a sacred link between families and, like the judge in our own culture, she has to remain above reproach. Thus it is usually necessary to take a second look at the more obvious differences in behavior because they often hide or grow out of more fundamental differences that are just beginning to be studied: differences which control behavior in a way that was never dreamed of, that are not conventions implying a choice but rules that are so constant that they are not recognized as rules at all.

(Hall 1959:144–5)

In fact in the whole Mediterranean world, the centrally located institution maintaining societal existence is kinship and its set of interlocking rules. The result is the central value of *familism*. The family or kinship group is central in social organization; it is the primary focus of personal loyalty and it holds supreme sway over individual life. Family integrity is to be valued above all. To understand familism better, to better develop the scenarios necessary to "read" Mediterranean communications better, we shall contrast it with the US central value of economic success. For Americans and a growing number of northern Europeans, the main social institution is economics.

Economics in the US

As US persons grow up they find that almost all the social arrangements which circumscribe the life of their community are centered on the single issue of the production and consumption of goods. Decisions about marriage are largely determined by one's ability "to afford to get married," and it surely costs exorbitant amounts of money to get elected to political office, even though the office itself is not bought! Adult self-worth is pivoted on income generation, and police logs are full of daily listings of thefts and burglaries, while a significant amount of attention is given to preventing the

45

possibility of private property transgression. A huge military machine is maintained at great cost largely to protect American economic interests all over the world. US foreign policy moves in the same direction, with little if any concern for the freedom, democracy and well-being of other peoples. The overall value of the illegal drug trade, so vital to the payment of Third World debt to US banks, is always assessed in terms of its street dollar value, never in terms of the number of families ruined, individuals crippled, persons dead.

The reason for this pervading awareness of property rights is that economics with its focal communicative behavior in quantitatively assessed production and consumption is central. The management of the economic area is not only linked to the sexual (kinship) and political areas, but also constitutes the very basis of all the strategies in these two domains. Credit means economic credit. Kinship, religion and politics are embedded in economics, i.e. the norms of kinship, religion and politics are determined directly or indirectly by economics. Here persons owning and/or controlling wealth ultimately make the laws that determine the social order; the wealthy rule. If the Reagan administration demonstrated anything from 1980 to 1988, it is the truth of the aforementioned observations. And the situation has not changed with Bush or Clinton.

All this cannot fail to create a definite self-image in the minds of both men and women, as well as a definite image of the physically and mentally incapacitated classes. The poor are judged to be poor largely, if not exclusively, because of their unwillingness to take up gainful employment and adhere to the rules of the economic game. Young people grow up believing that success means economic success, that profit orientation (called "greed" in the Mediterranean) is virtuous, that regardless of the demands of public communal well-being, private property is sacred. The present distribution of wealth is largely due to self-made individuals and their desire to "earn" more while keeping the competition at bay. Thus, were it not for the property rights of the wealthy classes, the rules for "fair" competition and the legal punishment that would be meted out to competitive individuals if caught in theft, burglary or market manipulation offense, all the prohibitions hammered into a person would be unable to inhibit him or her from realizing his or her greed orientation by acquiring and utilizing all the valued things he or she might encounter. And the young person comes to consider the US enculturated acquisitive drive (drive to succeed, success orientation) so strong that only the legal and social impediments to acquiring and consuming more prevents a person from further pursuit of his or her desire. The image which the young person has of the goods of youth (cars, money, clothing, etc.) complements this self-image. The drive to acquire such goods is equally strong, and should he or she but manage to acquire one of them, everything that youth can have and do would soon be his or hers. In fact, as the popular view has it, the status-giving quality of goods is greater than personal qualities by far. What one has, what one possesses, what one controls through ownership are far more important than what sort of person one is. Consider the moral and intellectual fiber of the publicly known wealthy, such as federal officials (for example, at HUD and the IRS in 1989), government appointees, ambassadors and the like.

The self-image of the producer/consumer is practically identical with this through various stages of life. A person is brought up to believe that once one has the consumer goods one longs for, one will be irresistible to others, successful and uncontrolled by anyone. Therefore one must never allow oneself to be found in a situation of want or lack. The average US person has been taught to believe from childhood that it is quantities that count; the good aspects of persons and the good things in life are those that are duly quantifiable. *How much* and *how many* are the best indicators of human meaning. And it is only external circumstances that can prevent a person from acquiring a portion that would significantly raise one's social standing. These views and expectations are, of course, self-fulfilling. In a society in which everybody believes that, unless prevented by circumstances, a person can in fact "make it" economically, they will behave accordingly. The wealthiest individuals in the country are duly listed annually (for example, in *Forbes*, while *Fortune* lists the most "successful" corporations).

Thus the acquisition of goods is both sought after and feared. While such acquisition is urgently sought after in the competition to "make it," once the goods have been acquired there is great fear in losing what has been acquired so dearly. Various sorts of savings plans and insurance policies are geared to allay such fear and to provide the security that ultimately counts, and that is economic security. Both emotions of guarding what one has and competing for more are experienced with considerable intensity. Perhaps this intensity can be taken as an indication of the intensity of childhood repression of acquisitive interest, i.e. being "selfish" or "self-willed." After adolescence this repression creates a strong sense of frustration for most US persons as they try to "make it." If, however, the social controls break down, or are eliminated, the repressed acquisitiveness engendered by the frustrated drive to have breaks through to the surface and seeks its expression for mainstream "good" Americans in white-collar crime, in petty thefts and tax cheating, as well as other property-focused aggression. Such aggression expressed as "greed" is also found in the attempt of the wealthy to acquire economic advantage through political control, i.e. through holding office, supporting those in office, influencing legislation, all focused on the amassing of ever greater wealth. The 110 or more cases in which members of the Reagan administration and/or their appointees were indicted and/or convicted point to such crimes in the name of wealth and wealth acquisition (a list of persons involved can be found in *Time*, May 25, 1987). Surely those cases are merely the tip of a pervading iceberg of behaviors deriving from US mainstream values.

That the foregoing considerations make sense to some extent to most Americans simply points to their presence in US society. The Mediterranean, on the other hand, does not share this central concern with money or with the economic institution(s) of society.

Kinship in the Mediterranean

Anyone living in the Mediterranean will quickly realize the heavy emphasis on and concern regarding gender-specific behavior as well as on the sinfulness of sex and its desirability. Traditionally, as Mediterraneans grow up, they find that almost all the social arrangements which circumscribe the life of their community are centered on the single issue of preventing the possibility of sexual transgression. While these arrangements have changed to a great extent in the cities of southern Europe, they are still alive in Mediterranean villages, European and non-European (see Gilmore and Gilmore 1979; Saunders 1981; Sabbah 1984). The reason for the traditional emphasis on the prevention of sexual transgression is that kinship, with its focal communicative behavior in cohabitation, is central. Here "the management of the sexual area is not only linked to the economic and political areas, but also constitutes the very basis of all the strategies in these two domains" (Sabbah 1984:15). Credit is more a matter of one's honor rating based on kinship than of collateral in goods. Even today, religion, politics and economics are embedded in kinship, i.e. the norms of religion, politics and economics are determined directly or indirectly by the kinship institution. Here well-born persons rooted in the "best" families control society in their role of patrons. Hence the constant concern to show that one is well-born and from the best of families (for example, Josephus, *Life* §1–6 Loeb; the genealogies in Matthew and Luke; Paul's pedigree in Phil. 3:5).

The extreme Mediterranean emphasis on the human genitals (for example, circumcision, phallus as evil-eye apotropaic, castration concerns), on sexual transgression and on the male's uncertainty of his maleness are part of the same scenario, as I shall describe subsequently. Here I wish to note that focus on legitimate cohabitation and the constant threat of sexual transgression fail to create a definite self-image in the minds of both men and women, as well as a definite image of the opposite sex. Young people grow up believing that were it not for the segregation of the sexes and the vengeance that would be surely meted out on the young man if caught in a sex offense, all the prohibitions hammered into him would be unable to inhibit him from having intercourse with the first woman he encountered. Young men come to consider their own sex drive so strong that only the physical impossibility of sexual access to the women of his social circle (because of their segregation, supervision, etc.) prevents them from satisfying their urges. The image young men are provided of girls and women complements this self-image. Of course, this image of females has been developed and maintained by males. According to this picture, the female sexual drive is equally strong. So should he but manage to corner any female alone, she might put up a wild show of resistance at first, but once he as much as kissed her, she would give in and readily become his. In fact, it is popularly assumed that a woman's lust is greater than that of a man, hence the even greater urgency to keep women duly circumscribed.

Women, in turn, are enculturated to believe this feminine self-image. Girls are brought up to believe that once they might find themselves alone with a male, they would be unable to resist his advances. Therefore the proper female must never allow herself to be found in such a situation. Girls are taught to believe from childhood that the central human being is the male – his honor replicated symbolically in his sexual drive. Thus from childhood, girls are led to believe that the mere sight of a woman is sufficient to arouse a man sexually, and only external, social circumstances can prevent him from having his way with her. These views and expectations are, of course, self-fulfilling. In a society in which

49

everybody believes that a man and a woman will inevitably have sexual relations unless prevented by circumstances, both of them will behave accordingly.

Sexual relations apart from marriage are invariably prohibited and therefore feared because of possible loss of paternal or fraternal honor. A young woman who has had sexual relations apart from marriage becomes unmarriageable, and hence an economic burden to her aging parents or brothers. Yet such sexual relations are spoken of as most desirable and therefore sought after. Both the fear of sexual relations and the desire for them seem to be experienced with considerable intensity. This feature can be taken as an indication of a desire for the mother that is especially strong and strongly repressed, as in areas where the father-ineffective family prevails (see Carroll 1986:222). The repression of this desire is tantamount to a childhood repression of sexual interest. After adolescence this repression creates an intense feeling of frustration which expresses itself in the agonistic aggression typical of the region.

Mediterranean families are structured variously, just as value preferences in the region differ from society to society. There are traditional endogamous communal structures typical of the Eastern sector as well as various nuclear family arrangements (see Hanson 1989a, following Todd 1985). Beyond these significant local variations, however, what Mediterraneans have in common relative to kinship is that inheritance follows the male line and that males represent the family to the outside (Hanson 1990), while females are expected to uphold the inside. Furthermore, there is a preference for marrying persons as closely related as possible; this is the well-known Mediterranean endogamy (Hanson 1989b). Finally, Mediterraneans are occasionally polygynous (legally, in Islam, illegally in Christian countries with a mistress system). We might say, then, that the Mediterranean family is patrilineal and rooted in a sharp gender division of labor. And since kinship is the focal institution, the family of this sort is the norm for understanding all other groupings. Thus any larger social aggregates are considered mere extensions of the family, enlarged super-families. All significant groups are usually the offspring of a single eponymous ancestor whose progeny have dwelt in a given land from time immemorial. Hence, in biblical perspective, note the ultimate unity of all Israelites, Romans, Arabs and any other chthonic people, and of all Mediterranean mankind from the original, single, Middle Eastern "earthling" (this is what the Hebrew 'adam means).

Given the principle of familism, individuals participate in all larger social groupings only through their family (domestic and political religion, occupation groups, political factions). All adults (those in middle or upper rungs of family hierarchy) would oppose any change that might disrupt or weaken the family since their social security is intimately bound up with the structure as it stands. Where familism is central and family the actual framework of life, a person learns to relate to others on a highly *social, ingroup-oriented* basis. A basic prerequisite for a truly social and ingroup-oriented exchange is for the interacting persons all to believe that they have some common bonds to tie them to the same group, from shared blood to mutual acquaintances to common heritage. They have to come to see that somehow they are members of the same group; they are "brothers" or "kinsmen." The family, the village or city quarter and the work group facilitate relations generally confined to group members in such social organizations of intense social interaction. In other words, without some sort of perception that a given individual and the person with whom he or she interacts are somehow attached to each other, somehow related to each other, interpersonal behavior remains extremely wary. Should there be nothing in common between them except common humanity, then the interaction is viewed as totally fraught with danger, like coming across a foreigner, an unfamiliar tree or dog or some other unexpected and unknown circumstance. On the other hand, given the dynamics of traditional Mediterranean demographics, apart from invasion, military occupation or enslavement, for such people to encounter an unknown person was an extremely rare occurrence in the past, and slightly more frequent today.

NO CHILDREN, ONLY SONS AND DAUGHTERS

Mediterranean parents do not beget children. Rather the babies born are immediately evaluated in terms of gender, as male babies and female babies, as boys or girls (cf. biblical birth announcements). The underscored gender differentiation of offspring from birth replicates the Mediterranean mode of marking off the world in terms of gender. Just as selves are male and female, so are the categories of others, nature, time, space and God(s). "For Providence made man stronger and women weaker . . . and while he brings in fresh supplies from without, she may keep safe what lies within" ([Ps.-Aristotle =] Theophrastus, *Oeconomica* 1344a4 Loeb). Males represent the family

51

to the outside; females keep it intact on the inside. Males own everything in the family that goes to the outside; females are in charge of what stays on the inside. Males defend the family from the outside; females maintain its integrity on the inside. The Mediterranean gender division of labor carries over quite emphatically into all spheres of life, unlike in US experience, where explicit gender division is confined, as a rule, to cosmetics, clothes and most public rest rooms.

Furthermore, since these male and female babies are enculturated into strong group families, they are quickly attuned to the fact that they are sons and daughters of certain fathers and mothers whose honor and shame engulf them. All the various members of the family will interfere in a person's life to steer or mislead. This is especially notable for males with their outward orientation. A male may not make decisions without consulting his near relatives and the senior members of his group. He lives in a compact organization in which everyone knows everyone else's business. From infancy on, males and females are trained to locate themselves securely within their group. Thus every utterance or deed goes through the censorship exercised by a person's ingroup orientation. Outgroup influences are minimal, and extraordinary behavior is rare. What might seem odd to non-Mediterraneans (for example, concern with the evil-eye, women with power to cast spells, sorcery accusations and the like) all fall within categories quite at home in the culture at large. The result is that all or most social contacts, as in any traditional society, are emphatically ingroup oriented and intense, with a resulting *personalization of problems*. This means that every obstacle is a person-related problem whose resolution marks a return to normalcy and whose non-resolution escalates an already wary, anxious way of living. Thus nearly all of life's problems are with "who's," not with "what's."

This emphasis on the ingroup-oriented, social dimensions of life is most vividly illustrated by the Mediterranean attitude toward space and the planning of residential quarters. Eickleman (1989:106) has noted that even a small town might have thirty to forty neighborhoods or quarters in the perception of its residents. One's neighborhood or quarter consists of households

> claiming multiple personal ties and common interests based on varying combinations of kinship, common origin, ethnicity, patronage and clientship, participation in factional alliances and spatial propinquity itself. . . . Only those clusters of households

evaluated as sustaining a particular quality of life are known as quarters. . . . [C]omponent households in a quarter assume that they share a certain moral unity so that in some respects social space in their quarter can be regarded as an extension of their own households. This closeness is symbolized in a number of ways: the exchange of visits on feast days, assistance and participation in the activities connected with births, circumcisions, weddings, and funerals of component house-holds, and the like. . . . Because of the multiple ties which link the residents of a quarter, respectable women who never venture to the main market can circulate discreetly within their quarter, since the residents all assume a closeness to each other.

(Eickelman 1989:106–7)

The point is that houses put together in a section of town do not form a neighborhood or city/town quarter. Residential space "is not prin-cipally in terms of physical landmarks but in shared conception of the social order" (Eickleman 1989:107). Perceptions and assessments of the spatial order are rooted and follow one's understanding of how people are situated and relate to each other; that is the social order.

In the Mediterranean world, infant boys are pampered, while infant girls are often treated strictly. More efforts are made to safe-guard and preserve the life of a boy child, who is more valuable, than that of a girl. In the first century, the Judean people consisted primarily of male ethnics, "the sons of Israel," "the sons of Abraham," "the house of Israel," with the woman's position quite ambiguous. The same held true of Christian groups: God did not talk *through* women unless when unmarried, their fathers were present (for example Philip's daughters in Acts 21:8–9) or unless when married, their husbands were present and duly respected (as Paul insists in 1 Cor. 11:2–16), or unless they were beyond childbearing age (as in Luke 2:36–7). That the angel of the Lord appears to Mary in Luke (and not to a male as in Matthew) concerning the birth of Jesus is not that extraordinary in the question of childbirth. For as a rule, God did not talk *to* women either, although there is a "biblical policy" which "allows women characters to hold direct discourse with God (or his agent) only in a 'procreative' context" (Fuchs 1982:153). And this is fully in accord with the "gender division of labor" char-acteristic of the circum-Mediterranean.

The traditional Mediterranean gender evaluation of offspring would seem to result in distinctive outcomes rooted in upbringing

(Bouhdiba 1977). Little boys learn that their maleness consists in not being female, with little more information than that. The reason for this is that for the first seven or more years of his life, the boy is always with women whom, he is later informed, he is expected *not* to be like. Adult males are not to be found around the house, as a rule, during most of the day. In such father-deficient arrangements role models are either not continually present or when present have little to do with children. Hence the boy is encouraged to live out a male role which is problematic and largely elusive. Consequently, as in other androcentric societies,

> masculinity must be won not only through internal and external struggle, but also through continual affirmation. Manhood therefore is not only "created culturally" in these societies, as has often been observed, but also culturally and publicly sustained. Inevitably both the conferral and maintenance of masculinity carry visibly competitive overtones, especially in societies which emphasize sexual distinctions, at least through invidious comparison. Conversely femininity may depend more often on natural functions and is therefore often less problematical.
>
> (Gilmore 1987:9)

Given the focus of the kinship institution and the familism rooted in it along with the male obligation to maintain the family and represent it to the outside, Sabbah's observation is quite apropos to envisioning economics embedded in kinship and its social psychological bearing:

> For example, given the exaggeration of the erotic dimension, certain economic problems are experienced as sexual problems. This is the case with a man's economic failure. The unequal distribution of wealth, widespread unemployment, the chancy character of jobs and wages reduces the buying power of males (if they have any). And since virility in patriarchal Muslim society is defined in terms of economic power, economic failure is experienced by the male as castration, as a problem with virility, as impotence. In the same way, the invasion by women of economic spaces such as factories and offices, which is an economic fact of development, is often experienced as erotic aggression in the Muslim context, where the female body, defined as *'urya* (nudity), has been neutralized by the tradi-

54

tional structuring of space (seclusion of women and the wearing of the veil when moving through male space).

(Sabbah 1984:17)

Furthermore, Nawal El Saadawi has perceptively noted an aspect of Arab childrearing that fits the Mediterranean in general:

> The tendency to exaggerate a boy's feeling for his own ego and masculinity will usually end in an inferiority complex, since he will always feel that he is unable to rise up to the image expected of him. On the other hand, a tendency to exaggerate the need for a girl to withdraw, and to shrink into an attitude of passivity (under the guise of femininity and refinement) tends to build up in her a form of superiority complex which results from the feeling of being better than the image that has been created for her. A superiority complex creates masochistic tendencies in women, and an inferiority complex breeds sadistic and aggressive tendencies in men. Both of these are compensatory mechanisms and are the two faces of the same coin.
>
> (Saadawi 1982:81)

If the evaluation and rearing of children in the eastern Mediterranean is in fact traditional, there is little reason to expect first-century persons not to have shared the tendencies described above. Males will tend to be sadistic and aggressive, willing to inflict pain on everyone except ingroup adult males (friends and family) in order to realize their goals, whether these others be children, wives or enemies. On the other hand, females will be masochistic, yet with an inflated sense of importance, especially after marriage and a son. And it will be sadism and aggression on behalf of the family that will be underscored as male virtue, while women will be lauded for their heroic masochism. The replication of these traits in Mediterranean values should bear out their controlling influence on behavior.

NO PARENTS, ONLY FATHERS AND MOTHERS

Just as offspring are rated in terms of gender, so too are parents. The roles of father and mother, just like the husbands and wives who play them, rarely if ever touch or overlap. The father dominates the family and represents it to the outside. Everything that relates the family outwardly is controlled by the father and is male: inheritance, land in the surround, jural relations (i.e. relations on the father's side), farm animals and implements, adult sons. On the other hand, everything that maintains the family inwardly is in the mother's purview and is generally female: the kitchen, non-jural relations (i.e. relations on the mother's side), milkgoats and other household animals, chickens, unmarried daughters, resident daughters-in-law, boys until old enough to be with the father.

Mothers and sons

While sibling relations are close, the mother–son bond is vaunted as the closest of Mediterranean affective relations. It is a distinctive by-product of Mediterranean childrearing practices. This mother–son attachment is based on mutual *need*: hers for a son to demonstrate her maturity and value to the ingroup, and his for a nurturing, caring figure in face of the general absence of adult males and the rather cruel process of "being a man." For what is distinctive of Mediterranean males is gender-identity ambivalence, revealed in their vehement abhorrence at or disavowal of everything "feminine." The result is a continued defense, through honor/shame polarities and prohibitions, against unacceptable female identifications.

According to contemporary Freudian psychology, the reason for this is that the primary (preoedipal) ego identification of children is with mothers, with the nurturing parent. Boys have to switch their gender identification to fathers during the oedipal stage (while girls do not), and this identification process involves a dis-identification from mother followed by a counter-identification with father. This process of dis-identification and counter-identification is impeded in the absence of available fathers or male surrogates who might act as counter-role models or psychic magnets (see Carroll 1986). In the Mediterranean, boys are raised under domestic arrangements excluding adult males, and hence lack discriminate male objects during this developmental period.

> This male remoteness has two important ramifications given the other related factors described here. First is that boys, confined to a female-dominated space, are denied an accessible male figure with whom to identify at the precise time that the primary gender-identity formation process is going on. Second is the consequent emotional closeness and affective "symbiosis" of mothers and sons – a pan-Mediterranean trait. In Portugal the "mother–son bond is thought to be the strongest possible

bond between two human beings" (Cutileiro 1971:112). In
Italy this bond is the "primary axis" of family continuity
(Parsons 1969:55); in Greece it is "indestructible" (Campbell
1964:168). Moreover, this uniquely powerful bond originates
in a domestic scene in which the boy often perceives the mother
– typical in Mediterranean societies – as dominant or "in-
charge" or as the "primary handler of the family's financial
resources" (Rogers 1975:734–735). One may argue reasonably,
therefore, that these widespread structural features impede a
solid male gender identity and promote early psychic identification with the more accessible parent, the mother.

(Gilmore 1987:14–15)

Plutarch tells us that once Alexander the Great received a letter from
Antipater denouncing Alexander's mother. But "after reading a long
letter which Antipater had written in denunciation of her, he said
Antipater knew not that one tear of a mother effaced ten thousand
letters" (*Lives: Alexander* 39.7.688 Loeb). On the other hand, there
is an abiding feeling that the world is secretly run by women, another
perpetual challenge to masculine autonomy.

Fathers and sons

Gilmore likewise makes a point, deriving from the previous one,
that has to do with the traumatic rupture of removal of the boy
from female society into the society of men. This removal takes place
without ritual and symbolism: there is no facilitating male initiation
ceremony or rite of passage for this stage. In societies where boys
are confined to the feminine domain until puberty or so, adolescent
boys are usually subjected to stressful or painful rites of passage
by which they "become" men and renounce female associations.
Mediterranean societies lack such formalized rituals. Hence, without
clear-cut consensual rupture with femininity and without biological
markers to signal manhood, each individual male must prove himself
according to group expectations. The male lives with the constant
threat of being considered feminine unless he can demonstrate otherwise. Hence the need for continual and unrelenting proof focused
on honoring the penis as repository of manhood and mirror of
masculine ego in the cult of phallic potency through sexual triumphs.
   The result is the Mediterranean hypermasculine syndrome, which,
as Gilmore notes, "almost always includes a distancing dread of the

feminine" and "a phallocentric worldview." The dread of and separation from the feminine points to the underlying belief that the masculine is both the overwhelmingly powerful self-definer and inherently endangered. Consequently males are ever vigilant and defensive when it comes to their maleness. Dread of the feminine derives from the residue of primary female identifications which are never fully eliminated. This dread and resulting separation from the female represent a "reaction formation" or masculine protest against unacceptable wishes to be like the mother, to be dependent, not to have a penis.

> The result is a distancing dread of the feminine and is the phallocentric worldview. . . . A major theme in this attitude is its defensiveness: it is a panegyric to what is, the phallus, since this contributes the minimal anatomical definition of a cherished manhood. But it is also a prophylactic stance, reflecting a fear of loss, or impairment, or diminishment of the male genital through the hostile action and shaming of other men or domineering women. . . . Hence the compensatory hypervaluation of the male genital and the almost priapic obsession with phallic assertion in the ethnomasculinities of the Mediterranean societies.
>
> (Gilmore 1987:13)

Relative to clarifying the social outcomes of the gender division of labor in the Mediterranean, Gilmore observes:

> [T]here is the unusual degree of absention of Mediterranean males generally from domestic affairs, reinforced by the rigid separation of public and private worlds . . . there is lack of institutionalized *rites-de-passage* from boyhood to a public conferral of masculinity in the Mediterranean cultures. . . . A rigid spatial and behavioral segregation of the sexes and the consequent domestic division of labor is probably the most striking physical characteristic of Mediterranean community life. . . . The virtual absence of males from the home implies that boys as well as girls are reared until puberty in an exclusively female environment.
>
> (Gilmore 1987:14)

It is unmanly for a father to stay around the house, to remain much in the house, to be concerned and involved with childrearing, not to avoid childrearing concerns, to give any child care, to act other than formally and distantly with his children, to stay remote from his children.

As for *fathers and daughters*, we might note here that their lives are rather completely separated. A daughter is subordinated to her father's authority, rarely sees him in a situation suitable for interacting and remains with him for but a short part of her lifetime. At the earliest marriageable age she is surrendered to her in-laws after proper ritual passage focused on the marriage transaction (on the social psychology of family relations, see Cuisenier 1975: 438–47).

TYPICAL PERSONALITY FEATURES

In comparison with mainstream US Bible readers, the Mediterraneans depicted in those texts were expected to be ever vigilant concerning their gender-based behavior. Here, given space constraints, I focus mainly on males since this is the general thrust in ancient Mediterranean literature. Males were free to express their feelings unreservedly. When they described themselves they tended to exaggerate. They believed that important events in their lives were caused by persons rather than impersonal causes. Finally, in their conversations, they felt it important to communicate how they felt far more than to articulate some interesting fact or other. Let us consider each of these features in turn.

Expression of feelings

Mediterranean cultures, as previously noted, usually provide a vent through which suppressed emotions can, at least occasionally, break into the open. This culturally approved outlet is the flare-up of temper, flashes of anger, aggression and violence, which are condoned by society and readily forgiven. This type of behavior tends to veer from one extreme to the other, being polarized between the two contrasting syndromes of self-control and wild outbursts of aggressiveness. While these seizures last, Mediterraneans are permitted to follow their feelings and go on a rampage. Hostility can thus easily become non-rational. Once they pass, sincere contrition follows, accompanied by bafflement and a total lack of comprehension of what one has done and how one could have done it. This sort of behavior, however, is generally confined to males, who are otherwise expected to show their emotions. Thus that Jesus felt sorry for various people is frequently noted (Matt. 9:36; 14:14; 15:32; 20:34; Mark 1:41; Luke 7:13). Herod (Matt. 2:16), Jesus' fellow villagers in Nazareth (Luke 4:28), the ten against James and John (Matt. 20:24), the chief priests and scribes (Matt. 21:15) and Jesus himself (Mark 10:14) are described as indignant, i.e. showing displeasure, indignation, for some reason or other. Paul's letter to the Galatians fits this category as well. Males who do not show their feelings are suspected of lacking a vital human trait, hence not dependable (Patai 1983:67). The show of emotion was an attribute of the honorable man. Thus we are told that Caesar pronounced a eulogy for his young wife (which was unusual since this was done only for older women) resulting in popular sympathy "so that they were fond of him, as a man who was gentle and full of feeling" (Plutarch, *Lives: Caesar* 5.2 Loeb). Caesar burst into tears when reading and thinking about Alexander's kingship as a youth (11.3 Loeb); and he wept at the death of his mortal enemy, Pompey (48.2 Loeb). Similarly, "Cato was the only one to commend his course [Pompey's], and this from a desire to spare the lives of his fellow citizens; for when he saw even those of the enemy who had fallen in the battle, to the number of a thousand, he burst into tears, muffled up his head, and went away" (41.1 Loeb). Finally, when Cicero took leave of his brother, "after embracing one another and weeping aloud, they parted" (Plutarch, *Lives: Cicero* 47.2 Loeb). Males read and write poetry (along with the poems in the Bible, note, for example, how Alexander the Great often sponsored poetry contests, mentioned by Plutarch, *Life of Alexander* 4.6.666; 29.1.681 Loeb). They are not expected to be too logical. They embrace and kiss in public (Matt. 26:48 and parallels; Luke 7:45; Acts 20:37; Rom. 16:16, etc.) and speak of their emotional attachment to each other (Phil. 1:8; Christians are urged to be emotionally attached to each other: Eph. 4:32; Phil. 2:1; 1 Pet. 3,8). Women are considered to be coldly practical (see Prov. 31:10–31).

Cathartic communication

As is generally known, the strong group persons described in the gospel narratives and Pauline letters are perceived as "endowed with a heart for thinking, along with eyes that fill the heart with data; a mouth for speaking, along with ears that collect the speech of others; and hands and feet for acting." In the abstract, human beings "consist of three mutually interpenetrating yet distinguishable zones of interacting with the environment: the zone of emotion-fused thought, the zone of self-expressive speech, and the zone of purposeful action" (Malina 1993:74). Lack of alignment or overemphasis of one of these three functional planes of human existence, thoughts, words and actions is often indicative of ill health (see Pilch 1985).

Relatively to communication, we might say that when Mediterraneans speak with each other, their main focus is interpersonal in that the purpose of their interchange, no matter what else is going on, is always to maintain emotional ties, to get along, to continue some personal interaction or ingroup relation. It would seem that the thought processes of Mediterraneans are relatively less focused on "what is really going on" than on how the group feels about what is really going on. Consider the trouble to which post-Enlightenment biblical scholars have gone to figure out the content, the intellectual message, of the gospel! What, in fact, is the message of the gospel? Is this a misstated question?

It would seem that our Christian sources themselves are instances of interactive, cathartic-oriented communication. We read that both Jesus and Paul were after people changing their attitudes, not information sharing. Their appeal was one of emotion-fused thought, and hence far more than a simple intellectual solicitation. And the change they sought meant largely a greater relationship of attachment and loyalty to the God of Israel (Jesus) or to God in Christ (Paul). Similarly, the gospel narratives themselves tell far less about "what really happened" than about how group members ought feel about what happened and so be further attached in loyalty to God. In this the gospels are quite true to their cultural environment. To use categories other than those from which the documents derived will only lead to dissatisfaction and frustration, as demonstrated by reaction to modern, post-Enlightenment scholarship.

Since catharsis is far more significant than the content of communication, the mere verbal expression of a state of affairs is taken by the speaker as if it were an actual fact in evidence. What this means is that rather frequently, conversation in a Mediterranean setting that is not pragmatically oriented (i.e. directed to some concrete outcome, such as buying and selling) generally has no focal, intellectual meaning, even no conceptual message at all. Such dialogue is a series of statements or expressions that shows conversation partners not what a speaker is thinking but what is in the speaker's heart, how a person feels about a situation. Thus conversation is expected to allow one to empty oneself out, to cleanse oneself emotionally. In literature, the genre of this sort of conversation is a diary or journal, while as an oral form it is not unlike soap opera monologues. A person thus thinks aloud, listening to himself or herself in an expression of feeling and attitude. Thus the Mediterranean custom of several persons speaking at once. The subject is always the collectivistic self, always put into situations of pressure by others. While US soaps have the individualistic self measuring its own claims to happiness, or stating its own consciousness, or simply letting off steam, Mediterranean conversations have the collectivistic self measuring its own claims to honor, stating its own feelings about authorities, letting off steam provoked by pressures of opposed groups. What matters in the Mediterranean perspective is not the actual state of things, but the emotions which the state of things arouses. This cathartic dimension of conversation might well account for numerous features of the Pauline letters as well as the dialogues that become monologues in John.

Since catharsis, emotion, and interpersonal loyalties are intimately bound up in communication, the limitations of the real usually do not serve as a check upon what is being ideally described. Consider the divine birth of Alexander the Great from Olympias and the God Zeus Ammon (Plutarch, *Lives: Alexander* 2–4 Loeb). Of the divine Alexander, Plutarch observes: "In general, he bore himself haughtily towards the Barbarians, and like one fully persuaded of his divine birth and parentage, but with the Greeks it was within limits and somewhat rarely that he assumed his own divinity" (28.1.681 Loeb). At death, Alexander's body stayed incorrupt: "Most writers, however, think that the story of the poisoning is altogether a fabrication; and it is no slight evidence in their favor that during the dissensions of Alexander's commanders, which lasted many days, his body, although it lay without special care in places that were moist and stifling, showed no sign of such a destructive influence, but remained pure and fresh" (77.3.707 Loeb). In the context of such biographical features, John's gospel does not seem terribly unsual.

There is thus among Mediterraneans a relatively greater discrepancy between thought and speech on the one hand and action on the other. In action, one is hemmed in by experience and the reality which it leads one to perceive. Yet for Mediterranean ingroup members, thoughts and words have higher and independent truth rating; they manage to retain a relative independence from reality (see Patai 1983:310–11). As the focus of ingroup interaction moves from the real to the ideal, the honor of all involved is duly maintained and protected, if not increased. The emotion generated serves to bind group members more closely over against outgroups and to fill them with the mutually felt esteem needed to carry on in an often hostile world.

Personal causality

In a setting where the value of group membership and personal causality far outweigh goods, things and objective or "scientific" explanations, nearly all significant dimensions of living are personalized as well. Patai cites Tütsch (1959:141–2), who notes:

> [T]he personalization of problems goes so far in the Arab countries that even material, technical difficulties accompanying the adoption of elements of Western civilization are considered as resulting from human malevolence and felt to be a *humiliation*. The Arabs, who have accepted Western law and European institutions, whose clothing, food, means of transportation, yes, life as a whole, are more and more determined by Western technology and science, of course experience always new "humiliations" which in other places would be considered normal difficulties of growth, and eliminated. Where the Arab encounters an obstacle he imagines that an enemy is hidden. Proud peoples with a weak "ego structure" tend to interpret difficulties on their life path as personal humiliations and get entangled in *endless lawsuits* or throw themselves into the arms of *extremist political movements. A defeat in elections*, a risk that every politician must face in a democracy, appears to be such a humiliation that an Arab can thereby be induced without further ceremony to take up arms against the victor and the legal government, or to ally himself with those who promise him success the next time.
>
> (Patai 1983:284)

What Tütsch says of Arabs holds for village Mediterraneans in general. The point is that the Mediterranean feels enemies and humiliations where Americans make allowances for material, objective and, in any event, impersonal difficulties. Similarly, successful outcomes when dealing with material, objective and impersonal difficulties such as lighting a fire, slaughtering an animal, finding something lost, or completing any task is considered triumph, a "victory" in which an enemy is vanquished.

Consequently, it would seem extremely important for the Bible readers to realize that to explain defeats and successes in terms of impersonal, objective factors instead of attributing them to personal factors would be to move into an unfamiliar terrain for a first-century Mediterranean. In other words, the explanatory models with which we are at home are totally alien to anything and anyone we might encounter in the Bible. The personages of the Bible keep personal factors operative, and this exclusively. And with personal factors operative, success indicates ability to overcome personal antagonists with the gratification that comes from this, while failure means personal impotence with the depression that this provokes.

CONCLUSION

This chapter is intended to provide a general orientation for the modern Bible reader as he or she attempts to imagine the types of persons found in the pages of his or her scriptural reading. I have suggested that first-century Mediterranean persons were strongly group-embedded, collectivistic persons. They were most concerned with family integrity. Since they were group-oriented, they were socially minded, attuned to the values, attitudes and beliefs of their ingroup. Because of their ingroup enculturation, they were used to assessing themselves and others in terms of stereotypes often explained as deriving from the geographical location of their group. Furthermore, since these persons were strongly embedded in a group, their behavior was controlled by strong social inhibitions along with a general lack of personal inhibition. Their prevailing social institution was kinship; familism was foremost in people's minds. And the primary way in which they made sense of the world was in terms of gender, by viewing persons as well as things, time and space in terms of male and female (for more information, see Malina and Neyrey 1991; 1996).

BIBLIOGRAPHY

Berman, Ronald (1987) *How Television Sees its Audience: A Look at the Looking Glass*. Newbury Park, CA: Sage.

Boehm, Christopher (1984) *Blood Revenge: The Anthropology of Feuding in Montenegro and Other Tribal Societies*. Lawrence: University Press of Kansas.

Bouhdiba, A. (1977) "The Child and the Mother in Arab-Muslim Society." pp. 126–41 in L. Carl Brown and Norman Itzkowitz (eds) *Psychological*

Dimensions of Near Eastern Studies. Princeton: Darwin.

Bowen, Murray (1978) *Family Therapy as Clinical Practice*. New York: Aronson.

Callan, Terrance (1987) "Competition and Boasting: Toward a Psychological Portrait of Paul." *Journal of Religious Studies* 13:27–35.

—— (1990) *Psychological Perspectives on the Life of Paul: An Application of the Methodology of Gerd Theissen*. Lewiston, NY: Edwin Mellen.

Carroll, Michael P. (1986) *The Cult of the Virgin Mary: Psychological Origins*. Princeton: Princeton University Press.

Cuisenier, Jean (1975) *Economie et parenté: leurs affinités de structure dans le domaine turc et dans le domaine arabe*. Paris/La Haye: Mouton.

Doohan, Helen (1984) *Leadership in Paul*. Wilmington: Michael Glazier.

—— (1989) *Paul's Vision of Church*. Wilmington: Michael Glazier.

Eickelman, Dale F. (1989) *The Middle East: An Anthropological Approach*. 2nd ed. Englewood Cliffs: Prentice-Hall.

Fuchs, Esther (1982) "Status and Role of Female Heroines in the Biblical Narrative." *Mankind Quarterly* 23:149–60.

Geertz, Clifford, (1976) " 'From the Native's Point of View': On the Nature of Anthropological Understanding." pp. 221–37 in Keith H. Basso and Henry A. Selby (eds) *Meaning and Anthropology*. Albuquerque: University of New Mexico Press.

Gilmore, David D. (1982) "Anthropology of the Mediterranean Area." *Annual Review of Anthropology* 11:175–205.

—— (1987) "Introduction: The Shame of Dishonor." pp. 2–21 in David D. Gilmore (ed.), *Honor and Shame and the Unity of the Mediterranean* (Special Publication of the American Anthropological Association #22). Washington: American Anthropological Association.

Gilmore, Margaret M. and David D. Gilmore (1979) " 'Machismo': A Psychodynamic Approach (Spain)." *Journal of Psychological Anthropology* 2:281–300.

Hall, Edward T. (1959) *The Silent Language*, Garden City: Doubleday.

—— (1983) *The Dance of Life: The Other Dimension of Time*. Garden City: Doubleday.

Hanson, K. C. (1989a) "The Herodians and Mediterranean Kinship, Part I: Genealogy and Descent." *Biblical Theology Bulletin* 19:75–84.

—— (1989b) "The Herodians and Mediterranean Kinship, Part II: Marriage and Divorce." *Biblical Theology Bulletin* 19:142–51.

—— (1990) "The Herodians and Mediterranean Kinship, Part III: Dowry and Inheritance." *Biblical Theology Bulletin* 20:10–21.

Malina, Bruce J. (1986) *Christian Origins and Cultural Anthropology: Practical Models for Biblical Interpretation*. Atlanta: John Knox.

—— (1993) *The New Testament World: Insights from Cultural Anthropology*. Rev. ed. Louisville: Westminster/John Knox.

Malina, Bruce J. and Jerome H. Neyrey (1991) "First-Century Personality: Dyadic, Not Individual." pp. 67–96 in Jerome H. Neyrey (ed.) *The Social World of Luke–Acts: Models for Interpretation*. Peabody, MA: Hendrickson.

—— (1996) *Portraits of Paul: An Archaeology of Ancient Personality*. Louisville: Westminster/John Knox.

Patai, Raphael (1983) *The Arab Mind.* Rev. ed. New York: Charles Scribner's Sons.

Pilch, John J. (1985) "Healing in Mark: A Social Science Analysis." *Biblical Theology Bulletin* 15:142–50.

Prochaska, James (1979) *Systems of Psychotherapy: A Transtheoretical Analysis.* Homewood, IL: Dorsey.

Räisänen, Heikki (1986) *The Torah and Christ: Essays in German and English on the Problem of the Law in Early Christianity.* Suomen Eksegeettisen Seuran Julkaisuja 45. Helsinki: The Finnish Exegetical Society.

Rappaport, Uriel (1976) "Josephus Ben Matitiahu [Flavius]: Remarks on his Personality and Deeds." *Ha-Umah* 15:89-95 (English trans. M. Mor).

Saadawi, Nawal El (1982) *The Hidden Face of Eve: Women in the Arab World.* Boston, MA:Beacon.

Sabbah, Fatna A. (1984) *Woman in the Muslim Unconscious.* Trans. Mary Jo Lakeland. New York: Pergamon.

Saunders, George R. (1981) "Men and Women in Southern Europe: A Review of Some Aspects of Cultural Complexity." *Journal of Psychoanalytic Anthropology* 4:435–66.

Seelye, H. Ned (1985) *Teaching Culture: Strategies for Intercultural Communication.* Lincolnwood, IL: National Textbook Co.

Selby, Henry (1974) *Zapotec Deviance.* Austin: University of Texas Press.

Stannard, David E. (1980) *Shrinking History: On Freud and the Failure of Psychohistory.* New York: Oxford University Press.

Stendahl, Krister (1963) "The Apostle Paul and the Introspective Conscience of the West." *Harvard Theological Review* 56:199–215.

Theissen, Gerd (1987) *Psychological Aspects of Pauline Theology.* Trans. John P. Galvin. Philadelphia: Fortress.

Todd, Emmanuel (1985) *The Explanation of Ideology: Family Structures and Social Systems.* Trans. David Garrioch. Oxford: Basil Blackwell.

Tütsch, Hans E. (1959) *Vorderasien in Aufruhr.* Zurich: Neuen Zürcher Zeitung.

Vanhoye, Albert (1986) "Personnalité de Paul et exégèse paulinienne." pp. 3–15 in Albert Vanhoye (ed.), *L'apôtre Paul: Personnalité, style et conception du ministère.* Louvain: Louvain University/Peeters.

3

THE MEDITERRANEAN SELF
A social psychological model

INTRODUCTION

Perhaps the most famous medieval New Testament hermeneuticist to translate the Synoptic gospels into the vernacular of thirteenth-century Italy was Francis of Assisi. His appropriations were dramatic, direct and dynamic rather than verbal, vapid and verbose. He sought positive, affirmative cultural equivalents in spite of the fact that he lived immersed in a society highly influenced by medieval Manichaeism. In his lifework, Francis would not allow that form of Gnosticism to filter out the basic humanity of the Good News that Jesus brought and was.

I mention Francis because of his interpretation of Jesus' invitation: "Whoever would be my disciple, let him deny himself, take up his cross, and follow me!" (Matt. 16:24). In St Bonaventure's description of Francis's dramatic appropriation of this injunction (I, 5 and II, 1–4, 1973:639–43), the climax comes when Francis physically cast off every piece of clothing that he wore since all he had was the property of the patriarchal authority controlling his life, his father. Naturally, he did this in public, since what sense would it make for a Mediterranean, even a medieval one, to undergo a symbolic stripping in private? We are then told that the local bishop, not to be outdone, took the opportunity to envelop Francis in his own cloak, thus symbolically subjecting him to churchly patriarchy in place of the previous kinship form.

The bishop's action apart, was Francis's interpretation of the gospel injunction on target? Or was it a medieval mirage so typical of the allegory of the period? What in fact would Jesus' injunction mean to his first-century Galilean contemporaries? The purpose of this chapter is to inquire into the meaning of Jesus' invitation to self-denial. Obviously such an inquiry requires clarification of the two terms involved: "self" and "denial." What is a self? Is the contemporary Euro-American self similar to the self of the ancient Mediterranean world? If the answer is positive, then denying or saying no to the self will be equivalent in today's world and in antiquity. If the answer proves to be negative, however, then the self-denial imaginable by persons today may turn out to be radically different from what Jesus and perhaps Francis had in mind.

Of course, in the area of self, it seems extremely useful to consider Francis of Assisi as a point of comparison with first-century Mediterranean selves. For Mediterraneans, whether ancient or medieval, rarely spoke in the psychological terms characteristic of individualistic cultures. Consider the total lack of personal information in such voluminous writers such as Bonaventure or Aquinas. The same is true for ancient writers in general, including those ancients connected with the New Testament writings, whether as authors or subjects. Instead of personal information, we are given stereotypical information about persons in terms of their family of origin, gender and geography, that is, about their kinship status and geographical moorings.

For Bonaventure, Francis's response to the gospel was rooted in the Synoptic invitation to self-denial. What was that passage about?

INVITATIONS TO SELF-DENIAL

The Synoptic passages that form the focus of this investigation are those statements about self-denial in Mark 8:34//Matt. 16:24//Luke 9:23. This set in the triple tradition is embedded in the context of Jesus' first announcement of his forthcoming death in Jerusalem, the first of three such announcements. The saying on self-denial comes as a climax to a previous saying about Jesus' death, as follows.

> From that time Jesus began to show his disciples that he must go to Jerusalem and suffer many things from the elders and chief priests and scribes, and be killed, and on the third day be raised. And Peter took him and began to rebuke him, saying, "God forbid, Lord! This shall never happen to you." But he turned and said to Peter, "Get behind me, Satan! You are a hindrance to me; for you are not on the side of God, but of men."
> Then Jesus told his disciples, "If any man would come after me, let him deny himself and take up his cross and follow me."
>
> (Matt. 16:24)

For whoever would save his life will lose it, and whoever loses his life for my sake will find it. For what will it profit a man, if he gains the whole world and forfeits his life? Or what shall a man give in return for his life?

(Matt. 16:21–6)

And he began to teach them that the Son of man must suffer many things, and be rejected by the elders and the chief priests and the scribes, and be killed, and after three days rise again. And he said this plainly. And Peter took him, and began to rebuke him. But turning and seeing his disciples, he rebuked Peter, and said, "Get behind me, Satan! For you are not on the side of God, but of men."

And he called to him the multitude with his disciples, and said to them, "If any man would come after me, let him deny himself and take up his cross and follow me.

(Mark 8:34)

For whoever would save his life will lose it; and whoever loses his life for my sake and the gospel's will save it. For what does it profit a man, to gain the whole world and forfeit his life? For what can a man give in return for his life?

(Mark 8:31–7)

But he charged and commanded them to tell this to no one, saying, "The Son of man must suffer many things, and be rejected by the elders and chief priests and scribes, and be killed, and on the third day be raised."

And he said to all, "If any man would come after me, let him deny himself and take up his cross daily and follow me.

(Luke 9:23)

For whoever would save his life will lose it; and whoever loses his life for my sake, he will save it. For what does it profit a man if he gains the whole world and loses or forfeits himself?

(Luke 9:21–24)

In the statement in question, the pattern is ABB'A': follow – self-denial – cross bearing – follow. Clearly, self-denial is parallel to taking up the cross. Now there is another tradition about taking up the cross that makes no reference to self-denial. Instead of reference to self-denial, there is emphasis on family denial. This is the Q tradition likewise cited in the *Gospel of Thomas*.

"Do not think that I have come to bring peace on earth; I have not come to bring peace, but a sword. For I have come to set a man against his father, and a daughter against her mother, and a daughter-in-law against her mother-in-law; and a man's foes will be those of his own household. He who loves father or mother more than me is not worthy of me; and he who loves son or daughter more than me is not worthy of me; and he who does not take his cross and follow me is not worthy of me."

(Matt. 10:34–8)

Now great multitudes accompanied him; and he turned and said to them, "If any one comes to me and does not hate his own father and mother and wife and children and brothers and sisters, yes, and even his own life, he cannot be my disciple. Whoever does not bear his own cross and come after me, cannot be my disciple.

(Luke 14:25–7)

Jesus said: He who does not hate his father and his mother will not be able to be my disciple (*mathetes*), and (he who does not) hate his brothers and his sisters and (does not) bear his cross (*stauros*) as I, will not be worthy (*axios*) of me.

(*GThom.* 55)

<Jesus said:> He who does not hate his fa[ther] and his mother as I (do), will not be able to be my [disciple (*mathetes*)]. And he who does [not] love his [father and] his mother as I (do), will not be able to be my [disciple (*mathetes*)], for (*gar*) my [mother] . . . but (*de*) she gave me life.

(*GThom.* 101)

Since renouncing one's kin group is parallel to taking up the cross, it would seem from this saying that such renunciation is equally much like self-denial. Further, kin denial and self-denial would both be equivalent to taking up the cross to follow Jesus. The collocation of this set, then, is very suggestive.

Many commentators pose the question of the source of these sayings (for example, Bultmann 1963; Langkammer 1977 *ad ver.* and their references). The Q and Thomas sayings would clearly antedate the Synoptic gospels. And it would seem that the block in Mark likewise antedates that gospel document since it is a compilation of disparate elements (Bultmann 1963:82) that cluster as part of the threefold announcement of Jesus' death. Such a threefold pattern is typical of oral lore. However, does any of the tradition derive from Jesus? That the triple tradition and Q/Thomas are pre-Synoptic suggests some reworking in those hidden halls of traditioning. In what direction? Some commentators call upon that one other passage in the Synoptics that likewise enjoins "taking up." This other tradition according to which Jesus equivalently asks people to take up something, not the cross, is that in M, dealing with what Jesus styles as "my yoke" (Langkammer 1977:215).

Come to me, all who labor and are heavily burdened, and I will give you rest. Take my yoke upon you, and learn from me; for I am gentle and lowly in heart, and you will find rest for your souls. For my yoke is easy, and my burden is light."

(Matt. 11:29–30)

There is a parallel of sorts to the first part of this statement in the *Gospel of Thomas*:

Jesus said: Come to me, for my yoke is benign (*chrestos*) and my rule is gentle; and you will find rest (*anaupasis – sic*) for yourselves.

(*GThom*, 90)

Since the *Gospel of Thomas* passage lacks any reference to "taking up" the yoke, the M saying about taking up the yoke is quite distinctive. The general consensus is that this M tradition is an Israelite Wisdom saying; "yoke" refers to behavior based upon distinctive Torah interpretation (see Suggs 1970:99–108; Bultmann 1962:159; both cite Sir. 51:23ff.; 24:19ff.; Prov. 1:20ff.; 8:1ff. as illustrative). To bear Wisdom's yoke means to keep to its ways of living out God's directives, to the Torah interpretation of Wisdom circles. To bear Jesus' yoke would mean, then, to keep to his way of living the Torah. The "easy" yoke is not one that is rather accommodating. Rather it is one that does not lead along misdirected pathways, but truly and directly leads to the goal of the Torah (Suggs 1970:108).

In sum, the primary data that serve as indicators of some original saying of Jesus in this tradition would include the triple tradition saying, the Q/Thomas saying and the M saying. How might we proceed to discover some original element(s) this regard? I base my suggestions on that famous principle of Bultmann's: "Conjectures are easy enough" (1963:161, n. 2).

First of all, the fact that Jesus was actually crucified, and that this datum was now applied to those bent on becoming members of the Christian movement group, would indicate that the mention of the cross was a later development of the tradition (although Langkammer 1977 thinks that it is an Old Testament reference to the *Tau* sign as, for example, Ezek. 9:4,6). Thus the feature of "taking up your cross" would be secondary. Likewise, it seems that reference to a yoke seems more indicative of Israelite custom rather than a pan-Mediterranean reference. The injunction to "Take up the yoke" would make as little general sense as that other famous M passage in which Jesus enjoins his apostles: "Go nowhere except to the lost sheep of the house of Israel" (Matt. 10:5).

71

Similarly, the mention of "becoming a disciple" also seems subsequent to simply following Jesus. Since Jesus was a faction founder, and the earliest traditions telling of how Jesus founded his faction consist of repeated "follow me" injunctions without "discipleship," the quality of the relationship of faction members to Jesus would not originally have been that of disciple to teacher. Initially, what Jesus' faction members were to do was proclaim the gospel of the kingdom and heal (as, for example, in Matt. 10:5ff.).

In the present forms of the tradition, the content of taking up the cross is defined by the preceding, parallel clause: to "deny self" in the triple tradition and to "leave family" in the Q/Thomas tradition. As I expect to indicate, there is really very little difference between the two. Given that the traditions about Jesus' teaching are invariably pictures or imaginable scenarios, however, I would opt for the description of the range of family members to be hated as original. Thus some original tradition would have run "If any man would come after me, let him hate father and mother [and other kin] and take up my yoke and follow me."

First in a context such as Matt. 10:36–7, with the rhythm of three occurrences of "is not worthy," a Wisdom *mashal* in a 2 + 1 form would run as follows:

> He who does not hate father or mother is not worthy of me; and he who does not hate son or daughter is not worthy of me; and he who does not take up my yoke and follow me is not worthy of me.
>
> (after Matt. 10:36–7)

Or in a context such as Matt. 11:28–30 coupled with Luke 14: 26–7:

> Come to me all who labor and are heavy laden, and I will give you rest. Take my yoke upon you, and learn from me; for I am gentle and lowly in heart, and you will find rest for your souls. For my yoke is easy, and my burden is light.
>
> If any one comes to me and does not hate his own father and mother and wife and children and brothers and sisters, yes, and even his own life, he cannot follow me. If anyone comes to and does not take up my yoke, he cannot follow me.
>
> (after Luke 14:26–7)

The point is that in the process of traditioning, the yoke falls out and the cross is put in. With this substitution, the saying takes on a broader scope. The yoke, bearing Jesus' interpretation of the Torah for the sake of the kingdom, is quite confined to Israel and the Torah. It undoubtedly belonged to the same stratum as the M saying:

"Go nowhere except to the lost sheep of the house of Israel" (Matt. 10:5).

In any event, it must have been a significant saying of Jesus for the practical life of Christian group members since it specified the conditions of following Jesus. This was subsequently called discipleship, the Christian way of life, that is, living in his way. What further underscores its significance is that it was reinterpreted early on, and this rather uniformly (unlike the saying on no divorce, for example, which has multiple interpretations).

The saying on taking up one's cross pointed to being ready to be shamed, to face shame, to be shamed even to death. The motivation for bearing such shame was for the sake of Jesus and the gospel, for the sake of professing the crucified Jesus. This reference to the cross and the motivation specified have wider scope. Shame fits into all the nooks and crannies of life. Following the Torah fits so many precepts or specific segments of life. "Take up your cross" thus generalizes a far more specific injunction or directive. Yet it surely fills out the meaning of Jesus' yoke by drawing the yoke's implications in terms of Jesus' actual fate.

In other words, while the yoke better fits the house of Israel, the cross could be universally amplified by Mediterranean experience, wherever Romans crucified, yet still relate to Jesus' distinctive yoke. Yet by whatever reading and regardless of whatever historical development be postulated, why would leaving the kingroup and/or taking up the cross be parallel to self-denial? What in fact is self-denial? To understand self-denial it is necessary to describe and define what is the self (as for asceticism in general, see Malina 1995). Here I intend to develop such a description and definition in the comparative way typical of social science criticism of the New Testament (see Elliott 1993).

CULTURE-BASED TYPES OF SELF

Descriptions of human behavior follow the paths of societal structures. Just as a computer has a disk operating system, so human groups have social structures which serve as humankind's operating systems. What makes the human system work at all, the electricity, so to say, is self-interest. And the goals, both proximate and ultimate, that social structures enable are values. There is close relationship among values, self-interests and structures. In individualistic cultures, self-interests are proper to single persons, while in collectivistic societies, self-interests are proper to ingroups.

Obviously, and not to be forgotten, the subject of the whole system that is operating is human beings in society, that is, persons in groups, individuals in environments, selves in relations. Persons in society are studied sociologically, individuals in environments are studied biologically, and selves in relations are studied psychologically (Harris 1989). This presentation deals with self/person in societal relations. This is the object of that fusion of perspectives called social psychology. Social psychology in fact "is about the mesh between the self and society" (Gamson 1992:53).

> The self here is defined as all the statements a person makes that include the word "I," "me," "mine," and "myself." This definition means that all aspects of social motivation are included in the self. Attitudes (for example, I like . . .), beliefs (for example, X has attribute Y in my view), intentions (for example, I plan to do . . .), norms (my ingroup expects me to do . . .), roles (my ingroup expects people who hold this position to do . . .), and values (for example, I feel that . . . is very important), are aspects of the self.
>
> The self is coterminous with the body in individualist cultures and in some of the collectivist cultures. However, it can be related to a group the way a hand is related to the person whose hand it is. The latter conception is found in collectivist cultures, where the self overlaps with a group, such as family or tribe.
>
> (Triandis 1990:77–8)

For the philosophical underpinnings of this enterprise, see Rom Harré (1980; 1984; 1989). Here we have the great help of social psychologists who have been working on descriptions of the self both specifically and generally, world-wide, for the past thirty years or so. The work of Harry Triandis and colleagues is most significant. It is on the basis of Triandis's masterful overview of research that I have developed the following contrasting descriptions of the individualistic and the collectivistic self. In their continuing investigation into social psychological types as matrices for culture, Triandis *et al.* have settled upon a continuum that runs from individualistic to collectivist. "Individualism," roughly speaking, means that individual goals precede the group's goals. "Collectivism" means that the group's goals naturally precede individual goals. With a view to comparison, I begin with a brief sketch of the individualistic notion of the self prevalent in the US. And then I move on to a description of the collectivistic self. The features laid out in sequence include the defining attributes of each cultural emphasis, the culture's virtues and other characteristic features, its socialization modes, self-conceptions, modes of social perception, advantages and disadvantages (of course, all in etic, comparative perspective).

Individualistic self and self-reliance

"Individualism" may be described as the belief that persons are each and singly ends in themselves, and as such ought to realize their "selves" and cultivate their own judgment, notwithstanding the push of pervasive social pressures in the direction of conformity. In individualist cultures most people's social behavior is largely determined by personal goals that often overlap only slightly with the goals of collectives such as the family, the work group, the tribe, political allies, coreligionists, fellow countrymen and the state. When a conflict arises between personal and group goals, it is considered acceptable for the individual to place personal goals ahead of collective ones. Thus individualism gives priority to the goals of single persons rather than to group goals. What enables this sort of priority is focus on self-reliance in the sense of independence, separation from others and personal competence.

For US individualists, freedom and self-reliance are important values, yet they are not the defining attributes of individualism. Rather the *defining attributes* of individualism are: distance from ingroups, emotional detachment and competition. Individualists, then, evidence much emotional detachment from others, extreme lack of attention to the views of others, relatively little concern for family and relatives and a tendency toward achievement through competition with other individualists.

Individuals do what makes sense and provides satisfaction rather than what must be done as dictated by groups, authorities, parents. While great guilt feelings might be triggered by abandoning the dictates of groups, authorities, and parents, the individual is above those dictates. The cardinal *virtues* of individualists include: self-reliance, bravery, creativity, solitude, frugality, achievement orientation, competitiveness, concern for human rights, pragmatism, freedom, competence, satisfaction, ambition, courage; and goals such as freedom and personal accomplishment. Success depends upon ability; the outcome of success is achievement.

Other characteristics include: sexual activity for personal satisfaction (rather than procreation), future orientation (but in terms of a short time perspective), emphasis on balanced reciprocity (that is, equal exchange), use of wealth to change social structures, instrumental mastery (need to dominate people, things such as the environment, events), exclusion of persons who are too different. Moreover, there is nearly exclusive emphasis on the nuclear family, with ready geographic mobility, the use of linear dance forms, a presumption of self-reliance and independence. Stress is placed on individual rights and individual privacy.

Consequently, *socialization* in individualistic cultures looks to what the person can do, to skills, and only secondarily to developing a sense of group identity. Children learn independence first of all. In child–mother relationships enjoyment and mutual satisfaction (having fun together) is what counts. Individualist socialization results in high scores in self–other differentiation. After parents, peer socialization is common, with a concomitant development of skills in dealing with peers (not with superiors or subordinates). Individualists perhaps never acquire skills to facilitate the functioning of a group.

Furthermore, in individualist societies, the individual's sense of insecurity is accompanied by large expenses for police and prisons. This feature is replicated by a national sense of insecurity with large military expenditures. Such cultures also display prejudice toward racial and religious groups that are too different, and toward unrealistic interpersonal relationships (and unrealistic international relationships), a significant amount of crime against persons (for example, sexual crimes, assault); more hospital admissions; and more drug abuse.

The *self* in individualist cultures is a bundle of personal attributes. Identity derives from what one has: skills, experiences, accomplishments, achievements, property. Attributes such as being logical, balanced, rational, fair, are considered important. Thus people define themselves by what they do in society, not by their ingroup memberships. Social functions are judged to be individually acquired attributes. So individualists often find the behavior of collectivists in intergroup relations quite "irrational." Individualists are emotionally detached from their ingroups and do not always agree with ingroup policies. Furthermore, individualists are extremely introspective and highly psychologically minded. Thus individual behavior is presumed to be best explained by internal psychological mechanisms rather than ingroup norms, goals and values. They perceive their ingroups as highly heterogeneous, and they experience little sense of a common fate with ingroup members. For they often have large ingroups (for example, the entire United States), with norms that are loosely imposed, and with boundaries that are not sharp and clear, but highly permeable.

The *social perception* of individualists is dominated by what others in some ingroup of significance are doing. Individualists belong to many ingroups, each of which controls only a narrow range of behavior (for example, some receive only organizational dues). Thus there is weak attachment to ingroups, with conformity to ingroup authorities determined by personal calculation; compliance can never be taken for granted. Language is low context, that is, the content of any communication is highly developed, spelled out in detail. In conflict, individualists side with horizontal relations (siblings, friends, equals) over vertical ones (government, parents).

Some of the *themes* distinctive to US individualist literature include: the dignity of humans, individual self-development, autonomy, privacy, the individual as the basis of society; individuals as used to analyze social phenomena, as the bases of political, economic, religious or ethical analyses; individuals as the sole locus of knowledge (Lukes 1973). In fact it has been demonstrated that US behavioral sciences, evolutionary biology and economic analyses are biased in favor of the scientists' own individualist culture, with little concern for broader human nature (Schwartz 1986).

The *advantages of individualism* include freedom to do one's own thing, maximizing satisfaction, self-actualization, creativity without having to pay the penalties of doing duty to the collective, of doing what the group expects, of meeting one's group obligations. In industrialized/information cultures, the advantage of individual action increases: independence, creativity, self-reliance. While individualists pursue an exciting life with a range of varied activities providing enjoyment and pleasure, at times such pursuit entails aggressive creativity, conformity and insecurity.

Thus some of the *negative concomitants* of individualism include the following. Interpersonal competition is often counterproductive (Rosenbaum *et al.* 1980) and can lead to distress and aggression (Gorney and Long 1980). Palmer (1972) finds individualism related to high competition concern for status, and violence. People in individualist cultures often experience more conflict within their families than people in collectivist cultures (Katakis 1978). The greater emphasis on achievement in individualist cultures threatens the ego (Katakis 1976) and causes insecurity. Insecurity leads to excessive concern about national security and feeds the arms race (Hsu 1981).

While in the contemporary world individualism can be found among the affluent and socially and geographically mobile, more modern segments of every society, individualistic cultures as a whole have emerged only where Enlightenment values have permeated society and agriculture has become the occupation of extremely few. The contemporary version of the individualistic self emerges rather late in human history. "The fundamental assumption of modernity, the thread that has run through Western civilization since the 16th century, is that the social unit of society is not the group, the guild, the tribe, the city, but the person" (Bell 1976:16).

Anthropological comparisons, however, indicate that contemporary hunter-gatherer peoples likewise fall on the individualistic side of the continuum, while modern agricultural primitives fall on the collectivistic. So Triandis postulates the stages of protoindividualism in ancient hunter-gatherer societies, collectivism in agricultural societies (presumably from sedentarization that began some nine thousand years ago), and finally neoindividualism in contemporary, post-agricultural societies beginning in sixteenth-century Renaissance city-states, with individualistic cultures underpinning the Industrial Revolution. The prime recrudescence of ancient individualism can be found in the neoindividualism that marks the industrialized, immigrant United States. The United States in nearly all examples – meaning immigrant, European United States – is emphatically individualistic, with all the typical traits of an exaggerated, overblown individualist culture.

In today's world, Triandis observes that 70 percent of the world's population are collectivistic, while the remaining 30 percent are individualistic (1990:48). As a matter of fact, individualism seems totally strange and esoteric, incomprehensible and even vicious to observers from collectivistic societies. Again, as Triandis notes, what is most important in the US, individualism, is of the least importance to the collectivistic cultures of the world (1990:50). Now, the point of all the foregoing observations is to demonstrate that any self that we might encounter in the New Testament, whether the Synoptic tradition or Paul, must necessarily be a collectivistic self.

78

Collectivistic self and family integrity

"Collectivism," in turn, may be described as the belief that the groups in which a person is embedded are each and singly ends in themselves. And as such these groups ought to realize distinctive group values, notwithstanding the weight of one's personal drive in the direction of self-satisfaction. In collectivist cultures most people's social behavior is largely determined by group goals that require the pursuit of achievements which improve the position of the group. The *defining attributes* of collectivistic cultures are family integrity, solidarity, keeping the primary ingroup in "good health."

The groups in which a person is embedded form ingroups in comparison with other groups, outgroups, that do not command a person's allegiance and commitment. Ingroups consist of persons who share a common fate, generally rooted in circumstances of birth and place of origin, hence by ascription. While individualists belong to very many ingroups, yet with shallow attachment to all of them, collectivists are embedded in very few ingroups. Collectivists are strongly attached to these few ingroups, and the ingroups in turn control a wide range of behaviors. A person's behavior toward the ingroup is consistent with what the ingroup expects; but behavior toward everyone else (for example, strangers) is characterized by defiance of authority, competition, resentment of control, formality, rejection, arrogant dogmatism, and rejection of influence attempts that have the outgroup as a source.

Collectivist *virtues* put the emphasis on the views, needs and goals of the ingroup rather than on single group members. These virtues include generalized reciprocity, obligation, duty, security, traditionalism, harmony, obedience to authority, equilibrium, always doing what is proper, cooperation, fatalism, pessimism, family centeredness, high need for affiliation, succor, abasement, nurturance, acquiescence, dependency, high superordination and subordination in the hierarchy.

Other characteristic features of collectivist cultures include the following. Sexual relations are exclusively for procreation, a fulfillment of social duty. The virtues extolled by collectivist cultures are social virtues, attitudes that look to the benefits of the group, rather than individualistic virtues. Thus we find virtues such as a sense of shame, filial piety, respect for the social order, self-discipline, concern for social recognition, humility, respect for parents and elders, acceptance of one's position in life, and preserving one's public image.

Thus anything that cements and supports interpersonal relationships is valued. The goal of life is ingroup (most often family) security and honor. The outcome of success in this enterprise is fame. Collectivist persons have many common goals with others in the group and engage in interpersonal relationships with a long time perspective (such as mother–son; while the child is growing, this is generalized reciprocity). They use wealth to maintain social structure.

Social norms and obligations are defined by the ingroup rather than determined by behavior to get personal satisfaction. Persons harbor beliefs shared with the rest of the ingroup members rather than beliefs that distinguish self from ingroup. And group members put great stock on readiness to cooperate with other ingroup members. In the case of extreme collectivism individuals do not have personal goals, attitudes, beliefs or values but only reflect those of the ingroup. Persons enjoy doing what the ingroup expects (Shweder and Bourne 1982).

Socialization patterns are keyed to developing habits of obedience, duty, sacrifice for the group, group-oriented tasks, cooperation, favoritism toward the ingroup, acceptance of ingroup authorities, nurturing, sociability and interdependence. The outcomes of such socialization produce persons with little emotional detachment from others, with broad concerns for family and greater tendency toward ingroup cooperation, and group protectiveness. Thus persons in such collectivist cultures will do what they must as dictated by groups, authorities, parents, rather than what brings personal satisfaction. The great temptation is to pursue some self-centered enjoyable activities. Should persons yield to such temptation and be found out, ingroup sanctions run from shaming to expulsion. In conflict, collectivists most often side with vertical relationships (parents, authorities) over horizontal ones (spouses, siblings, friends). Furthermore, collectivistic cultures often evidence language that is ingroup-specific (there are many local dialects), with people using context rather than content in conveying meanings; hence, high-context communication is prevalent.

The collectivist *self* is a dyadic self as opposed to an individualistic self. A dyadic self constantly requires another to know who one is. Thus the collectivist self is a group self that often internalizes group being to such an extent that members of an ingroup respond automatically as ingroup norms specify without doing any sort of utilitarian calculation. This is a sort of "unquestioned attachment" to the ingroup. It includes the perception that ingroup norms are universally valid (a form of ethnocentrism), automatic obedience to ingroup authorities and willingness to fight and die for the ingroup. These characteristics are usually associated with distrust of and unwillingness to cooperate with outgroups. Often outgroups are considered a different species, to be evaluated and treated like a different species of animate being.

Collectivist persons define self to outsiders largely by generation and geography: family, gender, age, ethnicity along with place of origin, place of residence. To outgroups, the self is always an aspect or a representative of the ingroup, which consists of related, gendered persons who come from and live in a certain place. To ingroup members, the self is a bundle of roles, ever rooted in generation and geography. One does not readily distinguish self from social role(s). The performance of duties associated with roles is the path to social respect. On the other hand, social perception is greatly prismed through who the other is, that is, to which group(s) he or she belongs.

Collectivist persons are concerned about the effects of their actions on others in the ingroup. They readily share material and non-material sources with group members. They are concerned about how their behavior appears to others since they believe that the outcomes of their behavior should correspond with ingroup values. All ingroup members feel involved in the contributions of their fellows and share in their lives. Thus individuals feel strong emotional attachment to the ingroup, perceiving all group members as relatively homogeneous, with their behavior regulated by group norms, based on acceptance of group authorities with a view to ingroup harmony and achievement at the expense of outgroups.

Collectivism is associated with *homogeneity of affect*; if ingroup members are sad, one is sad; if joyful, one is joyful (as in Rom. 12:15). Those in authority expect unquestioned acceptance of ingroup norms, and homogeneity of norms, attitudes and values. Interpersonal relations within the ingroup are seen as an end in themselves. There is a perception of "limited good" according to which if something good happens to an outgroup member it is bad for the ingroup, because "good" is finite and thus resources are always in a zero-sum distribution pattern. Finally, the ingroup is responsible for the actions of its members. This has implications for intergroup relations. Specifically, in collectivism one expects solidarity in action toward other groups. Joint action is the norm. Authorities usually decide what is to be done, and the public must follow without question. Good outcomes for the other group are undesirable, even when they are in no way related to one's own outcomes. Each individual is responsible for the actions of all other ingroup members, and the ingroup is responsible for the actions of each individual member. Thus, for instance, ancient Israelites related to Romans in response to Roman policies toward the house of Israel as if each Roman were the maker of those policies. The Romans, in turn, interpreted the actions of individual "Judeans" (the Roman outgroup name for the house of Israel) which fitted their general ideological framework as the actions of all "Judeans."

All things being equal, collectivists seek to maintain harmony with humans and things, and hence to live in harmony with the environment. They try to include those who are different, and tend to be non-competitive. With their emphasis on proper interpersonal relationships (all things being equal), they have less crime against persons (for example, sexual crimes, assault), fewer hospital admissions, less drug abuse.

Collectivists evidence high rates of social support when unpleasant life events occur. Naroll's (1983) review of the evidence suggests that the very positive social indicators characterize societies in which the primary group is a normative reference group that provides strong social ties, emotional warmth, and prompt punishment for deviance; is culturally homogeneous; and includes active gossip, frequent rites, memorable myths, a plausible ideology and badges of membership.

In the contemporary world, societies characterized by collectivistic cultures have low rates of homicide, suicide, crime, juvenile delinquency, divorce, child abuse, wife beating and drug and alcohol abuse and are characterized by good mental health. On the other hand, such societies are also characterized by dissatisfaction with the excessive demands of family life and by low gross national product per capita, and by poor functioning of the society in the political realm. Thus there is a trade-off between quality of private and quality of public life, which are kept quite separate.

Obviously, our Mediterranean ancestors in the Christian tradition were essentially collectivistic. Now when we read descriptions of the appropriations of New Testament injunctions in the past, my question is why did those people, who were equally collectivistic, appropriate those injunctions in the way they did? Where did they put their emphasis? How would their Christianity be distinctive in its own way? How would it matter in collective life?

PSYCHOLOGICAL FOCUS OF SELVES:
IDIOCENTRIC AND ALLOCENTRIC

The foregoing comparison contrasts two types of cultures, the individualistic and the collectivistic. The researchers who have gathered information about these types of culture would situate the "pure" types at opposite ends of a spectrum. For the fact produced by this research is that people are enculturated in terms of socialization patterns that run along an axis whose extremes are totally individualistic and totally collectivistic. There seems little to indicate that first-century Mediterranean societies were anything other than collectivistic. And the situation seems to have stayed this way well into the European Renaissance period (notwithstanding the unverifiable assertions of French philosophers quoted by Perkins 1992:245–7).

Along with the cultural setting of human socialization, Triandis *et al.* (1993) have further pointed out the value of taking note of the psychological bent of individuals within both individualistic and collectivistic cultures. For persons in all cultures reveal an individual psychological orientation that likewise ranges along a scale from idiocentric to allocentric. Idiocentric persons are, of course, self-centered, while allocentric individuals are other-centered. With this perspective, we can say that just as in our individualistic society, we have narcissistic, self-centered individualists as well as other-centered individualists, so in antiquity, there were self-centered collectivists and other-centered collectivists.

The value of this further nuance is to distinguish the self as socialized because of cultural cues (individualistic and collectivistic), and the self as oriented by interpersonal, psychological experience.

DEFINED SELVES: PRIVATE, PUBLIC, INGROUP

There is one more perspective on the self that specifically looks to the mesh between person and culture. While still in the context of the individualist and collectivist model, Triandis notes the various ways in which persons deal with the way their selves are specifically defined in the process of socialization and in later social experience. For a person's self is in fact defined by a variety of factors. Triandis distinguishes among the privately defined self, the publicly defined self and collectivistically defined or better, ingroup-defined, self. The outcomes of these processes of defining the self are as follows. First of all, there is a "private self" deriving from what I say about my traits, states, behaviors. Then there is a "public self" that refers to what the general group says about me. Finally there is a "collective or ingroup self" referring to what the ingroup says about me (Triandis 1990:77–83).

What is significant for understanding the self in terms of social psychology is the way the defined selves emerge in the contrasting cultural types. Thus people from collectivist cultures sample and take stock of ingroup self-assessments far more than people in individualist cultures. In collectivist cultures there is a general inconsistency between private self and public self. People do not tell you what they personally think, but what you need or want to hear. This split is required by politeness and face (for example, no public insult to a shameless person). Thus people are enculturated to think one way and speak another. For the most part, getting along with others is valued above all sorts of other concerns. Saying the right thing to maintain harmony is far more important than telling the truth above all. People are not expected to have personal opinions, much less voice their own opinions. It is sufficient and required to hold only those opinions that derive from social consensus. Social behavior derives from relative status where hierarchy is the essence of social order.

In individualist cultures, the public and private selves converge because two inconsistent selves cause the individual to experience dissonance as well as to undergo a sort of information overload. Furthermore, in individualist cultures, the public and private selves are influenced by the same factors. People are expected to be "honest" even if ignorant, "frank" even if brutal and "sincere" even if stupid. Here one must think and say the same thing. Social behavior derives from individualist choices based on one's class affiliation.

To summarize the perspectives on the self that have been presented up to this point, consider Figure 1.

Within prevailing individualistic or collectivistic cultures, single persons may turn out to be idiocentric or allocentric. When it comes to behavior springing from the ways in which the self is defined, however, individualists as a rule fuse private and public selves (the single line in the figure), while collectivists separate private and public selves while choosing a public self that is usually in harmony with the ingroup self (the shaded line). Deviations from such general orientations readily stand out. Consider the case of the prophet.

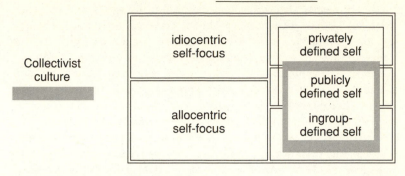

Figure 1 Perceptions of the self

PROPHETS

We learn of the prophetic role in the Bible as a collectivist cultural role. Now, from the point of view of defined selves, what is distinctive of prophets is their willingness to have their private self and their public self coincide. (This is also childish and childlike in collectivism – as in "The Emperor's New Clothes"). While people in these societies are to suppress their private self in favor of an ingroup-shaped public self, the prophets let private and public self coincide. Thus to individualist Bible readers, prophets sound honest, frank, sincere, direct. They "tell it like it is" or ought to be. This feature of a prophet's behavior, therefore, is not surprising to individualistic persons since this is normal individualist behavior. But that is not the case in collectivistic cultures.

One reason why prophets must make their private self coincide with the public self is that the burden of their message is rooted in a private experience of revelation. The same is true of experiences involving dreams, visions and stars, for example. Thus in collectivist contexts, prophets (and magi and astrologers) seem to fall into individualistic interludes in their normally collectivistic lives, interludes characterized by altered states of consciousness (see Pilch 1993a; 1995). Prophets, then, were good candidates for self-denial. But why would anyone else in the ancient world perceive themselves as capable of denying self?

As I have noted in a previous study (Malina 1992), collectivistic persons in antiquity believed that they had little if any control over their lives. They were controlled by various superordinate

85

personages. These include God, the gods, various sky-servants of God or the gods, demons, the emperor and his representatives, local kings and other elites, the well-born, tax collectors, toll collectors, the local military, older relatives, parents and the like. While people believed that they were controlled, they often sought patrons to control those who controlled them, and thus avoid some stressful situation. Furthermore, they may or may not have been responsible for the choices they made in such controlled contexts. Some believed that they were responsible; others believed that they were not.

Given this social arrangement, what sort of persons felt capable of changing their way of living? To whom would appeals for self-denial or another form of socially based conversion be directed?

DENYING SELF: SYNOPTIC TRACES

Simply put, denial is saying "no" to another. How does one say "no" to the self? If the self is collectivistic, self-denial is saying "no" to the collectivistic self. In this section, I shall flesh out the model of collectivistic self-denial while making reference to Synoptic resonances of Jesus' injunction in these documents. Of course the same could be done with the writings of Paul and his tradition. But here I stick with the Synoptic story-line.

Considering the previously sketched traits of collectivistic society, self-denial entails at least the following negations. First of all, there is the negation of the core concern of the collectivistic self: family integrity and all that the primary ingroup provides. Given the core value of family integrity in collectivistic structures, it is no surprise that self-denial and family-denial are almost parallel. In the ancient (and not so ancient) Mediterranean, females were enculturated to look forward to such dissolution of family integrity as they were handed over to another family in marriage (see Jacobs-Malina 1993). Cousin marriages turned this family-denial into greater family integrity, yet that does not seem to have been the case in Hellenism (see Malina 1993). For males, on the other hand, disattachment from the family of orientation would be quite abnormal. For in a collectivistic culture, so long as a person remains in society bereft of some primary ingroup, the person remains on the brink of actual death. In this context, Judas' death follows culturally from his break with the Jesus faction by his betrayal of the founder (Matt. 27:3–5).

In other words, survival in society after the negation of family integrity would require that a person move into some other actual

86

or fictive kin group. Women effected such a move without choice by marriage arrangements. On the other hand, widows were "free" (see Rom. 7:2–3). Males, on the other hand, could be enticed away from their families, honorably or otherwise (for example, the Prodigal Son, Luke 15:12). Jesus tells his self-denying followers to expect "a hundredfold now in this time, houses and brothers and sisters and mothers and children and lands" (Mark 10:29–30; see Mark 3:33–4 for Jesus). Another option would be to move out of society entirely – an option chosen early on by some creative Egyptian desert dwellers and the Qumran Essenes.

To stay with the Synoptic story-line, the outcome of such self-denial, then, would be a new ingroup consisting of affiliation to a fictive kin group. In the period of Jesus' activity, with focus on the revitalization of Israel, the new ingroup would consist essentially of the core group around Jesus plus faction supporters around the country, notably in Galilee (as in the "mission field" of Mark 6:6–12 and parallels). The general thrust of interpersonal relations in the new fictive kingroup would require that a new range of behavior fill the qualities described by traditional collectivistic virtues. For example, while concern for ingroup honor is a traditional collectivistic virtue, the new behavior qualifying as honorable in and for the ingroup is service (for example, Mark 9:35; 10:35), attachment to other ingroup members (= love; as in Mark 12:31–3), taking the last place (Mark 10:31) and the like (see Jacobs-Malina 1993). What is now required is the adoption of new goals that might direct the pursuit of achievements which improve the position of the fictive kin group. In this initial phase, since the Jesus group was a faction, the new goals would be those of Jesus. It might be good to recall here that a faction is a type of coalition, a group formed for a given time and for rather specific ends. What distinguishes a faction from other coalitions (action sets, gangs, etc.) is that a faction is personally recruited by a single person for the recruiter's own purposes. Those recruited join the faction in response to the invitation of the faction founder and to facilitate and implement the goals of the faction founder (see Malina 1988).

Now, in a collectivistic culture, the defining attributes of a faction's core group (here: the disciples) are loyalty to the central personage(s) (called "faith") and group solidarity (called "love"), enabling the new primary ingroup to develop survival ability until the central person's goals are realized. Jesus' goals are duly described, for example, in the "mission discourse" of Matt. 10:5–42 and parallels (also "for the sake of the gospel" in Mark 8:35; 10:29). Commitment to the new central personage is frequently emphasized ("for my sake," Matt. 10:18,39; 16:25; Mark 8:35; 10:29; 13:9; Luke 9:24). With this commitment at the forefront, persons can see themselves sharing a common fate, now rooted in circumstances of group affiliation as "brothers" (later in baptism, as in Matt. 28:19) and place of origin (for example, the first recruited are village mates from Capernaum, then presumably all Galileans), hence by ascription. Initial supporters were sought only in the house of Israel (as in Matt. 10:5) and the "towns of Israel" (Matt. 10:23; see also Luke 13:22). The new ingroup of fictive kin receives Jesus' total allegiance as his own family once did (Mark 3:31–5; Matt. 12:46–50; Luke 8:19–21). Now faction members owe similar allegiance to Jesus, at least, for one cannot serve God's goals and anything or anyone else (Matt. 6:24; Luke 16:11). A person's behavior toward the new ingroup is to be consistent with what the ingroup expects (see especially Matt. 18:15–18, 19–20). In the New Testament period this sort of norming is still under way as the Jesus faction develops into a set of Christian corporate groups.

Of course, behavior toward outgroups is characterized by the tendency toward maintaining distance (see the list of negative labels in Matthew compiled by Malina and Neyrey 1988:152–4). This list as well as various incidents in the story evidence defiance of authority (of the scribes of the Pharisees, of the Temple personnel; later of hostile Romans), competition (with Pharisees and Judaizers), resentment of control (by the scribes of the Pharisees), formality toward outsiders, rejection of other norms, arrogant dogmatism (compare Jesus' responses to his challengers in the Synoptic tradition; Paul's responses to his opponents) and rejection of attempts by outgroups to influence the new fictive kin group (beware of the leaven of the Pharisees).

Collectivist virtues put the emphasis on the views, needs and goals of the new ingroup. In the case of a faction, the emphasis falls on the views, needs and goals of the faction founder. These include generalized reciprocity with the faction founder (Jesus heals Peter's mother-in-law without request after Jesus "calls" Peter, Mark 1:30–1), obligation and duty to the faction founder ("for my sake," listed above), security and harmony of the group (for example, "stay salty and be at peace with one another," Mark 9:50), harmony with the faction founder (those who disagree are "Satan," as Peter in Mark 8:33; Matt. 16:23), obedience to the faction founder's goals ("for the gospel"), always doing what is proper (what comes "out of a person," Mark 7:20–3 and parallels), ingroup centeredness, high affiliation (followers are "brothers"), nurturance by the founder ("he saved others," Matt. 15:31, prays for Peter, Luke 22:31–2), dependency on the founder ("we are perishing," Matt. 8:25; Luke 8:24), high superordination and subordination alike as the core group members find their niches (arguments about who is greatest = more honorable in Mark 9:33–5; Matt. 18:1–5; Luke 9:46–8; greatest = oldest, hence precedence at Last Supper in Luke 22:24–7).

In other words, the virtues extolled by collectivist cultures will be attitudes that look to the benefit of the faction founder and his goals: the gospel of the Kingdom of God. These attitudes include a sense of honor vested in core membership (to judge the tribes of Israel: Matt. 19:28), respect for the faction founder ("for my sake"), other-centered behavior in support of ingroup members (service as criterion), satisfaction with one's status in the group, respect for older group members (as children in a kin group), acceptance of one's position in the group (greatness from service) and preserving the group's public image (honor–shame ripostes). Thus anything that cements and supports interpersonal relationships within the ingroup is valued (service, support, ceding place). The goal of life is the founder's goal for ingroup members, with their security and honor. Other characteristic features of collectivist cultures will be adapted to fit the life and goals of the faction. Since sexual relations are exclusively for the fulfillment of social duty, if the faction consists of adults, there will be no need for sexual relations given the temporary nature of a faction. However, once the faction takes on the more permanent form of a corporate group, such as the Pharisees had, then this area changes.

The "mission discourse" and its implementation point to how social norms and obligations are defined by the founder (Mark 6:7–13; Matt. 10:5–42; Luke 9:1–5) rather than determined by behavior to get personal satisfaction. Persons harbor beliefs shared with the rest of the ingroup members because of their allegiance to the founder, rather than beliefs that distinguish self from ingroup. And group members are to put great stock on readiness to cooperate with other ingroup members in fulfilling the founder's goals, with personal goals, attitudes, beliefs and values that reflect those of the founder.

There is nothing of personal satisfaction that might characterize behavior in collectivist factions. The process of resocialization within the new ingroup is keyed to developing habits of duty and obligation to the faction founder, sacrifice for the founder's goals, group-oriented tasks, cooperation, favoritism toward the ingroup, acceptance of ingroup authorities, nurturing, sociability and inter-dependence. The outcome of such resocialization is the production of persons with little emotional detachment from the faction founder, with broad concerns for the fictive kin group and greater tendency toward ingroup cooperation and group protectiveness. Thus members of factions in collectivist cultures will do what they must as dictated by the ingroup's founder rather than what brings personal satis-faction. In conflict situations, Jesus is portrayed as expecting his collectivist followers to side with him (vertical relationships – as faction founder) over others in the group who oppose, outside social equals, for example, Pharisees (horizontal relationships).

Affiliation with the Jesus faction and the resulting fictive kin group will have to be a dyadic decision rather than a personal decision. In this regard, one might note that the first followers of Jesus are actual brothers, while the third "call" is directed to a townmate (Matthew/Levi). Whether the others in the traditional core group were related or not is not specified (although John points in some interesting directions: brothers, townmates, a twin). Since the col-lectivist self is a group self that internalizes group identity to such an extent that members of ingroups respond automatically as ingroup norms specify, without doing any sort of utilitarian calculation, "conversion" will be possible only in terms of mini-groups and in public. John's baptism involved such groups, and Jesus belonged to one of them.

Thus Jesus calls his first followers in pairs and/or in public. Such conversion requires dislodging the perception that previous ingroup norms, the norms characteristic of Israel, are universally valid for those born in the house of Israel. And this can only be done by refashioning present ingroups into outgroups (thus "hating one's family" as noted above, opposition to Pharisees, opposition to the Temple and its personnel; "he who is not against us is for us," Mark 9:40). Along with rearranging group allegiances, new motivation for resocialization into the new fictive kin group has to be provided. The result will have to be distrust and unwillingness to cooperate with the previous ingroups likewise bent on "pleasing God" (Pharisees, Temple authorities). How would this be possible? It would seem that a number of Jesus' followers were motivated by the fact that Jesus had access to God's patronage (or Jesus himself offering patronage). This patronage was expended to control those who previously controlled people's existence (note the control exerted now by the core group: "authority over unclean spirits," Mark 6:7; or more fully: "authority over unclean spirits, to cast them out, and to heal every disease and every infirmity . . . to heal the sick, raise the dead, cleanse lepers, cast out demons" Matt. 10:1,8). Both those sharing in such authority and the recipients of benefactions would be the prime candidates for self-denial. In the gospel story, the disciples believe that they were responsible for their actions, and hence that their self-denial ought to be rewarded (Mark 10:28–31; Matt. 19:27–8). This is quite different from Paul's perspective, according to which people were really not responsible (as in Rom. 5:12–17; 7:1–25). They are "called by God" (1 Cor. 7:17 and *passim*), and hence both their self-denying behavior and its rewards are a patronage favor of God brokered by Jesus (see Malina 1988; 1992).

Since Jesus' problem is revitalizing "the lost sheep of the house of Israel" (Matt. 10:5), his faction produces a new ingroup that will be the true Israel. If the obstacle to this revitalization is kinship attachment, then the new Israel will be a new (fictive) kin group. If Israel's problem is obeying and pleasing the God of Israel, the new ingroup will have these tasks as its goal. If Israel requires revitalization, it will be because it deviated in its social structures and cultural values from what it was meant to be. Such deviance was apparent in styles of adherence to Temple and sacrifice rather than to God and obedience to God.

Since neither generation nor geography serves to define self any longer, the self must be a new collectivistic creature in repentant Israel. To outgroups, the self is always an aspect or a representative of the ingroup that consists of related, gendered persons who come from and live in a certain place. To ingroup members, the self is still a bundle of roles, yet generation and geography alone are not the key elements; rather repentance is crucial, even if confined to Israel. Even John knew that God could make children of Abraham, i.e. Israelites, from stones (Matt. 3:9; Luke 3:8), while Jesus insists that "many (Israelites) will come from east and west and sit at table with Abraham, Isaac, and Jacob in the kingdom of heaven" (Matt. 8:11), and disciples are to be made of Israelites in "all nations" (Matt. 28:19). Yet one does not readily distinguish self from social role(s); the first disciples are still fishermen, albeit "fishers of men" (Mark 1:16 and parallels). The performance of duties associated with roles is still the path to social respect. On the other hand, social perception is greatly prismed through who the other is, that is, to which group(s) he or she belongs. And the range of outgroup persons was still characterized by place of origin (for example, Judeans, Jerusalemites), group affiliation (Pharisees, Herodians, Sadducees) and social role (priest, scribe).

Collectivist persons are concerned about the results of their actions on others in the ingroup. The problem, of course, is the degree of self-identity with the new fictive kin group, in conjunction with the abiding (residual?) identity with the old kin group. Female relatives of Jesus' disciples are variously mentioned as present with the Lord and his entourage, including at the crucifixion (see Mark 15:40–1). Now ingroup members were to share material and non-material sources readily with group members. They were to be concerned about how their behavior appeared to others since they believed that the outcomes of their behavior should correspond with ingroup values. Again the problem that remained was which ingroup. All ingroup members felt involved in the contributions of their fellows and shared in their lives.

As in society at large, then, individuals would develop strong emotional attachment to the new ingroup, perceiving all group members as relatively homogeneous, with their behavior regulated by the founder's goals, based on acceptance of the founder's norms with a view to ingroup harmony and achievement at the expense of outgroups. Ingroup members were to treat each other like children, presumably of the same family (Matt. 18:1–4). Thus since collectivism is associated with homogeneity of affect, in the Jesus ingroup as well, if members were sad, one is sad; if joyful, one is joyful. The faction founder would expect unquestioned acceptance of ingroup goals and norms flowing from the goals, and hence eventual homogeneity of norms, attitudes and values. Interpersonal relations within the ingroup were seen as an end in themselves.

There is a perception of limited good according to which if something good happens to an outgroup member it is bad for the ingroup, because "good" is finite and thus resources are always in a zero-sum distribution pattern. Hence the concern about who is greatest (Mark 9:34 and parallels), and about being prominently first after Jesus (James and John wish this in Mark 10:35–7; while it is their mother in Matt. 20:20–1). Thus as a corollary, anyone for the outgroup is against us (see Mark 9:40; similarly: "He who is not with me is against me, and he who does not gather with me scatters," Luke 11:23).

Finally, the ingroup is responsible for the actions of its members. This has implications for intergroup relations. Specifically, in collectivism one expects solidarity in action toward other groups. Joint action is the norm. (Jesus is often attacked through disciples, Mark 2:16 and parallels, or disciples attacked through Jesus, Mark 2:18, 24 and parallels). Good outcomes for the other group are undesirable, even when they are in no way related to one's own outcomes (concerning the almsgiving, prayer and fasting of Pharisees in Matt. 6:1–18; or concerning Pharisee behavior in Matthew 23). Each individual is responsible for the actions of all other ingroup members, and the ingroup is responsible for the actions of each individual member (hence the need to address Judas' shameful behavior, notably in Matt. 27:3–10). Thus, for instance, even as regards the broad ingroup of regional residents, Galileans relate to Judeans in response to Judean policies in Galilee as if each Judean were the maker of those policies, and they interpret the actions of individual Judeans which fit their general ideological framework as the actions of all Judeans (the special note of Jerusalemite scribes at Mark 3:22; 7:1 and parallels; and the underscored hostility of Judeans throughout Matthew, with the climax coming when the Judean Jerusalemites answer: "His blood be on us and on our children!" Matt. 27:25; the final decree of Jesus is given in Galilee, not Judea, Matt. 28:16).

While collectivists sought to maintain harmony with humans and gods, and hence to live in harmony with the environment, Jesus' ingroup followers, with their commission to heal, were expected to control the environment in the area of illness (and perhaps others as well). To heal another is to control those forces which made the person ill (see Pilch 1993b). The purity orientation derived from Israel did not prevent new Israel from attempting to include those who were different, and to be non-competitive within their group.

Along with other collectivist cultures, one would expect the Jesus faction to evidence high rates of social support when unpleasant life events occur. The gospel story simply reports their remaining together after Jesus' death. Acts, in turn, describes how this fictive kin group became a primary group. As a primary group it was to become a normative reference group that provided strong social ties, emotional warmth and prompt punishment for deviance. Of course, it tended to be culturally homogeneous and included active gossip, frequent rites, memorable myths, a plausible ideology and badges of membership.

CONCLUSION

Mainstream US culture is one of self-denial by first-century standards. By those standards, the collectivistic self is dead. We, male and female, are taught to kill our collectivist inclinations by processes of enculturation and socialization. Note how our killing of the collectivistic self enables the individualist self to emerge in all its exaggerated glory. Thus instead of an over-bloated and exaggerated collectivist self, we find ourselves sporting an over-bloated and exaggerated individualism (see Malina 1995).

The confusions generated by perceptions typical of individualistic and collectivistic cultures are well illustrated, for example, in the eminently collectivistic new encyclical of Pope John Paul II, *Splendor of the Truth*. This document attacks individualism as something negative. It even advocates the elimination, debasing and rejection of individualism. Of course, the real question is: Individualism of what sort? If the document refers to idiocentrism or self-centeredness regardless of cultural type, it makes perfect sense and would win the consent of most individualistic Americans. But if the document means the US individualistic way of life, even in its allocentric dimensions, then it would be difficult to take the document seriously, to say the least. As noted previously, collectivistic cultures may have their merits, but these do not include political freedom and economic development. And collectivists, with their emphasis on family integrity, are usually quite inattentive to their idiocentrism when it comes to outgroup persons.

In an individualistic cultural context, it would be equally difficult to implement what Jesus expected of his followers. For while many find it imperative to remind Americans of the great value of family solidarity, family attachment and family commitment, it is the denial of such a family focus that is the burden of the self-denial required by Jesus "for the kingdom." As the Synoptic tradition itself reveals, self-denial is family-denial. Adherence to a fictive kin group centered on God and adhering to the teaching of Jesus was to characterize true Israel. St Francis acted out this self-denial quite well – and quite correctly in his collectivistic, medieval Mediterranean world.

REFERENCES

Bell, Daniel (1976) *The Cultural Contradictions of Capitalism.* New York: Basic Books.

Bonaventure, St (1973) *Major Life of St. Francis.* Trans. Benen Fahy. pp. 627–787 in Marion A. Habig (ed.) *St. Francis of Assisi: Writings and Early Biographies.* Chicago: Franciscan Herald.

Bultmann, Rudolf (1963) *History of the Synoptic Tradition.* Trans. John Marsh. New York: Harper & Row.

Elliott, John H. (1993) *What is Social Science Criticism?* Guides to Biblical Scholarship. Minneapolis: Fortress.

Gamson, William A. (1992) "The Social Psychology of Collective Action." pp. 53–76 in Aldon D. Morris and Carol McClurg Mueller (eds.) *Frontiers in Social Movement Theory.* New Haven: Yale University Press.

Gorney, R. and J. M. Long (1980) "Cultural Determinants of Achievement, Aggression and Psychological Distress." *Archives of General Psychiatry* 37:452–9.

Harré, Rom (1980) *Social Being: A Theory for Social Psychology.* Totowa: Rowman and Littlefield.

—— (1984) *Personal Being: A Theory for Individual Psychology.* Cambridge, MA: Harvard University Press.

—— (1989) "The 'Self' as a Theoretical Conception." pp. 387–417 in Michael Krausz (ed.) *Relativism: Interpretation and Confrontation.* Notre Dame: University of Notre Dame Press.

Harris, Grace Gredys (1989) "Concepts of Individual, Self, and Person in Description and Analysis." *American Anthropologist* 91:599–612.

Hsu, Francis L. K. (1981) *American and Chinese: Passage to Differences.* 3rd ed. Honolulu: University of Hawaii Press.

Jacobs-Malina, Diane (1993) *Beyond Patriarchy: Images of Family in Jesus.* Mahwah: Paulist.

Katakis, C. D. (1976) "An Exploratory Multilevel Attempt to Investigate Interpersonal and Intrapersonal Patterns of 20 Athenian Families." *Mental Health and Society* 3:1–9.

—— (1978) "On the Transaction of Social Change Processes and the Perception of Self in Relation to Others." *Mental Health and Society* 5:275–83.

Langkammer, Hugolin (1977) *Ewangelia według św. Marka: Wstęp, Przekład z Oryginału, Komentarz.* Poznań/Warsaw: Pallotinum.

Lukes, S. (1973) *Individualism.* Oxford: Blackwell.

Malina, Bruce J. (1988) "Patron and Client: The Analogy Behind Synoptic Theology." *Forum* 4/1:2–32.

—— (1989) "Dealing with Biblical (Mediterranean) Characters: A Guide for U.S. Consumers." *Biblical Theology Bulletin* 19:127–41.

—— (1992) "Is There a Circum-Mediterranean Person? Looking for Stereotypes." *Biblical Theology Bulletin* 22:66–87.

—— (1993) *The New Testament World: Insights from Cultural Anthropology.* Rev. ed. Louisville: John Knox/Westminster.

—— (1995) "Power, Pain and Personhood: Asceticism in the Ancient Mediterranean World." pp. 192–77 in Vincent L. Wimbush and Richard

Valantasis (eds.) *Aseticism*. New York: Oxford University Press.

Malina, Bruce J. and Jerome H. Neyrey (1988) *Calling Jesus Names: The Social Value of Labels in Matthew*. Sonoma: Polebridge Press.

—— (1996) *Portraits of Paul: An Archaeology of Ancient Personality*. Louisville: Westminster/John Knox.

Naroll, R. (1983) *The Moral Order*. Beverly Hills: Sage.

Palmer, S. (1972) *The Violent Society*. New Haven: College and University Press.

Perkins, Judith (1992) "The 'Self' as Sufferer." *Harvard Theological Review* 85: 245–72.

Pilch, John J. (1993a) "Visions in Revelation and Alternate Consciousness: A Perspective from Cultural Anthropology." *Listening* 28:231–44.

—— (1993b) "Insights and Models for Understanding the Healing Activity of the Historical Jesus." pp. 154–78 in Eugene H. Lovering Jr (ed.) *Society of Biblical Literature 1993 Seminar Papers*. Atlanta: Scholars.

—— (1995) "The Transfiguration of Jesus: An Experience of Alternate Reality." pp. 47-64 in Philip F. Esler (ed.) *Modelling Early Christianity: Social-Scientific Studies of the New Testament in its Context*. London: Routledge.

Rosenbaum, M. E. *et multi alii* (1980) "Group Productivity and Process: Pure and Mixed Reward Structures and Task Interdependence." *Journal of Personality and Social Psychology* 39:626–42.

Schwartz, Barry (1986) *The Battle for Human Nature: Science, Morality and Modern Life*. New York: Norton.

Schwartz, Shalom H. (1990) "Individualism-Collectivism: Critique and Proposed Refinements." *Journal of Cross-Cultural Psychology* 21:139–57.

Shweder, R. A. and E. J. Bourne (1982) "Does the Concept of Person Vary Cross-Culturally?" pp. 97–137 in A. J. Marsella and G. M. White (eds) *Cultural Conceptions of Mental Health and Therapy*. Boston, MA: Reidel.

Suggs, M. Jack (1970) *Wisdom, Christology and Law in Matthew's Gospel*. Cambridge, MA: Harvard University Press.

Triandis, Harry C. (1990) "Cross-Cultural Studies in Individualism and Collectivism." pp. 41–133 in John J. Berman (ed.) *Nebraska Symposium on Motivation 1989*. Lincoln: University of Nebraska Press.

Triandis, Harry C. *et multi alii* (1993) "An Etic–Emic Analysis of Individualism and Collectivism." *Journal of Cross Cultural Psychology* 24: 366–83.

4

MARY AND JESUS
Mediterranean mother and son

INTRODUCTION

The purpose of this chapter is to consider the mother of Jesus of
Nazareth through ancient Mediterranean eyes. Biblical scholars as a
rule wish to find out what some biblical author said and meant to
say to an original audience. In Christian theology this meaning of
the original human author is identified with God's meaning, what
God intended to express in his Word (for example, Vatican II, *On
Revelation* §12). Now, to find out what any text means, it is quite
apparent that the social system expressed in the text has to be of
prime interest since the meanings in the wordings in the spellings
that make up the written Bible derive from a social system (Malina
1991). And the social system in question for biblical studies is that
of the original author and his audience. For our purposes of entering
the world of the first-century eastern Mediterranean, we work with
a comparative model featuring mainstream American society on the
one hand (Williams 1970), and a model of preindustrial peasant
society outfitted with traditional Mediterranean features on the other
(Malina 1989; 1994). While these may not be the most perfect of
tools, nonetheless, to speak about Mary, the mother of Jesus of
Nazareth, as she is presented in the New Testament and subsequently,
one must use some model of the social system of the times.

However, that is not all. As anyone in the Christian tradition
knows, nearly everything claimed for Mary over the past two thousand years is simply not to be found in the New Testament. Aside
from the deafening New Testament silence about such current major
attributions as Mary's Immaculate Conception, Perpetual Virginity
and the Assumption, there is likewise nothing to be heard about
Mary's parents, birth, childhood, marriage, life in the holy family,

her role, if any, in early Christianity and her death. The attentive Bible reader will have noted that New Testament authors have little to say about Mary. What they do mention serves essentially to explain who Jesus might be.

The purpose of this chapter is to inquire into the bases for the traditional information about Mary, not simply to examine the extremely sparse biblical record relative to her. The fact is that the New Testament witnesses are never a norm for assessing devotion to the mother of Jesus. Why is this the case? Why is the symbolic understanding of Mary derived from elsewhere than the New Testament? And why are we willing to reexamine some of these dimensions of Marian faith with what might appear as irreverence and disrespect?

To answer these questions, I would first of all belabor the obvious by pointing out that the devotion to and understanding of Mary over the past two millennia are rooted in and ultimately derive from the Mediterranean cultural region. What is typical of this region is kinship as the focal social institution and concern for honor and shame within a gender-based division of labor (Malina 1994). It is rather easy for Americans to reflect upon traditional evaluations of Mary in a comparative way since those Mediterranean cultural traits sharply differ from mainstream, middle-class American values. Here economics is the focal social institution, and our concern is with measurable achievement based on "fair" competition. For us the individual person is the socially and legally sanctioned bearer of rights and obligations. Not so in the Mediterranean, past and present (Malina 1989; see the critique of the Mediterranean as cultural region by a Mediterranean ostensibly defending honor in De Pina-Cabral 1989).

SOURCES OF INFORMATION ABOUT MARY OF NAZARETH

Christian thinking about Mary of Nazareth is rooted in the infancy stories of the gospels. And these infancy stories are focused on Jesus, not on Mary. As stories of Jesus' birth and events that surrounded that birth, we may safely assume that the infancy stories are deduced from the fact that Jesus was crucified and raised from the dead. In antiquity, the description and assessment of the birth and childhood of notable personages inevitably derive from the adult status and roles held by that person. If Jesus of Nazareth was the Messiah to come, raised from the dead by the God of Israel, then obviously his birth and childhood would be just as the Synoptics described it. Wiedemann (1989:50) notes:

> The idea that personality can change was almost completely alien to Greek and Latin biography . . . a *vita* is an account of what sort of person he was, throughout his life. . . . Indeed, much Greek biography is not primarily about individuals at all: it is about character types.

I would suggest that the characteristic features of Greek and Latin biography applied equally to other Hellenistic works, including the gospels. Great personages were seen to have certain characteristics from the very moment of birth which remained with them throughout their life (Wiedemann 1989:51). Hence whatever is said about Jesus' mother in these stories is fundamentally stated as a function of underscoring the qualities of Jesus as person, and "preflection" of Jesus as Risen Messiah. For example, since Jesus' resurrection ushered in "the last days," it was expected that the "young men shall see visions and old men dream dreams" (Acts 2:17; see Kilborne 1987). True to the principle, it seems, Matthew's story features old men dreaming dreams with information from God (and vice versa: if they had dreams from God, they must have been old). Luke has the old Zechariah having a vision (a significant departure), while the young Mary has a procreation-related vision. This latter point is typical of biblical literature (and the Mediterranean) in that God bothers to communicate with women solely about their reproductive functions and subsequent gender-based roles.

In a society in which everybody believes that a man and a woman will inevitably have sexual relations unless prevented by circumstances, both of them will behave accordingly. So should a male but manage to corner any female alone, she might put up a wild show of resistance at first, but once he as much as touched her, she would give in and readily become his. Notice how readily Mary gives in when "cornered" by the angel! While obviously no lust is involved in Mary's case, the scenario still points to traditional Mediterranean urgency to keep women duly encompassed. And Mary's answer in this difficult situation is: "let it be to me according to your word" (Luke 1:38). What this means in typical Mediterranean fashion is: "As you like!"

Thanks to her vision Mary considers the son she conceives as quite special since she can take a trip alone from Nazareth to a city of

Judah (Luke 1:39). The fetus is apotropaic, clearly capable of warding off evil and even recognized by another fetus, Zechariah's son to be (1:41). The events preceding the conception of these fetuses and their subsequent in-womb behavior simply points to another typical feature. For God knows his prophets even before they are born, and he consecrates and calls them from their mothers' wombs. Thus, for example: "Before I formed you in the womb I knew you, and before you were born I consecrated you; I appointed you a prophet to the nations" (Jer. 1:5); and "The Lord called me from the womb, from the body of my mother he named my name" (Isa. 49:1; Paul believes the same must have been true of him since he functions as prophet: Gal. 1:15–16). And as might be expected, having been filled with the Spirit, Elizabeth proclaims Mary blessed because of her reproductive role: "blessed is the fruit of your womb" (Luke 1:42). Of course, since all children were swaddled, so Jesus was too; for Luke this feature is a sign to the shepherds (Luke 2:12). The practice of swaddling underscores the authoritarian quality of Mediterranean society (Lipton *et al.* 1965; Hudson and Phillips 1968; and photos in Weidemann 1989)

In the gospels, we find Jesus properly talking down to his mother (in Luke 2:49 and John 2:1–4), and even distancing himself from her and her Mediterranean claims on him: "Here are my mother and my brothers!" (Mark 3:31–5); "How honorable rather are those who hear the word of God and keep it" (Luke 11:28). Further, the attentive gospel reader will have noted that Matthew, Mark and Luke know nothing about Mary at the foot of the cross. The gospel of John, on the other hand, mentions the presence of the beloved disciple and the mother of Jesus at the cross (John 19:25–7). But who these last-mentioned personages might actually have been is quite unclear. For John does not seem to know anything of Jesus' Davidic pedigree, and he is equally ignorant of Jesus' birthplace (John 7:40–4). Finally there is no indication that the author of John's gospel knew the name of Jesus' mother, yet he does mention "the mother of Jesus" at a wedding in Cana (John 2:1–4). Without the Synoptic gospel tradition, the chances are that Mary of Nazareth would not be known or remembered at all. Yet as John's gospel indicates, such would not be the case for "the mother of Jesus" (for example, even Gal. 4:4 recalls Jesus "born of a woman"). What I mean is that regardless of the extent of our ignorance of the actual figure of Mary of Nazareth, the fact that Jesus had a mother would alone have sufficed to account for the Mediterranean-generated attitude toward that relatively unknown personage. And in fact it did suffice!

MARY IN SERVICE OF MEDITERRANEAN VALUES

From about the fourth century, with the Emperor Constantine's adoption of Christianity as a legal Roman religion, philosophically minded Christian leaders felt an urgent need to get their ideas about Jesus as Messiah quite clear. In this early philosophical phase of Christian theology, it was paramount to articulate the right ideas about Jesus. Since these philosophizing Christians were Mediterranean males, "naturally" concern for the mother of Jesus was part and parcel of their project. In the history of Christian theology, the study of the role of Mary, often called Mariology, developed from such a Mediterranean male application of the principle of fittingness or propriety. The idea was to speak of and act toward the mother of the Messiah in a fitting way. Since Christians presumably did not honor previous Messiahs with mothers, one did not know how to speak of and act toward the mother of the Messiah. Furthermore, while most Christians would agree that Jesus was Messiah, what it meant to be Messiah was quite confusing, especially for Hellenistic philosopher types who were somewhat confused by a Messiah who was human, born like a human being, not dropped from heaven. Thus the philosophical principle of propriety or fittingness. This principle ran as follows: *if it is proper or fitting, it must have been and therefore it was.* It is proper and fitting to call Jesus "God." Therefore, it is proper and fitting to call Mary "the mother of God," which she must have been, and therefore she was the mother of God. But what good is her status as mother of God if she is dead and buried? So it is proper and fitting for Mary to have been raised after her death; therefore, she must have been raised after her death, and she in fact was raised after her death. But it is equally proper that she be taken to heaven after her death and resurrection; therefore she must have been taken to heaven after her death; therefore she was taken to heaven after her death, and is in heaven right now. Once the principle of propriety was accepted, it produced a large number of "facts" that allowed any inventive and intelligent Marian devotee to seek out parallels in Jesus' life and status for the life and status of Mary. If Jesus was poor and suffered, so too Mary. If Jesus healed, so did Mary. If Jesus was Lord, then Mary must have been a lady of sorts. If Jesus is king, so Mary is queen. Mary thus becomes the feminine side of Jesus. In actual Christian practice, Jesus and Mary together formed the male and female dimensions of the incarnation of the one God of traditional Christian monotheism.

The elites of the ancient Mediterranean world proved themselves quite adept at philosophical reasoning. Psychology, however, was quite another matter. Mediterraneans were anti-introspective. Instead of judging people individually and psychologically, Mediterranean elites and non-elites utilized stereotypical descriptions and explanations.

For example, genealogy can be deduced from one's subsequent behavior and character (and behavior/character offer solid indication of one's genealogy). Social standing necessarily determines one's abilities or lack of them (and ability or inability is clear proof of one's social standing). A person who does something for all mankind is of divine birth (and divine birth points to benefits for all mankind). Kings necessarily perform valuable actions of benefit to many (hence actions that benefit many point to some royal agent). Magic is effective only among the ignorant and immoral; the ignorant and immoral are addicted to magic. Magicians are fearsome, threatening and suspicious persons; hence fearsome, threatening and suspicious person are almost certainly magicians. Good and honest persons are preoccupied with continuity and antiquity – they respect the past; hence those who advocate a break with the past, who advocate something brand new, are rebellious, outsiders and deviants (Malina 1986a: 35).

So it is fair to ask which stereotypical descriptions were fitting for Mary. In a philosophical mode, Mary played the role of ideological cipher for the feminine, specifically as virgin and mother. Given the available knowledge of biology and the lack of interest in psychology, Mary was given a significant symbolic role to serve part of the prevailing religious system. On the basis of their cultural experience of the feminine, of virgins and mothers, those Mediterranean theologians of Christian antiquity described the mother of Jesus in a way they felt necessary to fit into their system or to symbolize something significant for their cultural context. The qualities revealed by these theologians, their biological misunderstandings, their misogyny, their fear of the feminine, their degradation of everything normally female – all these features are effectively denied (psychologically speaking) in their attributions applied to Mary. In this they simply followed behavior evidenced by pre-Christian Mediterranean theologians in their assessment of the feminine and of their favorite goddesses: Isis, Cybele, Demeter and the like.

The way monotheism, as abstract philosophical system, got to permeate the awareness of western Europeans was through a monarchy that embraced the whole known world. Religion in the period was not a free-standing institution; there was no separation of religion and politics or religion and kinship. It was the norms of politics and kinship that largely controlled religion (see Malina 1986b; 1994; 1996). With Constantine and subsequently, the Christian movement became part and parcel of the imperial political institution. Doctrine and doctrinal positions replicated political ones. Thus to say that Jesus is God-man is to say that the emperor is God's single, human focus in the world, imbuing the role of emperor with divine attributes as well. After all, emperors are appointed by God, are they not? To say that Mary is the mother of God is to say that she has the same role toward Jesus as the emperor's mother or empress has toward the emperor. This is visible in early art (see Neyrey 1990). To say that Mary is queen is to raise the social level of queen to the supernatural, with subjects owing due respect, the same as saying Jesus is king. Similarly, to say that Mary is a lady is to raise the social level of the well-born aristocratic females of the Middle Ages to the supernatural, requiring the respect of their subjects. Interestingly enough, in the Middle Ages with the rise of new religious orders largely from aristocratic families, Mary was called the Bride of Christ. This was a Western perspective; in the process it extols the role of aristocratic virgins and puts their role in the realm of the supernatural.

This is Mariology in function of hegemony, doctrine as weapon of conflict. The Mariological titles of Mary, the experiences of Mary, serve the interests of those adopting the titles, using the titles, having the experience. Recent popes can say that Mary is the ideal mother, thus urging contemporary females to stay within their role of mother. They do not say that Mary is the ideal businesswoman, chief executive, career person, athlete, stockbroker, priest or bishop.

ON BEING A MEDITERRANEAN VIRGIN AND MOTHER

It is rather obvious in its taken-for-grantedness that Mary of Nazareth is always referred to in her gender-specific sexual roles of Mediterranean virgin and mother. Given the Mediterranean origins of the gospels, it is no surprise that Mary is portrayed in the stereotypical female role of Mediterranean mother. Without anachronism one will not be able to find anything psychological in the New Testament. Yet twentieth-century people look specifically for the psychological. In simple terms, there is just nothing psychologically known about Mary at all. However, modern Mariologists have not been stopped by this. They have been weaving their symbols of the feminine and attributed them to Mary for centuries, so why not another picture of Mary, this time duly psychological?

The fact is that Mary is presented in extremely few New Testament passages, specifically as stereotypical mother. All pious authors and theologians have said about her "fiat" would seem to be pure fabrication, often male fabrication, making Mary wonderful because she acted just as any male would like, with full obedience and subjection to God (the way any female should behave to her church leaders and to her husband). Once her "fiat" is uttered, she proves herself devoted to her natural role of mother, with all the virtues natural to feminine nature: gentleness, docility, forbearance, submissiveness, humility, modesty, silence, obedience, long-suffering compliance, charity, prudence, compassion, purity, praise, docility. Nothing like the macho Mediterranean ideal of controllable wife and daughter! Of course, none of this is in the New Testament texts, but made up according to the commentator's ideas of some ideal mother with cultural attributes most often denied to the normal flesh-and-blood women of his experience. In their methods and significantly, in their conclusions, these Mediterranean theologians simply followed the procedures evidenced by pre-Christian Mediterranean theologians in their assessment of the feminine and of their favorite goddesses: Isis, Cybele, Demeter, Artemis and the like. What, then, are some of the stereotypical features of a Mediterranean maid and mother?

In the Mediterranean, there are really no parents, although the word is occasionally used. Ordinarily people speak of their fathers and mothers (as in "Honor your father and your mother" in the Ten Commandments). As we saw in Chapter 2 above, the roles of father and mother, just like the husbands and wives who play them, rarely touch or overlap. Fathers are potent or impotent like seed, while mothers are fertile or barren like fields. Fathers alone generate offspring; the whole essence of a newly born boy or girl derives entirely from the father alone, and hence fathers alone "beget" (Matt. 1:1–16). The mother serves merely as passive nurturing agent who conceives and bears children (Matt. 1:21; Luke 1:13, 31); children are begotten of them (Matt. 1:16) or in them (Matt. 1:20) not by them. The father dominates the family and represents it to the outside (see Delaney 1986, 1987). Everything that relates to the family outwardly is controlled by the father and is male: inheritance, land in the surround, jural relations (i.e. relations on the father's side), farm animals and implements, adult sons. On the other hand, everything that maintains the family inwardly is in the mother's purview and is generally female: the kitchen, non-jural relations (i.e. relations on the mother's side), milkgoats and other household animals, chickens, unmarried daughters, resident daughters-in-law, boys until old enough to be with the father. "For Providence made man stronger and women weaker . . . and while he brings in fresh supplies from without, she may keep safe what lies within" ([Ps.-Aristotle =] Theophrastus, *Oeconomica* 1344a4 Loeb).

Similarly, Mediterranean husbands do not simply beget "children." Rather the babies born are immediately evaluated in terms of gender, as male babies and female babies, as boys or girls ("will bear a son ..." not a "child," Matt. 1:21; Luke 1:13,31). The underscored gender differentiation of offspring from birth replicates the Mediterranean mode of marking off the world in terms of gender. Just as selves are male and female, so are the categories of others, nature, time, space and God(s). The Mediterranean gender division of labor permeates all spheres of life quite clearly. In the US, such marked gender differentiation is largely confined to public restrooms, cosmetics and clothing.

How does this gender-based world look? At an abstract level we might look at sets of values. Consider these sets of values. Ends values (*yang*, *animus*): sense of independence, leadership, task orientation, outward orientation, assertiveness, self-discipline, impassivity, activity, objectivity, analytic mindedness, courage, unsentimentality, rationality, self-sufficiency, confidence, emotional control. Means values (*yin*, *anima*): dependence, non-aggression, non-competitiveness, inner orientation, interpersonal orientation, sensitivity, nurturance, subjectivity, intuitiveness, yieldingness, receptivity, supportiveness.

Which of these values are human? If they all are, how ought they be apportioned between males and females? In a gender-based society, ends values are locked onto males, and means values onto women. But this is still quite abstract. A second set of considerations, getting more concrete, has to do with the role of major social institutions, specifically the focal institution of kinship. Since males represent the family to the outside, while women maintain the inside, we find that male values look outward while female values look inward. A third set of considerations, getting even more concrete, has to do with social roles of males and females in the Mediterranean, specifically mothers and their boys and girls.

Mediterranean social pressure would have mothers pamper their boys but treat the girls strictly. More effort is expected to safeguard and preserve the life of the more valuable boy than that of a girl (see Wiedemann 1989:5–48). For it is the son's obligation to support parents in their old age (for example, see the Ten Commandments, whose provisions are directed to adult males). Girls will marry out as a rule anyway and have to support their husband's parents. As for the first-century "house of Israel," the community consisted primarily of male ethnics, "the sons of Israel," "the sons of Abraham"; the "daughters of Israel" belonged through the males. The main exceptions to gender definition for women were widows (as in Luke 2:36–7). Widows were social anomalies, no longer a "field" to be bounded by males. Should they not have sons, widows required some sort of social assistance (as in 1 Tim. 5:9–16).

The same was largely true in Christian groups. If a woman's husband was present, and she showed due respect to him, God might speak through her (as Paul insists in 1 Cor. 11:2–16). In the Bible, women characters generally hold direct discourse with God (or his agent) only in a procreative context (for example, the angel speaks with Mary in Luke 1:28–37). This behavior is fully in accord with the gender division of labor characteristic of the Circum-Mediterranean, and it endured for some time. For example:

> Returning home (from church) we prepare two tables: the table for nourishing the body and the table of Holy Writ. The husband repeats that which was spoken at the holy gathering, the woman educated, and the children listen.
>
> (Chrysostom, *In Gen. Sermo* 6,2; *PG* 54, 607)

Or again:

> Your mission as father continues and prolongs our episcopacy. ... Every one of you in your own home, of which you are the head, ought to consider yourself as fulfilling the function of bishop, to guard over the faith of those who are subject for this purpose, that no one should fall into heresy, neither the wife nor son nor daughter nor servant, for they were purchased at a great price.
>
> (Augustine, *Sermo 94*, *PL* 38, 580–1)

While Augustine might have the father guarding the faith of his charges, it is unmanly for a father to linger around his wife and children. For, as we saw in Chapter 2 above, the virtuous father knows that it is improper to remain long in the house, to be concerned and involved with childrearing, to accept childrearing concerns, to give any child care. The good father will not act other than formally and distantly with his children; he will stay psychologically remote from his children. In such a family, the sphere of childrearing is nearly exclusively female. Boys stay with the mother until it is time to move into the male world. Note how in Luke (2:48) it is Jesus' mother who deals with him when he pays no attention to the caravan's departure.

Furthermore, most adult males work at jobs that simply allow for the subsistence of the family. They are economically marginal producers (see Carney 1975 and Oakman 1986 for economic standards in antiquity). These two features, the absence of the father and his economically marginal role, produce what Carroll calls "the father-ineffective" family. "By definition, a father-ineffective family is a family-type characterized by the concentration of *de facto* authority within the home in the hands of the mother, and is usually considered to be a result of the widespread economic marginality of males" (Carroll 1986: 50). Proverbs (31:10–31) offers a glimpse of the female in the father-ineffective family. Gilmore observes:

> [T]here is the unusual degree of absention of Mediterranean males generally from domestic affairs, reinforced by the rigid separation of public and private worlds . . . there is lack of institutionalized rites-de-passage from boyhood to a public conferral of masculinity in the Mediterranean cultures. . . . A rigid spatial and behavioral segregation of the sexes and the consequent domestic division of labor is probably the most striking physical characteristic of Mediterranean community life. . . . The virtual absence of males from the home implies that boys as well as girls are reared until puberty in an exclusively female environment.
>
> (Gilmore 1987:14)

Psychologically, the father-ineffective family structure, with boys staying nearly exclusively with women "until they are old enough," directs a son to develop a sexual drive for the central controlling, adult female, nearly always the mother, and this drive "will not only be strong but also strongly repressed" (Carroll 1986:55). Until they join male circles, boys know only female behavior directly. Once with the men, they are regularly taunted that they are behaving like females. From then on, the boy's task is to behave "like a man," something he will remain permanently unsure of. The result is typical Mediterranean *machismo*.

> The *machismo* complex is a male-centered ideology that encourages men to be sexually aggressive, to brag about their sexual prowess and their genital attributes, and to dominate women sexually. It leads to a view of the ideal man as being a man totally under the control of his testicles.
>
> (Carroll 1986: 49; cf. Jesus' parable about eunuchs, males without testicles, Matt. 19:12)

The focus on the testicles is further underscored by the prevailing Mediterranean belief that males alone engender offspring. As previously noted, women simply serve as a field, bounded soil, into which the seed is planted. This is what the angel informs Mary of in Luke (1:30–8).

The extreme Mediterranean emphasis on the human genitals, on sexual transgression and on the male's uncertainty of his maleness are part of the same scenario. The cultural focus on legitimate cohabitation and the constant threat of sexual transgression fail to create a definite self-image in the minds of both men and women, as well as a definite image of the opposite sex. Young people grow up believing that were it not for the segregation of the sexes and the vengeance that would be surely meted out on the young man if caught in a sex offense, all the prohibitions hammered into him would be unable to inhibit him from having intercourse with the first woman he encountered. Young men come to consider their own sex drive so strong that only the physical impossibility of sexual access to the women of his social circle (because of their segregation, supervision, etc.) prevents them from satisfying his urges. The image of girls and women provided to young men complements this female self-image. The female sexual drive is equally strong and indiscriminate. "Left to herself, it is believed that a woman has no resistance, she is open to men" (Delaney 1987:41). Therefore the proper female must never allow herself to be found alone with an unrelated male. Girls are taught to believe from childhood that the mere sight of a woman is sufficient to arouse a man sexually (perhaps angels as well, as in Gen. 6:1–4). Only external, social circumstances can prevent him from having his will on her. These views and expectations are, of course, self-fulfilling.

Given the fact that there has been devotion to a female deity in the Mediterranean from time immemorial, Carroll asks why? Why the specific Mediterranean focus on virgin and mother (for example, Cybele in the first Christian centuries, and Mary especially from the fourth century on)? He offers the following hypotheses:

> Hypothesis 1. Fervent devotion to the Mary cult on the part of males is a practice that allows males characterized by a strong but strongly repressed sexual desire for the mother to dissipate in an acceptable manner the excess sexual energy that is built up as a result of this desire.
>
> Hypothesis 2. The distinctive features of the Mary cult over the centuries have been shaped primarily by the son's strong but strongly repressed desire for his mother.
>
> Hypothesis 3. Identifying strongly with the Virgin Mary allows women to experience vicariously the fulfillment of their desire for sexual contact with and a baby from their fathers.
>
> In summary, then, though the process works differently for males and for females, in the end the father-ineffective family intensifies Oedipal desires in both sons and daughters, and so promotes Marian devotion. The association of the Mary cult with southern Italy and Spain can therefore be traced to the prevalence of the father-ineffective family in these regions.
>
> (Carroll 1986:56, 59, 61)

MEDITERRANEAN KINSHIP UNITS

For Mediterranean people, the one great goal in life is the maintenance and strengthening of the kinship group and its honor. Those personality traits which tend to strengthen group cohesion are positive, encouraged and rewarded in childhood, approved and upheld as ideals in adulthood. Those personality traits which tend to be detrimental to group cohesion are considered faults; their manifestations are discouraged and punished in childhood, and met with strong disapproval and censure through the individual's life. Actions that strengthen ingroup cohesion are honorable; otherwise they are not.

The underlying Mediterranean value is kinship or family loyalty. Words such as Hebrew *hesed*, Arabic *'asabiyya*, Greek *agape* all refer to the social value of group-attachment. They connote familism, family spirit, kinship spirit, feeling of being tied together to persons by birth. Muhammad condemned it as contrary to the spirit of Islam, much as Jesus attempted to loosen family bonds because they proved contrary to the spirit of renewed Israel (see Matt. 10:34–6; Luke 12:51–3; Q; cf. also Mark 10:29–30 and par.). Such family commitment implies boundless and unconditional loyalty to fellow family members; parental claims on children are strong enough to make a husband give up his wife. This is ineradicable familial particularism. It assumes that the family is a unit by and of itself, a self-sufficient and absolute unity, with every other family as its legitimate victim and object of raiding and plunder.

While sibling relations may be close, *the mother–son bond* is perhaps the closest Mediterranean equivalent in intensity of what people in the US expect in the "love" of a marriage relation. Mother–son relations are a distinctive by-product of Mediterranean childrearing practices. For what is distinctive of Mediterranean males is gender-identity ambivalence, revealed in their vehement abhorrence or disavowal of everything "feminine." The result is a continued defense, through honor/shame polarities and prohibitions, against unacceptable female identifications.

According to contemporary Freudian psychology, the reason for this is that the primary (preoedipal) ego identification of children is with mothers, with the nurturing parent. Boys have to switch their gender identification to fathers during the oedipal stage (while girls do not), and this identification process involves a dis-identification from mother followed by a counter-identification with father. This process of dis-identification and counter-identification is impeded in the absence of available fathers or male surrogates who might act as counter-role models or psychic magnets. In the Mediterranean, boys are raised under domestic arrangements excluding adult males, and hence lack discriminate male objects during this developmental period.

> This male remoteness has two important ramifications given the other related factors described here. First is that boys, confined to a female-dominated space, are denied an accessible male figure with whom to identify at the precise time that the primary gender-identity formation process is going on. Second is the consequent emotional closeness and affective "symbiosis" of mothers and sons – a pan-Mediterranean trait. In Portugal

the "mother–son bond is thought to be the strongest possible bond between two human beings" (Cutileiro 1971:112). In Italy this bond is the "primary axis" of family continuity (Parsons 1969:55); in Greece it is "indestructible" (Campbell 1964:168). Moreover, this uniquely powerful bond originates in a domestic scene in which the boy often perceives the mother – typical in Mediterranean societies – as dominant or "in-charge" or as the "primary handler of the family's financial resources" (Rogers 1975:734–735). One may argue reasonably, therefore, that these widespread structural features impede a solid male gender identity and promote early psychic identification with the more accessible parent, the mother.

(Gilmore 1987:14–15)

This feature is rather ancient. For example, once after reading a long letter which Antipater, his vice-gerent, had written in denunciation of his mother, Alexander the Great said Antipater knew not that one tear of a mother effaced ten thousand letters (Plutarch, *Lives: Alexander* 39.7.688 Loeb). It is the most apposite Mediterranean value that accounts for the role of Mary as access to her son.

As for *fathers and daughters*, we might note again here that their lives are rather completely separated. A daughter is subordinated to his authority, rarely sees him in a situation suitable for interacting and remains with him for but a short part of her lifetime. At the earliest marriageable age she is surrendered to her in-laws after proper ritual passage focused on the marriage transaction (on the social psychology of family relations, see Cuisenier 1975:438–47).

The outcome of this style of childrearing is male sadism and female masochism. Males see little wrong with inflicting pain on other living beings or in watching such pain inflicted on others. Females, on the other hand, are led to believe that suffering and its endurance is simply the woman's lot. The curses of Genesis 3:16–19 and the behavior of Cain and the curse in Gen. 4:8–13 point in this direction. Similarly, biblical directives on childrearing and discipline focus on the inflicting and endurance of pain (see Pilch 1993). In this regard, the observations of Nawal El Saadawi are worth repeating:

The tendency to exaggerate a boy's feeling for his own ego and masculinity will usually end in an inferiority complex, since he will always feel that he is unable to rise up to the image expected of him. On the other hand, a tendency to exaggerate the need for a girl to withdraw, and to shrink into an attitude of passivity (under the guise of femininity and refinement) tends to build up in her a form of superiority complex which results from the feeling of being better than the image that has been created for her. A superiority complex creates masochistic tendencies in women, and an inferiority complex breeds sadistic and aggressive tendencies in men. Both of these are compensatory mechanisms and are the two faces of the same coin

(Saadawi 1982:81)

If the evaluation and rearing of children in the eastern Mediterranean are in fact traditional, there is little reason to expect first-century persons not to have shared the tendencies described above. Males will tend to be sadistic and aggressive, willing to inflict pain on others in order to realize their goals, whether these others be children, wives or enemies. On the other hand, females will be masochistic, yet with an inflated sense of their importance, especially after marriage and a son. And it will be sadism and aggression on behalf of the family that will be underscored as male virtue, while women will be lauded for their heroic masochism. The replication of these traits in Mediterranean values should bear out their controlling influence on behavior.

✓ CODEPENDENCE: MEDITERRANEAN MOTHERS AND SONS

The focal role of kinship, the gender division of labor, the way males and females are socialized into their gender roles, the central place of the family group over and against other groups – all these Mediterranean features point to what today is called codependence. Families in honor/shame societies are much like chemical dependence families in our society. The reason for this is that the main thrust in life is to acquire and/or defend honor in a gender-based society. Such honor and shame dependence can be defined as the need to deal with recurring trouble, problems or difficulties associated with acquiring or defending honor. The trouble in question is likely to occur in one or more of several areas where challenges to honor usually emerge: interpersonal relationships, legal dealings, commercial transactions, health concerns, spiritual concerns and occupational activities.

Codependence has been defined as "an emotional, psychological, and behavioral pattern of coping that develops as a result of an

112

individual's prolonged exposure to, and practice of, a set of oppressive rules – rules which prevent the open expression of feeling, as well as the direct discussion of personal and interpersonal problems" (Subby 1984, cited by Whitfield 1987:29). Thus codependence refers to "any suffering and/or dysfunction that is associated with or results from focusing on the needs and behavior of others" (Whitfield 1987:28–9). It develops from turning our responsibility for our life and happiness over to other people and to God as in fatalism or "trust in Providence," whether Israelite, Christian or Muslim.

From all that has been said about the Mediterranean family, it would seem that Mediterraneans, like other strong group people, are normally codependent if only from being raised in a family controlled by oppressive gender rules, focused upon its own honor and in conflict with other families. Furthermore, consider Mediterranean maidens and their initiation into motherhood. If Mary was an adolescent mother with her firstborn, she would have been mentally and emotionally impoverished to meet the range of basic human needs. As a Mediterranean female, it is highly likely that she ever had her needs met when she was an infant or small child, much less in her incipient adulthood. In order to survive, children who cannot develop a strong, true self compensate by developing an exaggerated false or codependent self. She would then be so in need that she would use others in an unhealthy and inappropriate way to get those needs met, as Mediterranean mothers usually do. Anyone in her immediate environment, anyone close to or near her, including her infant son, will be unconsciously used.

At first it might seem inconceivable that a mother would use a vulnerable, helpless, newborn infant to get her own needs met. Yet this invariably happens in the Mediterranean. And it occurs repeatedly in many troubled or dysfunctional families. One reason for this is that a female becomes an adult woman only through marriage (see Wiedemann 1989:143 *et passim*), and she maintains that status with honor only by childbearing, preferably by bearing a son. Any society that premises a girl's adulthood on marriage and male offspring must surely be viewed as primarily concerned with the mother's needs rather than the child's. In Luke, Elizabeth underscores this point by her greeting Mary as "the mother of my Lord!" If the infancy stories indicate anything, Jesus' birth was surrounded with lots of problems, questions, indecision, confusion and dysfunctions – albeit duly miraculous. Conditions in the story and in the culture point to parents and families that tend to promote confusion, regression and misdirection.

The genesis of codependence begins by the repression of one's own observations, feelings and reactions. In strong group societies, it is the group's needs and vision that override the individual's at every step. And in the Mediterranean it is a gender-based, kinship-focused vision that requires males and females to repress any idiosyncratic observations, feelings and reactions, even though the males are usually not given clear direction as to what is the ideal male, and females cannot be conceived of independently of their relations or lack of relations with males. In sum, others, usually parents, relatives and villagers, invalidate one's own observations, feelings and reactions – crucial internal cues of creative independence – so that the individual does the same and invalidates his or her own observations, feelings and reactions.

Early in the process, Mediterraneans are taught to keep all family secrets within the family, to deny them to the rest of the world, or in sum simply to deny them. Because one is to focus entirely on the needs of others, one begins to neglect one's own needs, and thus stifles normal individual psychological development.

But persons have their feelings, especially of hurt, and they are quick to learn to repress and deny those feelings. Mediterraneans thus learn at a rather early age to tolerate emotional pain increasingly, thereby becoming numb to that pain, and unable to grieve completely over everyday losses. In this way they learn to lose the ability to sympathize with the pain of others and are quite willing to abuse others physically, emotionally and spiritually. They abuse those in their group "for their own good," for example, their children, spouses and elderly relatives; and they abuse those not of their group simply to underscore their own social boundaries.

This sort of emotional stifling and constant attention to the cues of others leads to blocking one's own growth and development in the mental, emotional and spiritual aspects of one's personhood. In such situations, people find that compulsive behavior allows them a glimpse of what might be as well as a release of tension. But if the compulsive behavior is destructive to oneself or one's group, one feels shame and a resulting lowering of self-esteem. At this point one begins to feel more and more out of control and one attempts to compensate by the need to control even more. The result is a sense of delusion and hurt and often a projection of pain onto others (attacking, blaming and rejecting).

Tension in such a society builds to such an extent that stress-related illnesses manifested by aches and pains and by dysfunction of one or more body organs are quite common. This marks an advanced state of codependence, which can deteriorate to one or more of the following: extreme mood swings, difficulty with intimate relationships and chronic unhappiness (cf. Whitfield 1987:30). Hence if Mediterraneans believe that they live in a "vale of tears," that "all life is suffering," that "it is only human to have a difficult life," and this during periods when there is no war, it is probably codependence that puts them in that vale of tears.

Giovannini has noted:

> Despite considerable variation in the content of Mediterranean moral-evaluative systems, some striking parallels exist which cannot be ignored. One of these is the cultural emphasis on female chastity as an indicator of social worth for individuals and their respective kin groups.
>
> (1987:61)

Women fit into the general social scheme of things essentially in terms of their gender roles, not in terms of their basic human needs. And the ideal fulfillment of these gender roles requires that they be embedded in, encysted in or enmeshed in males: father, brothers, husband and sons. The woman symbols concern for the inside of the family, its internal goodness, honesty, trustworthiness and the like. In this sense, the woman is the focus and bearer of the kinship group's shame, i.e. its concern for its own honor, its own self-respectability and worth. What makes the role of women in the Mediterranean different has been noted by Gilmore:

> The difference is that in the Mediterranean lands women themselves are often nonproductive materially – ideally they are "excluded" from nondomestic work. Rather, they carry an immaterial or conceptual resource, their chastity, arbitrarily elevated to central position as an exchange value. This value is transmitted lineally through male vigilance, enhancing the family patrimony. So as Schneider has argued, female modesty is metamorphosed, almost in the manner of a fetish, into a pseudo-commodity, or more accurately a capital good.
>
> (1987:4)

Note, for example, how the Council of Trent rates virginity higher than marriage itself (Session 24, Canon 10, Denzinger and Schönmetzer 1963:1810). It is no wonder that even in marriage, for example, sexual purity is rated above any other quality such as health, vigor, industriousness, intelligence, beauty and the like. It would seem that female modesty as a capital good would derive from

> small, atomistic kinship units competing over scarce resources in the absence of effective state control. Given conditions of economic and institutional poverty, female chastity came to be considered a valuable component of each family's patrimony, and hence a means of acquiring useful affines in the struggle for survival.

> (Gilmore 1987:7)

Ideally women should not be seen alone by men. That is tantamount to a provocative flaunting of a scarce resource, behavior allowed only when the father or brother is present in the case of an unmarried girl, or the husband in the case of a married woman. After all, it is a resource that belongs to the male.

As noted previously, women believe themselves quite vulnerable to male sexuality. Their only protection is male tutelage and surveillance; hence, for their own good, they submit to male dominance, which is considered by all in the society as morally justified. The ideal woman is acted upon rather than acting. Her status depends upon her fecundity, especially in producing male offspring for her husband and his family. Her goodness is assessed in terms of her compliance with repressive norms, and hence by her acquiescence to the female status quo. As Saadawi has noted, female childrearing behavior produces masochistic women, largely with an inflated sense of their importance, especially after marriage and a son. The virtuous woman will be lauded for her heroic masochism, the stuff of Mediterranean holiness when coupled with gender roles of virgin, wife, mother. Furthermore, should she attempt to take on a male's role in certain circumstances, provided male honor is not at risk, the married woman is praised. There are no female equivalents of "effeminate," "unmanly" or "emasculated." Often strong "masculine" women are admired (see Gilmore 1987:9).

CONCLUSION

Why am I willing to use a different principle to interpret Mary in the gospels than the principle of philosophical propriety hitherto in vogue? A first reason is that philosophy derives from some social system and inevitably gives expression to its cultural moorings. Hence what I would consider philosophically appropriate is quite different from what a Mediterranean would. As I have shown (Malina 1989), Mediterraneans lived in a society in which the main social institution was kinship. The fact that Mary is celebrated as virgin and mother indicates as much. I live in a society in which the main social institution is economics. Kinship itself is much controlled by economic norms, by quantity orientation.

Marriages in the US are not arranged by parents who ask about dowry, who are concerned that the bride be a virgin, that if possible she be a first cousin, that the two sets of parents like each other and get along well. We do not expect to see the tokens of virginity displayed at the wedding party to prove the honor of the girl's family and the honor rating of the newlyweds, who underscore the honor of the uniting families.

Rather, we are concerned that the newlyweds, who choose each other, will not be an economic burden to us, that they have enough money to afford to get married, that husband and wife have the intellectual and social wherewithal to get and keep a good job with their car and eventually a house and enough savings to get their children into college to repeat this cycle.

Nowadays, given the shift in perception of time, a sense of history, a sense of culture, of psychological personhood, I propose a different principle for historical interpretation. It is like the principle of propriety, but on a concrete level. It runs as follows: If some feature exists in Mediterranean society and everything indicates that it always has been that way in the Mediterranean, it must have been in the past. This is quite different from the realm of ideas, the ideal realm, in which old Mariology moved. This new Mariology, if one can call it that, is based on an entirely different ideology. This ideology requires some positive evidence, some testable experience of an attribute applied to Mary in order to prove worthy of Christian faith.

For example, I would say instead that if Mediterranean mothers married in early adolescence have been and continue to be code-pendent persons, so Mary too. If it has been and still is that Mediterranean females are concerned about their shame, so Mary too. If it has been and still is that in the Mediterranean world the main division of life is gender-based, that the world is essentially male and female, it is into such an essentially male and female world that Mary and Jesus and the rest of the first generation of Christians lived and moved and had their being.

117

In our period of history, when people are moving toward a common language lectionary and hymnal in religion, when people are insisting on equal pay for equal work regardless of gender differentiation in business, when females are urged to realize their full potential regardless of gender stereotypes, it is curious to realize that the role of Mary, the virgin mother of Jesus, continues to be based exclusively upon gender-based sexual roles. For Euro-American women, such self-definition based exclusively on gender-based sexual roles would be an indication of psychopathology (Draguns and Phillips 1972:1). And yet some church leaders, largely Roman Catholic and fundamentalists, would urge this sort of "Marian" or "biblical" role on women. And they do this in spite of the fact that there really is absolutely nothing known about Mary except that she was a Mediterranean maid and mother.

> But it is this very cult of the Virgin's "femininity," expressed by her sweetness, submissiveness, and passivity that permits her to survive, a goddess in a patriarchal society. For her cult flourishes in countries where women rarely participate in public life and are relegated to the domestic domain. In countries like Ireland, Spain, Portugal, Italy and Belgium, women are not rallying for comfort to a symbol that holds out hope of something different from their lives. Mary is worshipped in places where the symbol of the subject housewife applies more readily, and therefore both reinforces and justifies the ruling state of affairs, in which women are expected to be, and are, men's devoted mothers and wives.
>
> (Warner 1983:191)

And it is only as true Mediterranean maid and mother that Mary effectively serves as this symbol.

REFERENCES

Carney, Thomas F. (1975) *The Shape of the Past: Models and Antiquity.* Lawrence, KS: Coronado.

Carroll, Michael P. (1986) *The Cult of the Virgin Mary: Psychological Origins.* Princeton: Princeton University Press.

Cuisenier, Jean (1975) *Economie et parenté: leurs affinités de structure dans le domaine turc et dans le domaine arabe.* Paris/La Haye: Mouton.

Delaney, Carol (1986) "The Meaning of Paternity and the Virgin Birth Debate." *Man* 21:494–513.

—— (1987) "Seeds of Honor, Fields of Shame." pp. 35–48 in David D.

Gilmore (ed.) *Honor and Shame and the Unity of the Mediterranean* (Special Publication of the American Anthropological Association # 22). Washington: American Anthropological Association.

Denzinger, Henricus and Adolfus Schönmetzer (1963) *Enchiridion Symbolorum, Definitionum et Declarationum de Rebus Fidei et Morum.* 32nd ed. Rome: Herder.

Draguns, Juris G. and Leslie Phillips (1972) *Culture and Psychopathology: The Quest for a Relationship.* Morristown, NJ: General Learning.

Gilmore, David D. (1987) "Introduction: The Shame of Dishonor." pp. 2–21 in David D. Gilmore (ed.) *Honor and Shame and the Unity of the Mediterranean* (Special Publication of the American Anthropological Association #22). Washington: American Anthropological Association.

Giovanni, Maureen J. (1987) "Female Chastity Codes in the Circum-Mediterranean: Comparative Perspectives." Pp. 61–74 in David D. Gilmore (ed.) *Honor and Shame and the Unity of the Mediterranean* (Special Publication of the American Anthropological Association #22). Washington: American Anthropological Association.

Hudson, Charles and Helen Phillips (1968) "Rousseau and the Disappearance of Swaddling among Western Europeans." pp. 13–22 in Thomas Weaver (ed.) *Essays on Medical Anthropology* (Southern Anthropological Society Proceedings No. 1). Athens: University of Georgia Press.

Kilborne, Benjamin (1987) "On Classifying Dreams." pp. 171–93 in Barbara Tedlock (ed.) *Dreaming: Anthropological and Psychological Interpretations.* Cambridge: Cambridge University Press.

Lipton, Earle L., Alfred Steinschneider and Julius B. Richmond (1965) *Swaddling, a Child Care Practice: Historical, Cultural and Experimental Observations* (Supplement to *Pediatrics* 35, 3/II March 1965: 521–67). Springfield, IL: Charles C. Thomas.

Malina, Bruce J. (1986a) "Miracles or Magic: II." *Religious Studies Review* 12:35–9.

—— (1986b) "Religion in the World of Paul: A Preliminary Sketch." *Biblical Theology Bulletin* 16:92–101.

—— (1989) "Dealing with Biblical (Mediterranean) Characters: A Guide for US Consumers." *Biblical Theology Bulletin* 19:127–41.

—— (1991) "Reading Theory Perspective: Reading Luke–Acts." pp. 3–23 in Jerome H. Neyrey (ed.) *The Social World of Luke–Acts: Models for Interpretation.* Peabody, MA: Hendrickson.

—— (1994) "Religion in the Imagined New Testament World: More Social Science Lenses." *Scriptura* 51:1–26.

—— (1996) "Mediterranean Sacrifice: Dimensions of Domestic and Political Religion." *Biblical Theology Bulletin* 26: (forthcoming)

Neyrey, Jerome H. (1990) "Mary – Woman of the Mediterranean: Maid and Mother in Art and Literature." *Biblical Theology Bulletin* 20:65–75.

Oakman, Douglas (1986) *Jesus and the Economic Questions of His Day.* Lewiston, NY: Edwin Mellen.

Pilch, John J. (1993) "'Beat his Ribs While he is Young' (Sir 30:12): A Window on the Mediterranean World." *Biblical Theology Bulletin* 23:101–13.

Pina-Cabral, João de (1989) "The Mediterranean as a Category of Regional

Comparison: A Critical View." *Current Anthropology* 30:399–406.

Saadawi, Nawal El (1982) *The Hidden Face of Eve: Women in the Arab World*. Boston, MA: Beacon.

Schaberg, Jane (1987) *The Illegitimacy of Jesus: A Feminist Theological Interpretation of the Infancy Narratives*. San Francisco: Harper & Row.

Triandis, Harry C. and Vasso Vassiliou (1972) "A Comparative Analysis of Subjective Culture." pp. 299–335 in Harry C. Triandis *et al.* (eds) *The Analysis of Subjective Culture*. New York: Wiley Interscience.

Warner, Marina (1983) *Alone of All her Sex: The Myth and the Cult of the Virgin Mary*. New York: Vintage Books (repr. of 1978).

Whitfield, Charles L. (1987) *Healing the Child Within: Discovery and Recovery for Adult Children of Dysfunctional Families*. Deerfield Beach, FL: Health Communications.

Wiedemann, Thomas (1989) *Adults and Children in the Roman Empire*. New Haven: Yale University Press.

Williams, Robin M., Jr (1970) *American Society: A Sociological View*. 3rd ed. New York: Knopf.

Part III

THE QUESTION OF SIGNIFICANT ROLES IN THE FIRST-CENTURY MEDITERRANEAN

5

WAS JESUS A CHARISMATIC LEADER?

INTRODUCTION

The origins of Christianity, according to the "Received View" (see Chapter 8), lie rooted in the charismatic leader Jesus of Nazareth (Gager 1975:20ff.; see also Malina 1986b; Gager's perspectives derive from Weber 1922/1968, who is also followed by Schütz 1974; Ebertz 1987; Mödritzer 1994). Subsequently the charisma of the leader was routinized (after Weber) or preserved (after Worsley 1968). The purpose of this chapter is to question the Received View. Did Jesus in fact have Weberian charisma? Was he in fact a Weberian charismatic leader? The basis for this questioning is the fact that there is little if any evidence from the earliest Jesus movement groups that would fit Weber's model of the charismatic leader. The information provided by the earliest sources offers nothing significant that might provide a fit or match with either Weber's original model or his preferred way of using that original model, or with the model developed by Weber's heirs and their preferred way of employing it.

WEBER'S CHARISMA

Weber developed the concept of charisma in order to explain a type of effect in behavior not rooted in traditional authority (for example, status) or legitimate authority (for example, office). If some persons have the socially recognized right to oblige others (this is authority), and this right cannot be explained by traditional warrants or rational principles (law, custom), then what can explain it? The "black hole" was called charisma. Weber's description of charisma might be summarized as follows, thanks to the recent, excellent study of Miyahara (1983). The term "charisma" occurs in two contexts of the Weberian corpus: that of the sociology of religion and that of the sociology of domination.

Charisma in the sociology of religion

In the sociology of religion, Weber distinguishes between magical, prophetic (or genuine) and routinized charisma. Briefly:

(a) Magical charisma refers to the attribution of special status to certain persons or objects because of a group's recognition of them as having extraordinary powers. Psychoanalytically oriented social scientists such as McIntosh (1970) and Camic (1980) view magical charisma as the only authentic charisma.

(b) Prophetic charisma refers to the attribution of special status to certain persons because of a group's recognition of them as having extraordinary claims deriving from definite revelations, missions or doctrines. Weber, in his sociology of domination, and scholars such as Tucker (1968) and Roth (1975) see prophetic charisma as genuine charisma.

(c) Routinized charisma refers to the attribution of special status to certain social institutions (for example, some office) because of a group's recognition of them as having extraordinary powers or doctrinal claims. Shils (1965, 1968) opts for routinized charisma as the real thing.

Charisma in the sociology of domination

In the sociology of domination, charisma is applied solely to "prophetic" charisma, and appropriately explained and adapted to fit a political institution. In this treatment the following features of charisma emerge:

- only *persons* can be called charismatic (unlike the use of the term in the sociology of religion);
- charisma entails a *relationship* between leader and followers (only recognition is required in the sociology of religion);
- the leader–follower relationship is marked by complete and personal *devotion* on the part of followers;
- the followers form a "*charismatic community*" in which the members are emotionally tied to each other;
- in its most potent forms, charisma is non-rational, value-free, disruptive of rational and traditional authority, inverting all

notions of holiness, of value hierarchies, of custom, law and tradition; in sum, charisma is *revolutionary*;

● charisma always has to do with *mission*, i.e. a normative image of the world, a new and normative worldview.

Miyahara sums up the idea as follows:

> The conception of genuine charisma in the sociology of domination is a generalization of that prophetic charisma in the sociology of religion. Both are a recognized quality of individuals, both tend to disrupt existing norms and rules of conduct, and both contain a mission or message. Weber's examples of genuine charismatics such as Jesus, Joseph Smith, and Kurt Eisner seem to confirm this point.
>
> (1983:371)

For Weber, routinized charisma is radically different from genuine charisma (and perhaps Weber would agree with Worsley's critique, that "strictly speaking charisma cannot, by definition, become routinized" (1968:xlix). Comparatively speaking, the main differences between the two are the following:

(1) routinized charisma is *no longer revolutionary*; rather it legitimates the existing institutional order;
(2) routinized charisma is *rooted in a social institution* (office, status) rather than in a person.

Yet Weber felt that he perceived a charismatic quality in the routinized since it had about it "an extraordinary quality which is not accessible to everyone and which typically overshadows the charismatic subject" (Weber 1922/1968:1135). Consequently, as Miyahara aptly notes (1983:372), "Weber is arguing that routinized charisma is charismatic since it contains an element of magical charisma."

What, then, is a charisma for Weber? The constants in his writings point to the following description: a charisma

> is the quality of extraordinariness inhering in some person, object or social institution imputed, ascribed and consequently recognized in that person, object or institution by a collectivity of people sharing an emotional form of communal relationship.
>
> (1922/1968:153, 1187–8)

Miyahara concludes his survey article with his own description of Weberian charisma in which he emphasizes the fact that charisma is a collective illusion, indicative of group alienation, that enables the "charismatic community" to ascribe a quality to some person or object regardless of their actual condition, and endow that quality with superhuman factuality. There can be no distinction between authentic and inauthentic charisma since all charisma is illusory; the only distinction to be found is that among the groups imputing it. Finally, as a concrete expression of alienation, charisma is neither necessary nor desirable (Miyahara 1983:383–4).

WEBER'S CHARISMATIC LEADER

Central, directive roles in social groups are usually held by managers. Not every manager is a leader. Managers may become leaders in crisis situations. For leadership depends upon an achievement on behalf of the group that finds itself in need of some quality, activity or object at a given time and place. In other words, leadership is not a quality of the individual, but a role dependent upon the presence of a number of variables, not the least of which is specific group need.

Leadership, then, is a form of crisis management that proves effective in a context of fateful enterprises, crucially significant campaigns and heavily meaningful movements. In line with the descriptions of charisma presented above, a charismatic leader would be someone whose personal qualities (of whatever sort) are highlighted, transformed and recognized as extraordinary by some cohesive group; that group then perceives the qualities as a source of effectiveness for mobilizing people for strenuous effort; and that effort focuses on change or maintenance of existing cultural values and/or institutional structures. This, of course, is the Weberian charismatic leader: a great man of authoritarian bent who is dedicated exclusively to radical change on the basis of his own personal virtuosity ("endowed with supernatural, superhuman, or at least specifically exceptional powers or qualities," Weber 1922/1968:241) in a situation of social crisis, especially one of political and/or normative vacuum. Dorothy Emmet (1958:233) has noted "that there is something rather Teutonic, suggesting the Fuehrer-Prinzip about Weber's description." And indeed there is. It is perhaps, more specifically, a reaction to a situation in which traditional values could no longer be verified in social experience within a cultural context of Germanic and/or north European tradition. In the same vein we might note with Schwartz (1983:30) how according to the German scholar Johannes Kuhn

(1932:142): "It is not easy for Europeans to comprehend the signif-icance of a man like Washington. We are too accustomed to seek human greatness in unusual talents and gifts of an individual nature." Would not the same hold for that culture's perception of Jesus? Drawing from this same intellectual tradition, a tradition which informed the leadership theories of Nietzsche and Freud, Weber could find in the leader's "specific gifts of the body and mind" the basis of his followers' "duty" to submit to his commands (1922/1968:1112). In this preconception, Jesus as central figure in the Christianity of northern Europe would obviously be perceived as a charismatic leader of the Weberian sort. It would seem, however, that such charismatic leadership contributed nothing to the devel-opment of the Christian movement groups (or to any Mediterranean movement at all).

In his recent study of Weberian charismatic leadership, Schwartz draws up a list of characteristics which might be profitably consid-ered here. These are presented in Table 2 below (adapted from Schwartz 1983:31). What marks off the charismatic leader is some extraordinary quality converted to effective power. Leadership, how-ever, emerges not simply and not always with extraordinary personal qualities. Given the crisis-context of the emergence of leaders, lead-ership often appears apart from extraordinary personal qualities yet always in extraordinary times and places. Consider the range of authority for a moment.

TYPES OF AUTHORITY RECONSIDERED

Authority can be defined as the social recognition of the right of another to oblige others. Such recognition is based either on an *ad hoc* standard (for example, in a given instance you do what I say because I am stronger, have more wealth, etc.), or on traditional and customary norms (for example, in a kinship group, the father has the right to dispose of his children's goods), or on a rule of law (for example, abstract rules, like the right to justice). Authority based on a standard would be simple authority, that based on traditional, customary norms would be legitimate authority, and that based on law would be legal authority (see Bohannan 1973; Selznick *et al.* 1968). Where does Weberian charisma fall into this scheme of things?

I suggest that charisma was introduced by Weber to deal with a type of legitimate authority rooted in traditional and customary norms. Legitimate authority is *ad hoc*, simple authority validated by some principle other than the *ad hoc*, simple authority itself. This validation is called legitimation. Legitimation rests upon some common, broadly encompassing norm recognized by members of a society. This norm constrains those members to conform to the wishes of a person 'or group considered superior, and who thereby becomes a legitimate authority, while acknowledging the subordinate status of the rest of the collectivity. Some examples of legitimating, broadly encompassing norms include: the will of God, hereditary succession or lineage, kinship, seniority, election by all the members of a group, election by only the devoted elite, election by only the propertied elite, ownership, special competence, and so forth.

Legitimate authority entails not merely tolerant approval but active confirmation and promotion of social patterns of behavior in terms of common values, whether preexisting social patterns or those that emerge in a collectivity in the course of social interaction. Consequently, legitimate authority is an ascribed right, a right to obligate others acknowledged by subordinates in a collectivity and sanctioned by some higher-order norm. It is the form of authority that is maintained by custom and that produces custom. This form of authority ranges from personal or traditional authority to impersonal or rational authority (see Malina 1981; 1986a).

Personal and impersonal legitimate authority

Personal legitimate authority inheres in the person, i.e. flows from circumstances that befall a person and are not under the individual's control. Such circumstances include birth, age, sex, physical size, status of one's family and the like. These features are culturally interpreted as directly related to one's capacity to exercise authority. Examples of personal legitimate authority would be hereditary rulership, hereditary priesthood, rights of the firstborn, aristocratic control of the polity due to inherited power, commitment, influence, wealth and the like.

Impersonal legitimate authority is acquired by a person by means of some skill or competence deemed pertinent and useful to the realization of the ends of the institution in which authority is embedded. Such authority is occupational, bound up with some sort of job, task or office and ceases with their termination or completion. For example, most US elective and bureaucratic positions are of this sort.

In sum, personal legitimate authority inheres in the person; the legitimated person automatically has the office or task. Impersonal legitimate authority inheres in the office or task; the office holder automatically has legitimate authority. These forms of legitimate authority are two ends of a scale, as it were. In the middle they may be mixed, for example, when an office depends on an examination (impersonal) open only to aristocrats, males, whites, etc. (personal).

Reputational authority

Along with personal and impersonal legitimate authority, however, there is a third form that belongs in this discussion. This is the authority that normally emerges in situations where cultural values cannot be realized in normal human living. This authority derives from the successful criticism and dislocation of the higher-order norms which legitimate the authority prevailing in a given society. This sort of authority may be called *reputational authority* because it is rooted in a person's ability to influence a change in the broadly encompassing norms that constrain recognition of legitimate authority. It is reputational authority that is often called "charismatic" authority; but that is misleading since very non-charismatic persons have acquired and wielded it without illusory extraordinary qualities (see Schwartz 1983; 1987 for George Washington). This authority emerges from a person's effective ability to convince members of a given society to recognize no longer some higher-order norm as binding. For example, if in a given society, office holders occupy their position because of divine will, a reputational authority will successfully demonstrate to the collectivity that divine will is not at issue at all, but force, chicanery, collusion, conspiracy, or some other principle.

In sum, reputational authority unseats the higher-order norms which stabilize and fix custom and thus calls existing custom into question. The Weberian charismatic leader would emerge under the following conditions:

- a group in fact rejects existing custom and grounds its rejection in some illusory quality of some person;
- this illusory quality serves as the basis for effectively questioning the higher-order norm legitimating the custom;
- actual ability apart, the person in question accepts the ascription and begins to wield power on the basis of the recognition of his or her illusory qualities.

But if the person in question is recognized as wielding legitimate authority because of a reputation rooted in socially verifiable

129

Table 2 Weberian charismatic leader and reputational legitimate leader

The charismatic	*The reputational*
The charismatic leader is self-appointed; he is "called" to a social mission and exudes self-confidence in his ability to carry it out	The reputational legitimate leader believes in mission but expresses no confidence in his ability to lead it. Seeks to avoid leadership role to which he is appointed by others
The charismatic leader is unattached to established social institutions and plays no part in their activities	The reputational legitimate social leader is a member of established social institutions, a representative of their values and protector of their central values
The charismatic leader is a radical who seeks to destroy existing traditions	The reputational legitimate leader is a conservative who is totally committed to existing traditions
The charismatic leader achieves and maintains authority by putting extraordinary talents to use in the performance of miraculous feats and/or the formulation of a new ideology	The reputational legitimate leader's talent are not extraordinary. He performs no unusual political feats and propounds nothing especially new in the way of ideology
The charismatic leader rejects rational administrative conduct. He dispenses power and justice in a "particularistic" manner, consistent with his personal interests and mission	The reputational legitimate leader is an incumbent in an accepted social role and administers power and justice according to accepted impersonal "universalistic" standards
The charismatic leader takes no part in institution building. His ideals and authority are routinized by disciples and successors	The reputational legitimate leader plays a direct role in both the creation and administration of new institutional structures
The charismatic leader derives his prestige by the seizing and effective use of power, thus demonstrating "strength in life"	The reputational legitimate leader derives his prestige from the avoidance and relinquishment and/or sharing of power, thus demonstrating "virtue"

130

influence (teaching) or beneficial power (healing), not in illusory charisma, then we shall have reputational legitimate authority in the normal and strict sense. Table 2, adapted from Schwartz (but not his terminology), offers a comparative perspective that may prove useful.

JESUS' CAREER

Which features of the foregoing typologies fit what is known of Jesus and the Jesus movement group? Given Weber's description of charisma, we may assume that charismatic attraction cannot be generated in a society whose definition of power relations precludes strong personal authority. And it would seem that the social climate of first-century Palestine described in the story of Jesus in fact precludes strong personal authority. It was a social climate characterized by inflated power, with Jesus exercising no power over people at all. His power was over demons just as with any other successful healer, including the demons of storms. And rarely does he exert power over nature. Weber's charismatic leader generates impassioned loyalties to himself. Consider the story of Jesus' "loyal" disciples: one betrays him, one denies him, the others flee from him in time of need – hardly indications of impassioned loyalties.

Hence, given Weber's definition(s) of charisma, the New Testament picture of Jesus poses two problems. Not only must the nature of the leadership which emerged in the Jesus movement groups be ascertained, but how any notion of charismatic leadership could have been conceived, let alone realized at the time, must be determined. Specifically, the question is how and why an attitude of awe formed around one man in: (1) a culture that was explicitly disdainful of the glorification of personality, (2) a culture in which complete deference to higher human authority was questionable, (3) a culture in which every form of power was deliberately and systematically scrutinized. Were such barriers to charismatic attraction in fact overcome?

As has been frequently noted (by, for example, Schüssler Fiorenza 1983:105ff.), the Jesus movement was a conservative revival, aspiring not to the creation of a new order but to the restoration of Israel and its previously held values and institutions. It was to the objective of the restoration of Israel that Jesus eventually committed himself. Jesus, therefore, did not employ his talents in a situation of chaotic disorder. Rather the situation was one in which traditional values could not be effectively realized, a normal situation for much of the history of Israel. As a healer he was not exactly extraordinary (see Hollenbach 1981). Extraordinary healers were considered magicians or wizards; and although Jesus was accused of being such, he denies it and the stigma does not take (see Mark 4:22–7). As an honorable teacher and master of riposte in the social quest for honor, he seems to have been as good as the best of his day (see Malina 1993:28–62). Rabbinic reports document similar abilities (see Neusner 1962). His proclaiming of a forthcoming theocracy ("the kingdom of heaven") was not so much an alternative to the political ideology prevailing in Israel as a hope for its radical realization. For as a staunch conservative revivalist he was devoted to the preservation rather than to the radical change of his society's political culture. Moreover, his leadership (not healing style, i.e. commanding demons) contained no authoritarian elements. He did not distinguish himself by feats performed to acquire power over others – his healings were attributed to God by his "amazed" and "astonished" contemporaries (see, for example, Mark 1:27; 2:12; etc.). Rather he distinguished himself by the lengths to which he went to avoid power (alternative Messianic power roles are repeatedly rejected: see, for example, Mark 8:11–12,33), and by the enthusiasm with which he empowered others (sending out the Twelve, see Mark 6:7–13; the Seventy, see Luke 10:1–12; asking the healed to return home and be followers there, see Mark 5:19, etc.). Finally, his core-group disciples certainly did not form a "charismatic" community with members emotionally tied to each other (they are concerned about their recompense for joining the movement group, Mark 9:28–30; and about their relative standing, Mark 9:35–9). And their commitment to Jesus was hardly unwavering, given their flight upon his capture (Mark 14:50). All these features point away from Weber's typology of charisma. These features along with the critique of Weber offered by Schwartz are totally ignored by recent German scholarship on the question (for example Ebertz 1987; Mödritzer 1994).

JESUS AS SYMBOLIC LEADER

Jesus' accession to local and regional acclaim was rather abrupt. Within the course of a year (in John three years) and on the basis of successful healings, proclamation, teaching and challenge-ripostes of honor, he gained the adulation of Galilean, Perean and Judean crowds. His fame spread even before he did anything for people;

they gathered to him on the basis of his growing prestige, either to be healed or to witness unsuccessful challenges to his honor. The transformation of the honorable Galilean healer into the revered ethnic Messiah is rather remarkable. To clarify this point, perhaps Durkheim can provide a point of departure:

> In the present day just as much as in the past, we see society constantly creating sacred things out of ordinary ones. If it happens to fall in love with a man and if it thinks it has found in him the principal aspirations that move it, as well as the means of satisfying them, this man will be raised above others and, as it were, deified. . . . And the fact that it is society alone which is the author of these varieties of apotheosis, is evident since it frequently chances to consecrate men thus who have no right to it from their own merit.
>
> (1912:243–4)

What, then, were the "principal aspirations" that Jesus despite his Galilean origins and non-elite standing seemed so well to satisfy?

The abruptness and intensity of Jesus' veneration after his successes in Galilee must be understood in the context of Israelite attitudes toward the social situation in Palestine in general. Although Jesus repeatedly doubted and denied his own capacities to lead his following to victory over the range of social, boundary-penetrating evils (for example, Roman taxation, usurpation by more powerful Israelites, demon infestations, illness, general situations of dishonor), those who followed him – from disciples to the crowds – were not so pessimistic. Israel's glorious political past as recounted in the Torah and its various updated versions had more than enough instances of successful reversals of the status quo and revivals of the past to warrant such moderate optimism. Thus what motivated Jesus' followers was sentiments rooted in Israel's glorious story of the past rather than technical considerations and analyses of the present. The use of the Torah to verify, clarify and highlight present hopes as well as the behavior of would-be Messiahs indicates as much (for a list from Josephus, see Betz and Grimm 1977:73–4). Jesus' successful healings and ripostes against ever more prestigious opponents inspired confidence, and this largely because public opinion ascribed significance to them on the basis of Israel's past: "Never was anything like this seen in Israel" (Matt. 9:33). Jesus' persistent successes developed a "collective effervescence," connected to him as hard and visible focus. Again Durkheim:

We are unable to consider an abstract entity. For we can represent only laboriously and confusedly the source of the strong sentiments which we feel. We cannot explain them to ourselves except by connecting them to some concrete object of whose reality we are vividly aware.

(1912:251)

Thus most Galileans, Pereans and Judeans of non-elite standing were, for various reasons, hungry for a living symbol of their willingness to endure a bleak present in face of a forthcoming reversal in the political economy in their favor. (Such a reversal in the political economy is what the term "redemption" means in Leviticus 25, and Luke records that this was what peasants expected of Jesus: "we had hoped that he was the one to redeem Israel," Luke 24:21). This hunger, of course, explains neither the choice of the symbol nor its legitimacy. The symbol was, in fact, chosen and legitimated by networking processes typical of the social situation at the time (see Lande 1977a, 1977b for models). Jesus' acknowledged healing ability and demonstrated defense of his honor against challengers from increasingly wider quarters – Galilee, Judea and even Jerusalem – helped to focus and reconcile regional interests and opinions in Palestine (see Hollenbach 1981).

THE MEANING OF LEADERSHIP IN ISRAEL

Jesus, of course, meant different things to different people. For some of his contemporaries he was simply a wizard (Mark 3:22) and upstart to be disdained by anyone with the sense to see what he was up to. The most important element of this criticism was its secrecy – conspiracy was the proper mode of dealing with the Jesus faction (Herodians and Pharisees conspiring at the beginning of Jesus' public activity, see Mark 3:6; Sadducees conspiring with Herodians and Pharisees to trap Jesus, see Mark 12:13; secret agreement with Judas, see Mark 14:10–11). Obviously this sort of secret behavior indicated that the critics of Jesus were in a minority (Mark 12:12), and they were right. It would seem that popular Israelite intuitive distrust of all centralized authority, especially political theocratic authority (Mark 11:27–33), led Jesus' followers to see no great value in specific technical qualifications for leadership, such as approval by Jerusalem authorities, by significant established Pharisee groups or the like.

Further, Israelite attitudes toward Jesus were shaped by another, more positive conception regarding factional leadership. Believing firmly in their divine covenant and in their own honor, Israelites looked to faction leaders (and "rulers" in general) mainly for exemplary leadership and inspiration. The tremendous prestige accorded Jesus was fundamentally based upon the conviction that God would come to rule Israel, as of old, because of the righteous honor of the individual Israelite (see Matt. 3:7–10: John the Baptist impugning the inherited honor of "many of the Pharisees and Sadducees"; the "brood of vipers" phrase is specifically an attack against the attitude of inherited righteous honor, on the lips of both John in Matt. 3:7 and of Jesus in Matt. 12:34; 23:33). The great factional leader was seen as one who by firmness and benevolence rather than public relations or technique or brilliance would harness and direct the individual Israelite's presumed righteous honor. That Jesus was assumed to have such traits to enhance the honor of his constituents can be seen in contexts where he is hailed as Son of David (see Mark 10:47–8; Matt. 21:9, 15). This attitude was such as to lift some of the responsibility for the delay of the arrival of God's rule from Jesus, for if that promised rule resulted from the character of men, then its delay could not be attributed to the leader alone. What mattered in the leader was motivation, and Jesus' followers hastened to acknowledge its priority.

Furthermore, Jesus did not have to be a vanquishing type of hero who wipes out all the enemies of the besieged group. In social conditions where cultural values cannot be realized in daily living, victory over enemies need not entail their destruction. The focus of victory here is on the preservation of one's followers from annihilation rather than on the eradication of enemies (for example, Moses in the Exodus; Joshua in Canaan). Salvation typically consists in rescue from difficult situations, not in the eradication of enemies. To preserve followers from annihilation is to shame enemies, to dishonor them while allowing the saved to enjoy the experience of their dishonor; this experience would not be available, of course, if the enemy were destroyed.

JESUS AS SYMBOL OF ISRAELITE VALUES

The prestige conferred upon Jesus during his ministry was more than just a form of "expressive symbolism." It was an interest-gathering deposit later drawn upon to sanctify the Christian movement (see the speeches in Acts 1–9). As is well known, the social context and basis for the Christian movement group in the period after AD 30 were not the same as for the Jesus movement group prior to AD 30. During the interval marked by the death and resurrection appearances of Jesus, public perception of Jesus underwent a profound change. As Galilean healer and honorable teacher, Jesus supplied his faction with a focal point for its aspirations for a re-newed Israel. After his death–resurrection, he becomes the group's central symbol of this renewal, actually effected by the God of Israel. To understand the transformation and to learn precisely what values Jesus symbolized to those who chose to believe in his enduring presence, some knowledge of the political values of the period is necessary.

The ideology of the Jesus movement drew from many sources: contemporary Israelite biblical interpretation, post-exilic Israelite social forms, the Hellenism of the Roman *oikoumene*, and positions marking it off from other movements, notably the Baptist move-ment and the Pharisee movement. The last two sources provide many of the metaphors through which the veneration of Jesus was expressed. From the Baptist movement derives the notion of Jesus as the "One who is to come," the one who "baptizes with the Spirit," and perhaps "Prophet." From the Pharisee movement specifically – and Israelite ideology in general – comes "Messiah." But neither the Baptist movement nor Pharisaism contributes directly to the veneration of Jesus or even to the ideology of the Christian movement itself. Rather the "mind" of the Christian movement was shaped by the experience of God as "he who raised Jesus from the dead," and by the many unknown interpreters of the meaning of this experience. It was on the basis of this experience that they came to understand Jesus' life, death and resurrection both before and after the writings of Paul (perhaps the only known interpreter of Jesus whose first-century writings we in fact have – the other writings are anonymous although labelled).

To explain which of Jesus' characteristics and achievements had the most significance for his countrymen, and to show why the veneration of these qualities eventually became so intense, persistent and widespread, an understanding of first-century Mediterranean estimates of power and honor are necessary.

POWER AND HONOR

While the terms "political power" and "politics," are not buzz-words in the Jesus movement, the proclamation of the Kingdom of Heaven and of the Rule of God and talk of Sadducees, Herodians and Romans were all concretizations of the selfsame focus, political power. The disposition of this sort of power was central to every political (hence religious) controversy before, during and after the Jesus movement. Whatever one's attitude to anything else, given Roman political ascendancy, power was dwelt upon by first-century Mediterranean conquered peoples rather endlessly, almost compulsively, for its natural prey was liberty. For members of the house of Israel, this meant specifically national liberty and its attendant perception, the Kingdom of God.

In other words, any discussion of the Kingdom of God (or Heaven) presupposes contemporary forms of political power as its opposing realities. The concrete dimensions of the Kingdom of God would undoubtedly take on qualities opposed to contemporary power uses. What in contemporary uses of power was so negative, so deleterious to Israel in particular? In Palestine at least, one feature of such power was that it was wielded over God's own people in God's own land and often in God's own name by Israelite aristocrats unconcerned with the provisions for a political economy willed by the God of Israel (see, for example, Leviticus 25). And the sons of Herod the Great who actually ruled were not covenanted with God, i.e. not of the line of David, subject to the God of Israel (as per covenant promise of 2 Sam. 7:13). And even if Roman taxation practices in Palestine might be interpreted as God's punishment or God's mysterious ways, how long would such a condition last? Has it not endured too long already? For Israel the problem was not that of men in authority (as in the US tradition: see Schwartz 1983:26), but first, of the pedigree of the men wielding the power, and second, of their moral qualities in enabling the rest of the populace to live under God's covenant with his people (as per covenant promises and directives of the Torah), i.e. their honor rating.

Next to Israel's concern about power and power-wielders (the Kingdom of God/Heaven) puts its focus upon righteousness: proper interpersonal relations between man and God and man and fellow man – as determined by the Torah. Unlike the US tradition, where virtue saves human beings from their own innate depravity, in Israel, human beings are not depraved; rather their social institutions are.

Righteousness enables a person to tolerate such institutions, even work for their destruction and transformation, while pleasing the God of the covenant. The righteous person in Israel is the honorable person. While Americans believe that social structures do not maintain themselves but rest ultimately on the qualities of the people who occupy positions within them, first-century Mediterraneans did not share the same analysis. For them social structures do in fact maintain themselves, regardless of the qualities of the people who occupy positions within them. "Original" sin, the condition of sin in Rom. 5:12ff., the controlling negative power in Romans 7, and the internal negative inclination of Rabbinism are examples of such structural deficiency. If the Kingdom of God is not realized, the problem is with the enduring structures controlling the good and the wicked persons occupying positions in them. The problem is how to transform those structures. If structures are beyond human control, then only God can in fact transform them. The Kingdom of God is about the transformation of social structure.

SOME COMPARATIVE PERSPECTIVES

Most Americans today take it for granted that their government has the ability to outlive its unscrupulous leaders and protect individual liberties. The British tradition, on the other hand, was obsessed with the abuse of power and took seriously the conviction that government stands or falls on the virtues of its leaders. First-century Israelites, however, took it for granted that foreign peoples outlive their leaders and can exert continual control over the collective existence of Israel.

That the Kingdom of God might be ushered in with an Israelite king was equally a possibility. The rules of the priestly Hasmoneans, Herod the Great as well as his successors, undoubtedly fostered rather deep public distrust in the office of king. But Jesus repeatedly demonstrated indifference to personal power over others. In popular estimation, this would have enabled him to become a stronger king than a more ambitious incumbent could have hoped to become. And this all the more so, as Jesus continued to reject kingship aspirations entirely. (Yet in the crucifixion narrative, Jesus' tormentors treat him with the contempt typical of deep distrust in the office of king: see Mark 15:17–18.)

Against a background of almost paranoid concern over the use and usurpation of power and an ideology which attributed to social

138

institutions an inherent "corruption," and to kingly claimants a "lust for power," it is no wonder that Jesus was looked upon as a most extraordinary moral hero. In those authoritarian contexts which give rise to the Weberian model of charisma (i.e. charismatic leadership), it is the successful taking and exercise of power that evokes admiration. But in first-century Judaism it was just the opposite: refusal to assume power when it was offered by circumstances characterizes persons committed to the Kingdom of God. On the other hand, in the US it is hesitancy to seek and assume office and haste in giving it up that are the ingredients going into political spectacles.

CONCLUSION

Grounded in a different set of social circumstances, the perception of Jesus in Christian movement groups was not something that could be read from the way he was perceived during the early part of his career. The honor accorded Jesus in Galilee with his successful healing activity, teaching and riposte to challengers was generated in a context of great and growing emotional fervor. Since the excited expressions of honor attributed to Jesus preceded any concrete claim to power on his part, it is fair to assume that anyone filling the role of healer and successful public teacher would have been as much esteemed as he was. In this sense, the initial phase of Jesus' career as Israelite symbol was "role-based." In contrast, the post-resurrection praise of Jesus invariably made references to what he did from the perspective of what the God of Israel did to him. This God of tradition somehow was in the death of Jesus and subsequently raised him. The resurrection marks a new revelation of the nature of God. As the Burning Bush and Sinai served for Moses and Israel as revelation of God, so now the Raised Jesus serves as revelation of God, whose new name is: "He who raised Jesus from the dead." Consequently, Jesus' honorable "passive" role in interacting with people, his "disinterestedness" in power and his inevitable accumulation of honor stand out all the more clearly. In this sense the second phase of Jesus' veneration was "performance-based," and significantly, God's performance with Jesus was passive.

In both phases of Jesus' career, the correspondence between his veneration and the concerns of his countrymen is mediated by a kind of "venerational reason," a form of encoding based on metaphoric appreciation (see Schwartz 1983:30). Jesus' commitment to the Kingdom of Heaven was a commitment to a set of political values, to a political culture (with religion, economics and kinship embedded). And such commitment on his part shows up in the form of devotion to him. To see Jesus in this way is to see him as a "collective representation," a visible symbol of the values and the tendencies of his society rather than as a source of those values and tendencies. Jesus thus personifies the values and goals of those who followed him. He was a first-century reputational, legitimate leader and the very antithesis of Weber's charismatic leader.

While the great charismatic leader à la Weber exudes confidence in his extraordinary abilities, thrives on power and glorification and, lacking ties to the established social order, seeks to effect its radical change, the great reputational, legitimate leader, exemplified in Jesus, affirms the traditional values and structures of his society by repudiating personal power. Thus if the Jesus movement (and the subsequent Christian movement) was an essentially revivalist, conservative development – a struggle not to create but to restore and maintain a society willed by God – then the image of Jesus may be its perfect symbolic expression.

Weberian charismatic leadership celebrates the decisive deed and the historical significance of a leading figure's initiative by stressing change over tradition, assigning priority of action over structure, and focusing on the possibility of sudden social transformation by extraordinary men. In contrast, the traits characteristic of what is known about Jesus reflect a political ideology more respectful of institutional restraints and procedures, one which conceives of power not as a prize to be seized from the community but as an obligation imposed by it. Accordingly, whoever personifies this ideology must be the model public servant, and in the context of the kingdom, the "servant or slave of God," who overcomes and/or sidesteps the authoritarian potential inherent in his own glorification (see Mark 10:45; Matt. 20:28; Luke 22:27). He must be distinguished from the Weberian, "Caesaristic" leader who exploits mass support for the purpose of establishing charismatic dictatorship. Against the Weberian conception with its emphasis on entitlement, privilege and strength, the ideal of leadership in first-century Palestine emphasized the Mediterranean qualities of honor, righteousness and service of the God of Israel. It would seem that the leadership of Jesus of Nazareth as described in the earliest sources describes this latter sort of ideal rather than Weberian charismatic leadership.

REFERENCES

Betz, Otto and Werner Grimm (1977) *Wesen und Wirklichkeit der Wunder Jesu: Heilungen, Rettungen, Zeichen, Aufleuchtungen.* Arbeiten zum Neuen Testament und Judentum 2. Frankfurt-on-Main: Lang.

Bohannan, Paul (1973) "The Differing Realms of the Law." pp. 306–17 in Donald Black and Maureen Mileski (eds) *The Social Organization of Law.* New York: Seminar.

Camic, Charles (1980) "Charisma: Its Varieties, Preconditions, and Consequences." *Sociological Inquiry* 50:5–23.

Durkheim, Emile (1912) *The Elementary Forms of Religious Life.* New York: Free Press (repr. 1965).

Ebertz, Michael N. (1987) *Das Charisma des Gekreuzigten: Zur Soziologie der Jesusbewegung.* WUNT 45. Tübingen: Mohr [Siebeck].

Emmet, Dorothy (1958) *Function, Purpose, Power.* London: Macmillan.

Gager, John G. (1975) *Kingdom and Community: The Social World of Early Christianity.* Englewood Cliffs: Prentice-Hall.

Hollenbach, Paul W. (1981) "Jesus, Demoniacs, and Public Authorities: A Socio-Historical Study." *Journal of the American Academy of Religion* 49:567–88.

Kuhn, Johannes (1932) "Address to the George Washington Bicentennial Banquet, Dresden." pp. 142–3 in *History of the George Washington Bicentennial Celebration.* Washington: US George Washington Bicentennial Commission.

Lande, Carl H. (1977a) "Introduction: The Dyadic Basis of Clientelism." pp. xiii–xxxvii in Steffen W. Schmidt, James C. Scott, Carl Lande and Laura Guasti (eds) *Friends, Followers, and Factions: A Reader in Political Clientelism.* Berkeley: University of California Press.

—— (1977b) "Networks and Groups in Southeast Asia: Some Observations on the Group Theory of Politics." pp. 75–99 in Steffen W. Schmidt, James C. Scott, Carl Lande and Laura Guasti (eds) *Friends, Followers, and Factions: A Reader in Political Clientelism.* Berkeley: University of California Press.

McIntosh, Donald (1970) "Weber and Freud: On the Nature and Sources of Authority." *American Sociological Review* 35:901–11.

Malina, Bruce J. (1981) "The Apostle Paul and Law: Prolegomena for an Hermeneutic." *Creighton Law Review* 14:1305–39.

—— (1986a) *Christian Origins and Cultural Anthropology: Practical Models for Biblical Interpretation.* Atlanta: John Knox.

—— (1986b) "Normative Dissonance and Christian Origins." pp. 35–59 in John H. Elliott (ed.) *Semeia*, Vol. 35: *Social-scientific Criticism of the New Testament and its Social World.* Decatur, GA: Scholars.

—— (1993) *New Testament World: Insight from Cultural Anthropology.* Louisville: Westminster/John Knox.

Miyahara, Kojiro (1983) "Charisma: From Weber to Contemporary Sociology." *Sociological Inquiry* 53:368–88.

Mödritzer, Helmut (1994) *Stigma und Charisma im Neuen Testament und seiner Umwelt: Zur Soziologie des Urchristentums.* Novum Testamentum et Orbis Antiquus 28. Göttingen: Vandenhoeck & Ruprecht.

Neusner, Jacob (1962) *A Life of Rabban Yohanan ben Zakkai: Ca. 1–80 C.E.* Studia Post-Biblica 6. Leiden: Brill.

Roth, Guenther (1975) "Socio-historical Model and Developmental Theory: Charismatic Community, Charisma of Reason and the Counterculture." *American Sociological Review* 40:148–57.

Schüssler Fiorenza, Elisabeth (1983) *In Memory of Her: A Feminist Theological Reconstruction of Christian Origins.* New York: Crossroad.

Schütz, John H. (1974) "Charisma and Social Reality in Primitive Christianity." *Journal of Religion* 54:51–70.

Schwartz, Barry (1983) "George Washington and the Whig Conception of Heroic Leadership." *American Sociological Review* 48:18–33.

— (1987) *George Washington: The Making of an American Symbol.* New York: Free Press.

Selznick, Philip, Leon H. Mayhew, Phillippe Nonet and Jerome E. Carlin (1968) "Law." In David L. Sills (ed.) *International Encyclopedia of the Social Sciences* 9:49–78. New York: Macmillan and Free Press.

Shils, Edward (1965) "Charisma, Order and Status." *American Sociological Review* 30:199–213.

— (1968) "Charisma." In David Sills (ed.) *International Encyclopedia of the Social Sciences* 2:386–90. New York: Macmillan/Free Press.

Tucker, Robert C. (1968) "The Theory of Charismatic Leadership." *Daedalus* 97:731–56.

Weber, Max (1968) *Economy and Society.* Trans. G. Roth and C. Wittich. Berkeley: University of California Press (German orig. 1922).

Worsley, Peter (1968) *The Trumpet Shall Sound: A Study of "Cargo" Cults in Melanesia.* New York: Schocken.

6

PATRON AND CLIENT
The analogy behind synoptic theology

INTRODUCTION

The people of Palestine at the time of Jesus formed a traditional peasant society (see Carney 1973:100–3). Such societies invariably have extremely wealthy landowners who provide the landless with land (and other items, such as tools and seed) to work in return for a specified share of the harvest (and other items, such as labor). This relationship and its obligations, called tenancy, is established by contract, written or unwritten, in conformity with custom, and more unusually, with law. In practice, such institutional arrangements often fall short of what they are intended to realize. Tenants may face emergencies ranging from family illness to drought. They may have to make provisions for the following year, yet lack certainty of tenure. The landowner can see to such needs of his or her tenant, but he or she is not obliged to do so under the tenancy agreement. Any help afforded beyond the bare bones of the contract is favor (bene-faction, grace). The tenant, in turn, is under no obligation to show respect, affection or friendly feelings to the owner of the land he works. Yet in peasant societies, landowners look for respect since what counts to them as well as to their tenants is honor; landowners need the "status support" that only their tenants can give them. "The establishment of special relationship between a landowner and *some* of his tenants, and an assurance of conspicuous deference and loyalty to the landlord, constitutes the patron–client addendum to the insti-tutionalized landlord–tenant relationship" (Landé 1977:xxi).

The patron–client relationship is a special type of personal, vertical, dyadic relationship. According to Eisenstadt and Roniger (1984:48–9), the features that all patron–client societies have in common are the following:

1   Patron–client relations are particularistic and diffuse (usually).
2   Patron–client interaction involves the exchange of a whole range of generalized symbolic media: power, influence, inducement, commitment.
3   The exchange entails a package deal, so that generalized symbolic media cannot be given separately (for example, concretely useful goods must go along with loyalty, solidarity).
4   Solidarity here entails a strong element of unconditionality and long-range social credit.
5   Hence patron–client relations involve a strong element of interpersonal obligation, ranging from high to low salience, even if relations are often ambivalent.
6   These relations are not fully legal or contractual, but very strongly binding, i.e. they are informal and often opposed to official laws of the country.
7   In principle, patron–client relations entered into voluntarily can be abandoned voluntarily, although always proclaimed to be lifelong, long-range, forever, etc.
8   Patron–client relations are vertical and dyadic (between individuals or networks of individuals), thus undermining the horizontal group organization and solidarity of clients and other patrons.
9   Patron–client relations are based on strong inequality and difference between patrons and clients. Patrons monopolize certain positions of crucial importance to clients, especially access to means of production, major markets, and centers of society.[1]

Special patron–client relationships invariably emerge in social systems in which the institutionalized order is considered inadequate to realize a meaningful, social, human existence. This inadequacy is rooted in a perceived lack of trust and confidence in other persons as well as in the institutional arrangements themselves. Where politics is focused solely on the well-being of office holders, including priests, where public religion is focused exclusively on the well-being of office holders, especially priests, where public economics is focused only on the well-being of the seller and office holders as well, there the governed, believers and buyers see little if any concern for their welfare in institutional arrangements (for the Roman empire as an instance of this situation, see Carney 1975:101ff.). The values touted by society and the realization of those values stand miles apart. Mutual trust is perceived as inflated and unreliable. One cannot know who is a neighbor, a friend, an ally. Social relations are agonistic, central authoritative personages are weak, and traditional values are upheld while being constantly subverted by agonistic boundary building.

Such a scenario inevitably entails adult males, usually, busily at work setting up direct relationships of personal attachment involving some form of interaction with a single other individual. This is a dyadic relationship (see Malina 1993:63ff.) Part of a meaningful, social human existence requires males to enter such relationships in a spirit of nothing ventured, nothing gained, with as many other willing partners as necessary to maintain a family with due honor. Such relationships are formed with peers, and hence are horizontal, or with a social superior, and hence are vertical. The patron–client relationship is of this latter sort.

The larger social goal pursued by means of such dyadic relationships is favor, "something received on terms more advantageous than those that can be obtained by anyone on an *ad hoc* basis in the market place or which cannot be obtained in the market place at all" (Landé 1977:xv).[2] Favoritism is the main quality of such relationships. The New Testament is heavily sprinkled with the vocabulary of favoritism, such as benefaction (see Danker 1982), reward, gift, grace and the like.[3] Horizontal dyadic relations between individuals of equal status, power or resources involve the exchange of favors and help in time of need. Invariably these are of similar quality. On the other hand, vertical dyadic relations, i.e. patron–client relations, between individuals of highly unequal status, power or resources involve the exchange of favors and help of a qualitatively different sort: material for immaterial, goods for honor and praise, force for status support and the like.

Such patron–client relations are commonly employed to remedy the inadequacies of all institutions, to cushion the vagaries of life for social inferiors. In our own day, for example, Third World preindustrial markets fail to protect ordinary customers against the risk of paying a higher than necessary price for goods of lower than normal quality since there are no fixed prices and no standardized quality (much like our technology repair: auto, computer, washer, TV, etc.; for the grammar of haggling see Hall 1959:151–3). To remedy this there are regular buyer–seller relations in which being a regular customer is exchanged for assured lowest possible price without haggling for the highest-quality goods available. This is favoritism in the marketplace. Similarly, one can find a favorite priest or saint offering assured understanding and help without effort for the highest-quality meaning possible; a favorite policeman offering an assured outcome without bribery for the highest-quality power possible; a favorite friend offering assured nurturing and support without begging for the highest quality commitment possible.

In the world of the New Testament, patron–client relations might be added to the legally sanctioned subordination of a slave to his or her owner just as in the legally sanctioned subordination of tenant to landowner. Thus the slave might be protected against the risks of being sold, killed or beaten, while the slave owner obtains the trust and commitment of the slave in question. Other examples of such personal subordination besides slavery include domestic service, "religious" service or worship, indentured labor, military occupation, apprenticeships of various sorts, including discipleship in philosophical schools, various tenancies (agricultural, bureaucratic, non-elite military rank). These institutions consist of essentially vertical dyadic relations. What the inferior lacks is assurance of aid in various emergencies and guarantee of permanent access to resources. This lack of assurance bespeaks a lack of and need for commitment on the part of one who might help (= special favor). No superior is obliged to provide such assurance and guarantee. On the other hand, the subordinate has no obligation to treat the superior with respect or affection or to accept any offer of abiding commitment.

What patron–client relations essentially entail is endowing and outfitting economic, political or religious institutional arrangements with an overarching quality of kinship. Such relations "kin-ify" and suffuse the persons involved with the aura of kinship, albeit fictive or pseudo-kinship (see Pitt-Rivers 1968). And since the hallmark of kinship as social institution is the quality of commitment, solidarity or loyalty realized in terms of generalized reciprocity, patron–client relations take on these kinship dimensions. Thus economic, political and religious interactions now take place between individuals bound together by mutual commitment, solidarity and loyalty in terms of generalized reciprocity, rather than the balanced reciprocity of unconnected equals or the negative reciprocity typical of superiors to their subordinates.

Just as law is the double institutionalization of custom, so patron–client is an addendum to custom (see Malina 1986a:112–38). It adds the qualitative symbol of commitment to politics, economics and religion and thus moves political, economic and religious relations into the realm of kinship. In ancient societies (as in most traditional societies) institutionalized relationships between persons of unequal power status and resources were highly exploitive in nature. They are based on power, applied vertically as force in harsh and impersonal fashion. Superiors sought to maximize their gains without a thought to the gains of those with whom they interacted. Thus, "the fact that even though a patron–client relationship connects persons of unequal status and power, it requires that they treat each other, and especially that the patron treat the client, equitably and with a special concern for each other's welfare" (Landé 1977:xxiii).

GOD THE PATRON

If Jesus called God "Father,"[4] then what he did was apply kinship terminology to the God of Israel, the central and focal symbol of Israel's traditional political religion. This sort of "kin-ification" is typically patron–client behavior. God, the "Father," is nothing less than God the Patron. It would seem, then, that in order to obtain adequate scenarios for understanding God's relationship to humankind as described by Jesus, a set of patron–client models should prove invaluable.

God as patron

The theme of God as Patron is heavily and explicitly underscored in Matthew.[5] More than 70 percent of his sixty-four uses of the word "father" refer to the God of Israel. Since "father" here does not mean "father" in any actual first-century, Mediterranean social sense, I suggest that the closest translation into contemporary English, mirroring first-century Mediterranean behavior, is "patron." The "Kingdom of God/Heaven" would be God's patronage and the clientele bound up in it; "to enter the Kingdom of God/Heaven" would mean to enjoy the patronage of God, the heavenly Patron, and hence to become client; and the introductory phrase: "the Kingdom of God/Heaven is like" would come out as "the way God's patronage relates and affects his clients is like the following scenario." Aalen (1962:226) described Jesus' conception of the Kingdom of Heaven as: "a new state of affairs, a definitive outpouring and sending of powers of deliverance and salvation, a restitution of mankind, a fulfillment of the world, or the beginning of this fulfillment." "Kingdom" is not "kingship or reign" but a realm, a community,

147

a "house" (240). Aalen mirrors the confusion in the gospel story-line. For the political religion proclaimed by Jesus (i.e. the kingdom) is in fact a fictive kin group (i.e. clientele, brothers and sisters), as emerges in the early Christian movement. Here I shall simply heighten the focus so that "kingdom" emerges as "clientele" in a patronage relationship.

All the Synoptics agree that Jesus proclaimed the Kingdom of God/Heaven, i.e. the proximate enjoyment of the benefaction of God as king. And they all have a heavenly voice witness to Jesus as beloved son, i.e. one who enjoys special divine patronage. It is no surprise, then, that in the narrative Jesus' essential emphasis was on the readily available benefaction of the God of Israel for all his subjects. Since God is "Father," these subjects are in fact clients. Of course, the place "to see God" (Matt. 5:8) was the Jerusalem Temple. There the immediate staff and entourage of God, his contracted servants, were the priests. Their task was to act as functionaries and facilitate interaction with the great God of Israel, a veritable heavenly Monarch. The ready availability of God's patronage apart from the Temple meant that Temple services, the official protocol to be followed to enjoy God's favor, was no longer required. Instead of subjects approaching the Monarch through functionaries, clients now approach the divine Patron without officialdom, and regardless of the clients' social standing. For example, in Matthew the Beatitudes (Matt. 5:3–12) offer first indications of the benefits of this patronage: the ready enjoyment of God's patronage, i.e. the Kingdom of God/Heaven itself, actual possession of the Patron's land, comfort and satisfaction meted out by the Patron, ready availability of the Patron to realize his part of the dyadic relationship (= mercy), acclamation by the Patron of being a favored recipient of patronage (= called sons of God) and recompense for maintaining the patron's honor (= your reward is great in heaven). Matt. 10:5 indicates that the original clientele was meant, initially, to be restricted to Israel. Clients were to show appreciative service on their Patron's behalf, bearing the "yoke of the kingdom of heaven," i.e. loving God with one's whole heart, life and wealth (Deut. 6:4). The divine Patron, like any patron, required to be honored publicly, i.e. to be glorified by his clients (Matt. 5:16). This is what Jesus' benefactions lead to (Matt. 9:8; 15:31; and Luke often). Yet as we shall see, Jesus did not behave as a patron, but as a broker; this is indicated in the gospel story by the fact that he gives power to his disciples, brokering God's power on behalf of other clients (Matt. 10:8).

148

Favor and favoritism

People have patrons because they need favors at certain times. They expect to be dealt with in terms more advantageous than those that can be obtained by anyone else as needs arise. The parable of the grumbling hirelings (Matt. 20:1–15), if it points to anything, it points to the fact that those hired are contract hirelings, not clients of the vineyard owner. Since they are contract workers, they should have no complaints. Their sense of injustice is rooted in the belief that they are clients, and the rude awakening in the story is that they in fact are not. Similarly, they expect, in time of need, to receive favors that are otherwise not obtainable. Favoritism is one of the purposes of dyadic alliances. Showing favoritism is a main means of maintaining the personal attachment that patron–client relations require. Such favoritism is a public display of the alliance to potential friends and actual and potential foes. And it often entails exchange of unwanted or unneeded favors. This latter exchange is ceremonial, celebrating those within an alliance. When favor exchange ends, the alliance is over. Hence the client's need never to express termination of the patron–client arrangement.

JESUS THE BROKER[6]

Patron and broker: social entrepreneurs

Another way to understand patron–client relations is with the model of a social entrepreneur. An *entrepreneur* is a person who, in some discernible form, initiates the manipulation of other persons and resources in the pursuit of personal benefits. Obviously the patron who makes his or her goods and services available to select clients is such an entrepreneur. But there is also a class of persons who can put prospective clients in touch with significant patrons. These are *social brokers*. Both patrons and brokers are entrepreneurs. Both roles often require risk and innovation. And their main expertise or specialty is social network relations.

Those central persons who become social entrepreneurs are individual replications of those social forms called villages, towns and cities. Where communication channels such as roads and rivers meet as transportation network centers, there social forms such as villages and cities develop. So also where "important" social networks meet, the meeting point is invariably a person, a symbolic center, about whom a range of social forms develop. The social forms of interest here are patron–client relations and factions.

As Boissevain has noted (1974:148–9), social entrepreneurs deal with two types of resources: (1) First-order resources such as land, jobs, goods, funds, power, information, all of which the entrepreneur controls directly. Such entrepreneurs are called *patrons*. (2) Second-order resources which are largely strategic contact with other people who control first-order resources or who have access to those who control first-order resources. Such entrepreneurs are called *brokers*.

Just as the analogy of patron is but one among the many available analogies for describing the God of Israel and need not be employed at all (king, lord, shepherd, etc. might do as well), so too not all potential patrons or brokers actually take up the role. People in the first-century Mediterranean knew quite well that centrally situated people become symbolic centers only under certain conditions: if they have interest in and talent for cultivating relations with strategic persons; if they can manipulate these relations for some benefits; if they can stay ahead of competitors; and that they take up the role because they are innovative and willing to take risks.

Jesus proclaims the ready enjoyment of God's patronage, and in fact by means of his healing and teaching takes up the role of broker relative to the patronage offered by the God of Israel. And in his preferred description of God, Jesus focuses on God as Patron. Consider the God of Israel as Patron in terms of the qualities of a Mediterranean patron:

1 He has interest in and talent for cultivating relations with strategic persons. (The initiative of the God of Israel in choosing Abraham, Isaac, Jacob and their descendants in Egypt for the conquest of Canaan and subsequent occupation, kingship, exile and the like admirably illustrates this God's interest in choosing a people and cultivating relations with its strategic persons.)

2 He can manipulate these relations for some benefit. (The pay-off which the God of the Fathers seeks in freeing Israel from Egypt is worship – proper recognition, honor and subservience.)

3 He can stay ahead of competitors. (The God of Israel insists on staying ahead of competitors, disallowing any other gods, while social interpreters such as prophets continually indicate God's control of the fate of Israel.)

4 This he does because he is innovative. (The social form of covenant with individual males of non-elite status along with a

range of Torah directives for the well-being of the people in the land point to such innovation.)

5   He is willing to take risks. (This theme of risk-taking is poignantly underscored in those prophets who point up the people's practical and theoretical rejection of God's initiative.)

If the only adequate analogy for describing God in biblical tradition is that of person, obviously God is a central person *par excellence* and can be none other than a social entrepreneur. As creator and covenant God, he clearly controls first-order resources, and hence can be readily understood as Patron. Within this scheme, Jesus with his proclamation of the Kingdom of God/Heaven and activity with relation to it occupies the position of broker of the Kingdom, offering second-order resources of strategic contact with God as Patron, the heavenly Father. Consider Jesus as broker in terms of the foregoing entrepreneurial features.

To begin with, as a broker Jesus too is a social entrepreneur with interest in and talent for cultivating relations with strategic persons, at least in Capernaum. He moved from the tiny hamlet of Nazareth (ca. 100 persons) to bustling Capernaum (ca. 8,000 or more?), and made contact with persons with lakeside transportation facilities, and information flow (tax or toll collector), as well as building up a fund of credit by healing. Then he manipulated these relations to his own benefit, obtaining honor as well as material support since he could dedicate himself to this brokerage once his contacts were firm. His competitors, local Pharisees and scribes, quickly took note of his success while he remained ahead of them, at least in Galilee. Jesus, by all accounts, was indeed innovative both in ideology and in program, while his insight into the fact that if he continued he would die points to his willingness to take risks.

Jesus the broker

In the gospel story, Jesus takes up the role of broker, not patron (as attributed to him in the later church, certainly after Constantine). In general a social broker places people in touch with each other, directly or indirectly, for some personal benefit. Brokers appear in a variety of guises, such as marriage brokers, real estate brokers and Mafioso dons, as well as letter writers in antiquity. In the gospel story, Jesus launches on a far more serious task, given the embedded quality of religion in the first-century Mediterranean (see Malina

1986b; 1994). He is a broker of the Kingdom of God/Heaven, offering to put people in contact with a heavenly Patron who, in turn, is ready to provide first-order resources of a political, religious and economic sort. Hence, as Yoder once noted, "Jesus' proclamation of the kingdom was unacceptable to most of his listeners *not* because they thought it could not happen but because they feared it might, and that it would bring down judgment on them" (1972: 88–9). They would not pay the price of such patronage. The price, of course, was willingness to enter dyadic alliance with the God of Israel.

A *social broker*, by definition, is a professional manipulator of people and information who brings about communication for personal benefit. Note how those early Christian roles of traveling apostle, prophet, proclaimer or preacher fit the description of broker. They manipulate people and information. And they also seek personal gain (for example, the benefits they are promised in Mark 10:29 are 100 percent in the present and participation in the soon to be transformed world). The reason for their reward is that they serve as agents of the central broker, Jesus. If Jesus and those who were commissioned by him were effective to any extent (Mark 6:30), that would be due to their social credit rating since the effectiveness of the broker depends upon his social credit rating.

According to one model of communication, a sender (source) sends a message to a person receiving along some channel to have some effect in a given time and place. The main task in communication is for the sender to get the message on the channel, and for the receiver to get it off the channel, while the sender receives a tariff, some personal benefit. In line with this model, the social broker is the sender or source who is to get the message on some appropriate channel(s). His or her success in doing so depends upon his or her social credit rating and the anticipated tariff. The channels are role relations in the broker's personal network, his or her set of relatives, friends and other "connections." Networks consisting of well-placed relatives (for example, in John 18:16) are high capacity/low tariff. Jesus does not employ such networks, although they do come into play in the Jerusalem community in Acts. Other networks are high capacity/high tariff, for example, a faction core group. It is this sort of network that Jesus builds in Capernaum, with outreach throughout Galilee.

Why Jesus became a social broker

People choose to become social brokers, as a rule, when two necessary and sufficient criteria are met: First, the structure and content of a person's social network must be sufficient to allow for brokerage; and second, a person must be willing to use that social network for personal gain, as a profession or means of livelihood.

To consider the first aspect, the features of network structure and content that assist in successful brokerage include centrality, time and power. Centrality refers to a person's occupying a bridge location between two clusters, cultures or organizations, for example, between bureaucrat and uneducated peasant, between Roman conqueror and conquered populace. It seems that from John the Baptizer, Jesus learned of God the Patron with a renewed and growing clientele. And from John, Jesus likewise learned of his own ability to occupy the position between that patron and his traditional clientele, Israel (see Hollenbach 1982). At the time John was imprisoned, Jesus devoted himself to this brokerage full-time. Relations have to be serviced; hence they take time. One who has more time to devote to servicing social relations is more likely to have a wider range of social relations and to be better informed than others. By recruiting a faction to participate in the brokerage, probably during a period of low occupation, Jesus puts himself in a good position for servicing relations with excellent opportunities for success. Finally, the power required for a successful social broker is power in the sense of control over first-order resources. Jesus' healing ability, his success at exorcism and his teaching renown "not like the scribes" all point to access to first-order resources, to the heavenly Patron, as the acknowledgement of the crowds indicates. Since manifest power affects the quality of the signal, the more power points to less noise and more relays triggered underscoring prominence.

What sort of benefits did Jesus acquire as broker

All commentators agree that patron–client relations are rooted in reciprocity (see Boissevain 1974; Eisenstadt and Roniger 1984; Landé 1977; Rouland 1979; and the people they cite). Patrons provide favors to their clients, while clients know and feel themselves in debt to their patrons for whatever the patron might wish, whenever the patron might wish. This sort of open-ended debt of gratitude marks generalized reciprocity (see Malina 1986a:101–22). It is such

153

an accumulation of debts of gratitude, with the culturally sanctioned awareness that they may be called in, that serves as gain for a patron. And the same is true of brokers. The main way in which brokers gain personal benefit is by accumulating debts of generalized reciprocity, hence by amassing debtors. Their motto might be said to be: "Do much for people, ask little in return." Social brokerage is a business consisting of a service. To the best of our knowledge, it was the chief occupation of the last period of Jesus' career. From our etic viewpoint, we might note the follow features of this, Jesus' business:

(1) *Capital*: Jesus' capital, like that of any other social broker, consisted of his personal network of relations with people. In the gospel story, this network must have been good in Capernaum since those whom Jesus summons to form his coalition do so quite readily.

(2) *Tariff*: Tariff is the value which Jesus, like any other broker, derived from the reciprocal transactions entailed in his brokerage. The tariff involved included services (invited to people's houses, funds contributed), information ("who do people say that I am?"), standing ("and his fame spread"), good will ("and they brought all their sick, possessed," etc.), honor, *but as a rule* the tariff will be a debt of generalized, interpersonal obligation for services rendered (cf. Matt. 11:28: "Come to me all you who labor," etc.). "Communicate with the patron now and pay me later," or "Pay me now and communicate with the patron later." In order to keep the relation open, the tariff is never paid in full. A "Thank you" would mean "No more, thank you," and hence that the broker's services would no longer be required.

(3) *Credit rating*: Credit in this context is the degree of faith which people have in the broker's ability to have a patron work on their behalf or against them. A credit rating, then, is what others think a broker's "capital" is. These consist of expectations and future possible services rather than certainties, i.e. they consist of faith and hope. Jesus the healer, exorcizer and teacher provided effective communication services (i.e. mediation, brokerage) to the God of Israel since it was the God of Israel who in fact healed, controlled demons and revealed himself to Moses in the Torah.

(4) *Debt*: Debt is an obligation to a broker incurred by his or her rendering service, i.e. using his network on behalf of another. An offer of service to one in need establishes credit in that it also makes the other liable. With every service performed, those helped and/or taught incurred a debt of gratitude. Jesus thus increased his

own credit because each debt was an open communication channel for return of services. In effect the one helped owed both the heavenly Patron and his broker Jesus. Thus debts owed a broker are in fact a listing of the broker's credit. Summaries such as: "In the evening . . . he healed many," etc. (Mark 1:34) provide a list of credit in the story. The debts owed Jesus the broker were proof that a large number of creditors had faith in the broker to provide services.

God the Patron and Jesus the broker

How does the role of the patron compare with that of a broker? A patron must *give* out first-order, non-expandable, limited resources, while a broker deals in *promises* to consult "patrons." In normal social interactions, a patron's credit is more limited than that of a broker. Yet the God of Israel had no limits. Unlike Graeco-Roman deities, this God found all things possible. Hence his credit exceeded that of his broker. As patron, God dealt in power (and politics) and inducement (and economics). His broker, Jesus, on the other hand, dealt in influence (and religion) and commitment (and kinship).

Since in normal social interactions, a patron's credit is more limited than that of a broker, religious, political, economic or kinship leaders are usually able to recruit a greater following by playing the role of broker rather than that of patron. The prophets and messianic claimants of Israel all played the role of broker.

Jesus as broker had his career interrupted in quite untimely a fashion by his shameful death. The gospel story does not provide a description of the *profits* he might have derived had this business continued, although in a sense Acts does provide some such information. For a broker normally reaps *interest*. This refers to the broker's ability to decide when and what will be repaid in generalized reciprocal obligation. The Risen Jesus in Matthew's commission and in Luke's advice seems to be asking that previous debts be paid to the core group. As broker, Jesus can do this more effectively than God the Patron since first-order resources are quantifiable, limited and not easily recoverable, while second-order resources are expandable and amenable to inflation/deflation. In fact, the charge to make disciples of Israelites situated among all nations and to preach to Israelites in Jerusalem, Judea and Samaria and to the ends of the earth points to expanding the network. Further, in Acts we read of conversion in the sense of the broker's ability to convert capital (network, contact with the Patron) and credit (people's faith in the broker's ability for or against them) into first-order resources such as property, goods, donations, political influence and the like. People who promise such conversion but refuse are treated quite violently (Ananias and Sapphira). Whose power was behind these deaths, the heavenly Patron's or the broker's? What stands behind this question is the normal social problem with conversion. Conversion makes a broker into a patron. If first-order goods come to Jesus' group because of their brokerage, this will make Jesus unequivocally tied to his *promises to make first-order resources available*, and not just information and commitment. Thus if his promises cannot be realized by his own provisioning of goods and services, his credit rapidly diminishes, and the broker's focus on the future and probabilities is lost; credit inflates.

Jesus' job description as broker

Jesus' job description as broker, like any broker's actual job description, was drawn in terms of his social *niche*. This refers to his position in a network marking his location relative to resources (centrality, prestige, time to service relations), competitors and clients. The ordinary problems faced by anyone embarking on a career of social brokerage include, first of all, the problem of acquiring customers, users of his or her services. This is normally done by getting a powerful patron. The broker's influence is then limited by and to the resources of his or her patron, and the broker is quite closely bound to the powerful patron in question. On the other hand, a broker might connect up with another broker, as, for example, Jesus joining John the Baptist. This is better for the broker since messages can be varied. The pool of users/debtors expands more rapidly since the newer broker can share in the pool of the other broker, which he or she adds his or her own. And the newer broker is less bound to the other broker. Now, in the story of Jesus we find both procedures. Initially both John and Jesus are connected, and this to the same powerful patron, the God of Israel. Soon Jesus goes on his own and recruits his own core group, developing his own faction.

A broker can fail in his or her efforts, and this too is a problem. Theoretically, blame for lack of success is or can be passed on to the patron (it was not God's will), or to a more powerful broker. In the gospel story, the disciples' inability to heal results in the case being handed on to Jesus (Mark 9:17ff.). Their failure reflects on them as brokers specifically in their inability to have the patron work on behalf of those with difficulties. Hence their standing with the heavenly Patron or their mode of approaching the Patron is put in doubt.

A final problem relates to the location in the social network at which the broker's niche gets consolidated. A successful, unchallengeable broker is one who has developed a range of contacts who control first-order resources so that other brokers are not needed. The result is to have effectively destroyed rival communication networks. Jesus' conflict with Pharisees, their scribes and the Jerusalem priests might be viewed as competition to gain monopoly control of access to the heavenly Patron. Jesus' core group believed that he had in fact gained such a monopoly position (as in Peter's answer to Jesus' "Who do people say that I am?," Mark 8:29). From that position, Jesus could now convert his second-order resources into valued ends such as the office of Messiah with power for himself and administrative jobs and offices (judging the tribes of Israel, Matt. 19:28; Luke 22:30) for his core group. The normally latent goal of a brokerage career is some other social position, such as a prominent role in the existing hierarchy or becoming a patron and heading a hierarchy of one's own. One might say with good reason that by embarking on a career of brokerage for the heavenly Patron, the God of Israel, Jesus in fact did intend to acquire some significant role in the social order headed by the God of Israel, for example, if not to become Messiah with power, then to have some comparably significant role such as prophet like Moses. The *social* psychology of the brokerage role in its first-century Israelite situation would require as much.

THE JESUS FACTION:
FROM CORE GROUP TO CHURCH

The problem of interpersonal relations

Basic forms of social organization that organize production, enable effective collective action and provide protection from psychological and physical threats include: kinship groups, coalitions, elective associations, local governments and, the state. As previously mentioned, the main problem which most persons experienced in the first-century Mediterranean world was that of reliability in obtaining the ends that social institutions were expected to produce. The insurance which these people took out was patronage, if they could get it. And those who facilitated that insurance for them were brokers. The resulting cluster of persons around a patron or around a broker and the network of connections among such central personages formed *non-corporate groups*.

Non-corporate groups are distinctive of peasant societies in general, and hence also of the first-century Mediterranean. Pharisaic ingroups (called *haburoth*) as well as the Jesus movement group were such groups. On the other hand, the *ethnos* or people of Israel, structured after its leadership in the Temple and in relationship with that leadership, formed a *corporate group*. For an understanding of patron–client relations as well as for an understanding of early Christian movement groups, a description of corporate and non-corporate groups should prove useful.

Corporate structures predominate "where the community as such can provide security and thus can protect individuals as well as their enterprises. Such protection is accorded in societies with a high level of integration, such as certain small-scale societies and some highly industrialized Western societies" with greater homogeneity of values and integration of institutions, with smaller differences of relative power (Boissevain 1974:203). Such conditions did not apply in the first-century Mediterranean except for minuscule ruling elites. These elites perceived society in terms of elegant pyramid structures with rankings deriving from ascription. (This is strong group/high grid society; see Malina 1986a:13–67.)

On the other hand, the non-corporate group, most often called a "coalition," is at home in non-individualistic societies where values and experience do not match. (This is strong group/low grid society.) Coalitions thrive

> where security cannot be guaranteed by the community at large. This is the case in fragmented plural societies or highly strat-ified societies, such as peasant societies, frontier areas and colonies, where a heterogeneity of values and a great differ-ences in relative power exist between social groups.
>
> (Boissevain 1974:203)

The *corporate group* of strong group/high grid society might be defined as a collection of people forming a corporate body with a permanent existence recruited on recognized principles with common interests and rules or norms giving the rights and duties of the members in relation to each other and to these common interests.

If "property" is very broadly defined as the right to something or someone in some exclusive way, then the common interests can be called property interests. Obviously such property interests are sacred by definition, and therefore are perceived as divinely sanctioned. The resultant structure is rightly called a *hierarchy*.

The coalition

The coalition, in turn, might be defined as a collection of people within some larger, encapsulating structure consisting of distinct parties in temporary alliances for some limited purpose. The coalition is the polyadic network relation typical of strong group/low grid dyadic personalities. Coalitions are of many types. Boissevain (1974), for example, distinguishes between a coalition of intimate kinsmen, cliques, gangs, action-sets and factions. Common names for one or another of these include: salon, coterie, entourage, machine, social circle, team, clientele, following, school, etc. Consider the foregoing definition of the coalition in terms of its parts while contrasting the social structure of Israel rooted in the Temple and the Jesus movement group in Galilee:

(1) *A collection of people*: The coalition is a social entity, like the corporate body or any other social unit. Thus both the non-corporate group of Jesus and his disciples and subsequent followers as well as corporate Israel centered in the Temple and priesthood leadership are social entities.

(2) *Within some larger, encapsulating structure*: The coalition never forms the general social structure of a whole society. This perhaps is the easiest way to distinguish non-corporate groups from encompassing structures. Thus the Baptist movement group and the Jesus movement group as well as Pharisee ingroups were such non-corporate groups. On the other hand, Israel rooted in the Temple was the overarching corporate body. Perhaps the Qumran community, isolated and intent upon being true Israel, was in fact a corporate body. As non-corporate groups, coalitions are embedded, encysted or encapsulated in some broader social structure, and by their very presence have effect on that structure. Hence the need of the encapsulating structure to take coalitions seriously.

(3) *Consisting of distinct parties*: These distinct parties in non-corporate groups may be individuals (members of the Jesus movement group), other coalitions (the Pharisees and Herodians joining together to have Jesus killed), even corporate groups (various

ethnic groups together under the aegis of the Roman empire), usually organized concentrically with core and peripheral members. We might note relative to the gospel story:

> It is no accident that societies such as those of the Mediter-ranean region, which place a high value on favoritism and give it form through dyadic alliance building often are also described as societies characterized by strong feelings and expressions of distrust, envy and vindictiveness. Many such societies institutionalize the spirit of vengeance through the development of clearly recognized rules concerning the right, duties, form and proper participants in the act of vengeance.
>
> (Landé 1977:xxxii; on feud and vengeance see
> Black–Michaud 1975 and Boehm 1984)

Thus instead of hierarchy, we find core and periphery. Such core and periphery arrangements, relative to individuals, have some notable features.

First of all, individual identity in the coalition does not usually replace more fundamental group identity; people still belong to the overarching corporate group (Israel), their village society and their occupation cohort and can always return to them (for example, Peter in John 21:3ff.).

Second, individual commitment to the coalition usually does not replace ideological commitment to a uniform set of rights and obligations; joining the Jesus movement group does not absolve a member from rights and obligations in Israel. On the other hand, membership in a corporate group and in basic social institutions in general requires total commitment to the group's set of rights and obligations. In other words, there are no hyphenated Israelites (or family members belonging to more than one family of orientation), but there can be hyphenated members of the Jesus movement group (for example, priests join the group in Acts 6:7). However, should a coalition develop exclusivise features, it will become a corporate group. The end result of such a process is to be seen in Christianity becoming the official Roman political religion with Constantine.

Third, another significant feature of core–periphery arrangements is that the nature of the commitment to the task as well as the resources committed to it differ from member to member. Total dedication of time and resources is not required of all members, only core group members (cf. Luke 9:57–10:11). Members participate largely in terms of their own agendas rather than that of their fellow members or of the group, which really has no agenda as a group. It is not a corporate group.

Fourth, depending on whether the group has a leader or not there will or will not be coordination of social action since this is based on the goals, ends or values of the central person. The Jesus group, like the Baptist group, had a central person with social action deriving from the goals, ends and values of that central person.

Finally, there are no clear-cut rules of recruitment for a coalition, and hence it is impossible to indicate "objectively" all its members. This is where the crowds which followed Jesus fit in. There are nearly always peripheral figures about whom it is difficult to decide whether they are in or out of the group, in favor or against the basic agenda. Yet subjectively, each member has a clear idea about who is and who is not a member, although all members would probably not agree (Boissevain 1974:201). To return to our definition,

(4)   *Temporary*: The duration of a coalition varies with the time necessary to realize its purposes. Since the Kingdom of Heaven was at hand, the Jesus movement group would not be expected to endure. The heavenly Patron would transform Israelite society within a human lifetime (Mark 9:1 and parallels). Because of its temporary quality, the coalition is unstable. While the core might have greater staying power, the same is not true of the periphery. Furthermore, this instability also derives from the fact that distinct parties join for different reasons. Some would seek the protection of their rights, others the advancement of their private interests, and still others help in the performance and execution of their individual duties (for example, healing for children). What Peter sought (Mark 10:28) and what the brothers James and John wanted (Mark 10:37) differed from what Jesus' relatives decided upon in the "caliphate" of Acts (Acts 12:17; 15:13; 21:18).

Reasons for joining the Jesus movement group would vary. The pragmatic goals of individual members may and do differ widely from the coalition's normative, general aim adopted by the central personage, i.e. proclaiming the coming heavenly kingdom. As we see in the example of Jesus himself in his leaving John the Baptist, as soon as one member attains his limited aims or sees a more expeditious way of achieving them, he will be ready to drop out, and hence to remove his resources! Thus the story of Judas' departure is not about his leaving the coalition; the others also left Jesus at his arrest. The Judas story is about the betrayal of a person to whom he was so indebted (Mark 14:10).

(5) *Alliance*: The alliance quality of the coalition presumes joint use of resources relative to the coalition's goal, but resources are always linked to the owner, who may remove them at any time. That, of course, is not the case with corporate groups which usually levy taxes or dues, as did the Temple-based priestly governors of the *ethnos* of Israel.

(6) *For some limited purpose*: The general purposes of a coalition do not include refashioning the whole of society as the inauguration of a new religious ideology might entail. Rather, within the general ideology of Israel – how to be finite and free, subject to the God of Israel and fulfilling his directives in the Torah – the Jesus movement group proclaimed the ready access of patronage from the heavenly Patron of Israel who would transform life with new structures enabling the realization of the traditional ideology. The problem was with the existing structure rooted in the Temple and the Temple hierarchy. This was not a patronage structure based on a fusion of

Corporate group	*Non-corporate group*

(1) a discrete
• multi-member aggregate
• having property
• aims and duties
  • which inhere in the group as such
  • which are distinct from those of its individual members
	(1) an indistinct and poorly defined multi-member aggregate
	• without common property
	• without specific aims and duties
	• tasks assigned to core group and immediate periphery
	• as incumbent on individual members

(2) Each member has rights and duties with respect to the group	(2) Each member has rights and duties with respect to central personage only
(3) All members are bound together • by virtue of their shared membership in the group and • by virtue of their common obligation to protect its interests and fulfill its obligations	(3) All members are not bound together, but each is bound to a central personage by virtue of individual call • by virtue of obligation to protect the interests of the central personage and fulfill obligations toward him or her

kinship plus religion and power. Rather, it was a dominance structure, consisting of religion embedded in politics alone. It was the
sphere of the Lord, heavenly Monarch of Israel. Thus what the Jesus
movement group sought was to add patronage qualities to the
embedded religion of Israel. The result would be to render life in
Israel more acceptable in that the God of Israel would be experienced as treating his clients equitably and with a special concern for
their welfare. Traditionally, it was the welfare of office holders (kings,
administrators and their entourage) and the priestly group that was
God's concern. Life for God's clients would thus grow more meaningful in terms of relationship to God and fulfilling his Torah. Thus
ordinarily unpredictable situations might become more predictable
by recourse to a trustworthy and reliable heavenly Patron on whose
favor clients could rely. In Landé's presentation (1977:*passim*), corporate groups such as the Temple relate to non-corporate groups such
as the Jesus movement group as shown in the columnar text on page
162.

The person-centered faction: the Jesus movement group

Of the major coalition types called cliques, gangs, action-sets and
factions, the one most befitting the Jesus movement group is the
faction. A *faction* is a coalition of persons (followers) recruited personally, according to structurally diverse principles by or on behalf of
a person in conflict with another person(s) with whom they (coalition members) were formerly united over honor and/or control of
resources and/or "truth." Thus, the significant features of factions
include the following:

(1)   Factions are recruited personally by or on behalf of a person
in conflict with another. The gospel story underscores how Jesus
recruited his original core followers. While for motivation, the story
simply states "I will make you fishers of men," contemporaries would
understand that what was involved was help in conflict with others.
Either the audience knew the group with whom Jesus was in conflict
(because their group was still in conflict with that group), or they
would await further details in the story. The point is that in first-
century Mediterranean society for a person to call followers meant
to seek aid in conflict.

Another distinguishing feature setting off a cohesive faction from
a corporate group is the focal position occupied by the leader of a
following, whether patron or broker and his clientele. He is more

important to his combination than is the head of a corporate group in three main ways: First, he makes a greater personal contribution than does the head of a corporate group to the common effort of his organization: he creates a clientele in the first place, and provides external connections, maintenance and special personal obligation to the clientele; the healing of Peter's mother-in-law as well as Jesus' break with his mother and brothers point up his seriousness about his special personal obligation. Second, a leader has more discretionary power than does the head of a typical corporation. As a matter of fact, the client "accedes to the patron the preponderance of power to decide how the two of them shall interact and collaborate. That is to say, he gives leadership to the patron and accepts followership for himself. This last gift, as will be seen, is of crucial importance to the structure of clienteles" (Landé 1977:xxviii); thus he is entitled to set goals for the clientele, including his own private goals. And the core group dutifully accedes, as in the gospel story, though not without hesitation. Third, he holds the central position in the social structure of his clientele; hence followers find greater security in their personal attachment to the leader than in membership in the circle of their fellows, unlike a corporate group. Followers belong to the leader, the recruiter, rather than to a corporate group or institution. They belong to Jesus (or Paul or Apollos or Peter) rather than to a church.

(2) Rivalry is basic to the existence of factions, for a faction supports a person engaged in a hostile competition for honor and/or resources or access to the "truth" (ideological base). Factions are thus always politically oriented in that they look to effective collective action. The gospel story fully underscores the agonistic, rivalry-rooted reality of the Jesus movement group. Pharisees, Herodians and Sadducees stand opposed to the program launched by the Jesus faction. And the apostolic age is followed by a long period of the age of apologetes, which is quite normal since rivalry continued as the norm until Constantine.

(3) Unlike other types of coalitions, factions compete with other coalitions for the same prize. "The goal of the faction is clearly to acquire scarce resources for which others are competing. This sometimes involves prestige and so may involve the destruction of resources commanded by a rival in order to reduce his prestige and honor" (Boissevain 1974:201). For the Jesus faction and its rivals, the prize was "pleasing the God of Israel," namely enjoying the practical, actual, real benefits of the patronage of Israel's God. It would seem that Temple personnel believed that they already adequately

enjoyed those benefits, while Pharisees left that enjoyment to some distant future, while focusing on the present as guided by the past. The Jesus faction, on the other hand, focused on the present as a broad area, encompassing the lifetime of all present, that would see the intervention of the heavenly Patron and the transformation of society in terms of Torah promises.

(4)   Factions are conflicting units formed within a larger encapsulating social entity. The Jesus faction fits within the polity of Israel with its embedded religion and economics. It emerges within a village, spreads to a region, and with Jesus' trip to Jerusalem, looks to the whole polity.

(5)   The structure of factions varies, notably in the complexity in which core members are bound to each other (for example, as brothers, villagers, regional persons, same experiences, etc.) within the faction and to the degree to which persons bound in such complex ways form the core around the leader and relate to him (relatives, townmates, etc.). Boissevain notes:

> Where there is a strong core, the faction often acquires a number of corporate trappings. Among the most important is the permanence of the group, for if the relation between the members of the core is many stranded and based on moral (ideological) factors as well as transactional ones, they may stay together longer. The longer the faction remains united, the more corporate characteristics it acquires. These may include a common ideology, property, and bureaucratic organization. These in turn lead to and follow from persistence in time. The relative strength of the leader is another important variable. This varies according to the importance of his own resources relative to those of his followers. Where he is strong he can direct the conflict of the group more accurately.
>
> (1974:195)

(6)   The structure, development, number and strategy of factions depends upon several aspects that boil down to two: problems of management and problems of new resources.

Management problems involve, among other things, how to build up as large a following as possible with a minimum of expenditure of limited resources. The number of followers is limited because recruitment is on a transactional basis; people have to be personally called by the faction leader or core group members in his name. Then individuals joining have to be serviced by the leader, requiring time and energy that are limited. Further, if the conflict concerning which the faction has been recruited remains unresolved, resources must be expended to satisfy followers. Perhaps, though not exclusively, the story of the feeding of the multitude is about this facet of faction life (much as Paul asks the better-to-do to see to the needs of their fellow clientele). Finally, the longer the followers are actually linked to the central person, i.e. mobilized, as are the core group and Galilean women on the way to Jerusalem, the greater the likelihood that they will establish contacts with each other independently of the leader. In the process they will compare benefits with each other and compete and/or conflict with each other over the leader's limited benefits with the leader having to become judge (the story of the Greedy Young Man, of Peter asking what disciples will receive, of James and John's mother asking on their behalf). If the leader is unsuccessful, results can be discontent, loss of allegiance, defection to another faction, formation of a coalition challenging the leader. In the gospel story, we find discontent and loss of allegiance (with Judas; with Paul we find loss of allegiance and formation of challenging coalitions). The second management problem looks to controlling the size of the following in the sense of keeping its allegiance as clientele. This does not seem to have been a problem for Jesus, since his career comes to an abrupt end. That is not the case in Acts, however.

The size of the following can be expanded beyond the limit imposed by resources (a sort of credit system), by introducing a distinctive ideology and establishing a bureaucracy. In Acts the initial preaching of Peter articulates such an ideology, and the structure of the Twelve serves as requisite bureaucracy. *Ideology* or moral content added to the quality of the leader's relationship with his followers as broker with the Patron, God of Israel, establishes an extra hold by subsequent leadership. This is done by using tried *causes* which provide a collective symbol and sense of purpose (for example, motivation deriving from the Torah). Leadership might also have recourse to *innovations*, but these are riskier. For example, the decision to allow a non-Israelite to join the faction leads to all sorts of difficulties. Torah and vision are required to adjust ideology which binds followers to God the Patron in a range of moral links. This means that peripheral members continue in the faction for pragmatic (instrumental, what's in it for me) reasons, for value attainment and moral reasons, and for altruistic and distinctive ideological reasons (which provides a common moral cause). Ideology allows the leader and the faction to be defended against criticism and attack as well as for the expression of allegiance in moral terms, in terms of moral purpose.

Furthermore, the *bureaucracy* or structured and stable organization of the relatively sedentary Twelve allows for expansion. They can attract big men and their following (for example, Jerusalem priests and elders), but usually at the cost of their losing control. Acts mentions nothing of this. To deal with greater numbers, leadership can delegate time-consuming tasks (recruitment, allocation of resources, judgment, mediation, brokerage, ritual) as Acts in fact mentions with the appointment of deacons. In this way, the Twelve become coordinators. In terms of management, the problem that may arise is that specialists may learn and perform their task so well that they outdo the leadership (compare Paul with the Twelve in Acts). We might conclude this section with the comment of Boissevain:

> The most efficient solution to the management problem is to introduce an ideology and a specialized bureaucracy. This is one way political parties come into being. But with this solution there is always the danger of the means becoming the end. That is, the group rather than the leader makes the first claim upon the loyalty of its members. Rivals then challenge the leader and defend their right to do so by claiming it is good for the group.
>
> (1974:198)

Group centered factions: the church of Acts

The story in Acts seems to verify a hypothesis suggested by Boissevain to the effect that in a relatively stable situation (i.e. where the environment of the factions remains constant), if the factional conflict persists, the coalitions will become increasingly structured. In time, factions become permanent competing structural units that are not leader-centered but group-centered, and that indeed is the case for early Christian groups. Note Matthew's insistence on group-centeredness (Matt. 23:8–12); similarly Paul (1 Cor. 1:13ff.); and groups known simply as "Pharisees" or "Herodians" or Judeans in general; note as well the rise of Rabbinism in the face of Christianity.

This phase of the development of the Jesus movement group is marked by *resource problems*, clearly underscored in Acts with the stories of donations laid at the feet of the apostles. The problem is how to develop and maintain resources for the availability of new resources affects: (a) the intensity of the conflict, (b) the structure of the factions, (c) the permanence of the factions and (d) the number of factions. Of course, a growing Christian group indicates adequate resources.

Now, there are two main resources: new techniques (means) for fighting or attacking a rival, or for recruiting followers (for example, new ideology, sources of employment, funds), and new prizes (ends) for which persons (leaders) compete (for example, political or administrative offices, jobs with honor, power, etc.). Among new Christian techniques is the ideology articulating the role of Jesus, the Messiah with power soon to come, along with the developing Torah basis clarifying Jesus' career; there was also a type of redistribution of resource along with continued conflict with Israelite groups. As for the new prizes, there were new offices or roles, behavior patterns ostensibly borrowed from Israel and a shifting situation of those attempting to wield power and commitment.

To understand the post-70 scenarios of Christian groups, it is important to note that in situations of social change, there is an increase in factionalism because there is an increase in new resources (ends and means). The period of the Judean war was such a situation of social change. And the new resources become available for four reasons:

(1) Social change creates conditions of uncertainty that produce new resources because conflicting parties in the change process cannot be fully aware of how to use a new technique or strategy or how to combat it. New technique or strategy in this period consists in heightened expectations of intervention by the heavenly Patron, in writing down traditions previously left oral, and in developing new literary forms, such as the loose-list form of the Mishnah and the gospel story form of Mark. For other groups in the period, such as the Zealots, one finds an overcommitment of other resources and the rapid elimination of a rivals. In the end, the Sadducean hold on the Temple vanishes, as does the centrality of the Temple itself. If the technique backfires (for example, the requirement that Gentiles become Israelites before entering the Jesus movement group), then we may see the elimination of the user of the new technique or strategy.

(2) The introduction of new political and religious ideologies and systems not only provides new moral symbols for antagonists to use, but often also provides new spoils. For Christians the

destruction of the Temple affirmed their group-centered coalition with greater outreach to non-Israelites, the spoils here being the increase in membership among non-Israelites.

(3) New spoils, such as increase in coalition membership, in support and respect, in broadened ideology in Israel and the like, very often cannot be exploited successfully by existing *corporate* groups, such as the priesthood in Israel and the aristocracy of the Sadducee party. The reason for this is that such corporate groups are not flexible enough to take advantage of changing situations. Corporate group members in such situations can be subverted by factional leaders; that was the situation even during Jesus' career during his trip to Jerusalem. Because of rigid membership rules corporate groups cannot expand fast enough to compete for new prizes. It is significant that the early Christian, group-centered factions altered their original membership rules, clearly at the behest of the heavenly Patron himself.

(4) The very introduction of new resources divides people into two camps: those who see the new resources as desirable and useful, and those who regard them as a threat to their traditional moral order and/or their political or economic position. The result is conflict as groups focus on the need to make and hold resources available for protection against rivals. Conflict involves competition for scarce resources (of any sort). Some people inevitably control more of whatever than others, especially symbolic goods such as power, influence, inducement and commitment. With this more, they are able to occupy or control all or most of the social roles from which others can be made to do what one wishes. People in control of such symbolic goods may be called "the haves," the *status quo* or establishment. People lacking such control are identified as the poor, the failures, the weak, the eccentrics, the drop-outs, the social misfits and, often, the young. These form the "have-nots," or the non-establishment. They form the social category from which coalitions may be recruited *by more powerful rivals of the establishment*. Clearly it was among such have-nots that Jesus practiced his brokerage.

CONCLUSION

The story of Jesus indicates that while there may be a number of opposition coalitions, they usually and eventually coalesce, with a resulting formation of two competing and asymmetric coalitions.

169

Establishment	*Opposition*
Defends tradition	Opposes, questions or redefines tradition
Has vested interest in maintaining status quo	Has no such vested interest
Tradition provides a charter for its existence	Tradition provides no such charter
It claims to interpret the norms and defend the moral order	It offers new norms with a new interpretation of the moral order
Because it controls most of the formal offices, it can often make use of legally sanctioned physical force, public funds, office and ritual to recruit followers and to defend itself	Because it does not control any formal offices, it cannot make use of legally sanctioned physical force, needs private funding, and cannot use office and ritual to recruit followers and to defend itself
It monopolizes the most important ideological symbols (because it defines, defends and interprets tradition and the moral order, and has more resources at its disposal than its rival)	It must coopt ideological symbols from its rival and redefine them in a sort of hand-me-down usage, a sort of "common" symbol reinterpreted, rather than a distinct and unique symbol of its own
Is secure in superior position, control of resources and maintenance of followers through patronage	Is insecure in secondary position, with no control of resources, and must recruit as many followers as possible through new techniques and ideologies
Techniques and ideologies are traditional	Techniques and ideologies are new, often invented by faction recruiter himself or herself
Is on the assured defensive, with presumed strong leadership and tightly organized structure	Must be on the attack, with developing strong leadership and streamlined organization
Is conservative	By merely challenging conservatives, is progressive

170

This is why factions and other conflict groups most often appear in pairs, with, for example, the Jesus group versus the Pharisees and Herodians. In Jerusalem it is the Jesus group versus Temple authorities, Pharisees and Herodians. Clearly the Jesus faction emerges as the opposition, at least in its version of the story.

Secondary and competing coalitions that abide by "the rules of the game," such as the Pharisees, do not do so because they see those rules as legitimate or morally necessary. They do not agree with the rules, but they are obliged to accept them because they are constrained by wielders of power and their sanctions, i.e. the Temple authorities. Opposition coalitions, such as the Jesus group, strive for power and honor by underscoring the power and honor of God, the heavenly Patron. They seek to bend, modify and innovate laws and customs that restrict their behavior in ways which *benefit themselves rather than their rivals*. Consequently, as Boissevain has noted (1974), in every conflict there is a built-in dynamism which can lead to change, for the competitors seek greater effectiveness. The opposition can and did grow bitter because it saw itself as obliged to obey owing to the resources controlled by the Jesus movement group, notably the crowds. The Jerusalem crowds, however, were not the Galilean crowds; and as the crowd's protection waned, the establishment opposition quickly put an end to the brokerage career of Jesus. The story of Jesus' death underscores how the heavenly Patron abandoned his chief broker. The appearance stories point to a reversal and the emergence of a group-focused coalition.

NOTES

1   As a rule patron–client societies are extensive and extractive in economies; leadership is concerned with plundering rather than developing, and taxation exists for the benefit of elites and not for the common good. Embedded economic activity looks to the expansion of control of ever larger domains or territories rather than looking to internal improvement. Other aspects include intensive exploitation of a fixed resource base; low level of specialization; and trade oriented outward and regulated by rulers or conscripted external groups. (Eisenstadt and Roniger 1984: 208; Carney 1973).

2   Of course, the vocabulary of "grace" (*charizomai, charis, charisma*) belongs to the favoritism of patronage. I suggest that *charizomai* refers to showing patronage, *charis* to willingness to be patron, and *charisma* to the outcomes of patronage. This is what Paul (and the rest of the New Testament) means with this set of terms. As for *charisma*, from the frequency of usage of the word (Rom. 1:11; 5:15,16; 11:29; 12:6;

1 Cor. 1:7; 7:7; 12:4,9,28,30,31; 2 Cor. 1:11; 1 Tim. 4:14; 2 Tim. 1:6; 1 Pet. 4:10) and by comparison with contemporary literature, it seems certain that the word was little used before Paul, and that Paul was the first to give it a technical meaning. What would the ordinary meaning of the word be? I begin with the verb form (because *-is*, for example, *charis* = grace, nouns refer to the action of the root, while *-ma*, for example, *charisma*, nouns refer to the result of the action of the root – the root being in the verb form).

(a) *Charizomai*: is a middle deponent verb, and means literally to give-in, hence to yield, forgive, donate; to bestow patronage. It is most often translated: to give freely or graciously as a favor. The problem with this frequent version is one of cultural anachronism, since until St Augustine there was no formalized notion of human freedom, except in the political social sense as the opposite of slavery. Further, it is questionable whether first-century AD society knew of anything like a "free" gift, considering the cultural presuppositions of "all goods are limited" and the "debt of gratitude" involved in giving (see Malina 1993:90–116). In other words, all "gifts" implied obligations and were made culturally with strings attached. This is what patronage is about, for this is how generalized reciprocity worked.

(b) *Charis*: refers to the action of giving-in to someone, i.e. giving-in-ness, readiness to act as patron. This is the word normally translated "grace." Culturally it implies vertical social standing since only the "haves" can give-in to the "have-nots," since giving-in presupposes a want or need on the part of the one given-in to. Dyadic alliance among equals erases the social perception of verticality, placing the behavior in the category of generalized reciprocity with the hope that all would equal out in some undefined future; this would actually be balanced reciprocity if it ever worked out that way. It further presupposes the idea of "all goods are limited," i.e. every available good belongs to someone since the only way the "have-nots" can share in the good is by the "haves" giving-in to them (see Malina 1993:90–116).

(c) *Charisma*: refers to the result of an action of giving-in, hence patronage, i.e. a gift-with-strings-attached by someone in an upper social stratum to one of a lower stratum; a donation-with-strings-attached because all goods are limited.

In sum, the area of social life in which the word functions seems to presuppose that persons who "give-in" are in a position to do so, i.e. in some way superior to the ones they give-in to either because of possession of something desirable and necessary (such as resources, power, information), or because of the importance of their role in social life (for example, they must grant forgiveness to stabilize a social group to avoid tension and conflict). The very fact of "giving-in" is in fact a "giving" which requires reciprocity, i.e. the donor must "give up" something and the recipient too must "give up" something, at least closed-ness to receive the needed gift.

From this it would seem that the God of Israel never simply "gives" in his interpersonal relationships with humans in history. He always "gives-in," because the God of Israel is Patron in a vertical dyadic relation with his arbitrarily chosen client. While God may have a need to give-in since he is honorable, he really has no need to give. And he really cannot "give" since "to give" necessarily presumes sheer equality, truly balanced reciprocity (Malina 1986a:98–111). Compare gift-giving in an affluent society and in a non-affluent society. If "to give freely" means to want nothing in return, then the God of Israel does not do this – and neither do people in peasant societies or in the contemporary Third World. "To give-in first" means at least to want the goodwill, the openness of the one wanting or needing the "giving-in." The Kingdom of Heaven announced by Jesus indicates that the God of Israel is ready "to give-in again," as divine Patron. In the Pauline tradition, of course, the main difference between *charis* and *charisma*, is that *charis*, God's readiness to be Patron, is shown to all men, while *charisma*, actual favor or patronage, comes to those "in Christ Jesus."

3   In this regard, consider the Torah and the Qur'an:

> Deut. 7:6–8: "For you are a people holy to Yahweh your God; Yahweh your God has chosen you to be a people for his own possession, out of all the peoples that are on the face of the earth. It was not because you were more in number than other people that Yahweh set his love upon you and chose you, for you were the fewest of all peoples; but it is because Yahweh loves you and is keeping the oath which he swore to your fathers."

> Deut 9:5–6: "Not because of your righteousness or the upright-ness of your heart are you going in to possess the land; but because of the wickedness of these peoples Yahweh your God is driving them out from before you, and that he may confirm the word which Yahweh swore to your fathers, to Abraham, to Isaac, and to Jacob. Know therefore, that Yahweh your God is not giving you this good land to possess because of your righteous-ness; for you are a stubborn people."

> Surah 3, 110: "You are indeed the best community that has ever been brought forth for [the good of] mankind: you enjoin the doing of what is right and forbid the doing of what is wrong, and you believe in God. Now if the followers of earlier revela-tion had attained to [this kind of] faith, it would have been for their own good; [but only few] among them are believers, while most of them are iniquitous: (111) [but] these can never inflict more than a passing hurt on you; and if they fight against you, they will turn their backs upon you [in flight], and you will not be succored."

In the Pastoral Letters ascribed to Paul: "For the grace of God has appeared for the salvation of all men, training us to renounce irreligion and worldly passions, and to live sober, upright, and godly lives in this world, awaiting our blessed hope, the appearing of the glory of our great God and our Savior Jesus Christ" (Titus 2:11–13).

4   The use of the word "father" for God is as follows in the gospels: Matt. 45/64 = 70.3 percent; Mark 5/18 = 27.7 percent; Luke 17/56 = 30.4

173

percent; Acts 3/35 = 8.6 percent (Luke Acts = 22 percent; John 123/137 = 89.8 percent. John undoubtedly refers to God as some actual father; given the situation of the group he represents, John would prefer to speak that way (see Malina 1985). The Synoptics, on the other hand, refer to God as Patron, i.e. they import kinship terminology to refer to the ultimate and only divinity. It is Matthew for whom this is an emphatic theme, while Mark and Luke (including Acts) offer no particular emphasis. The Synoptics trace back this usage to Jesus.

5 In terms of the prevailing French model of story roles (see Barr 1987: 29–31) the gospel story roles include the following:

```
                                              axis of
patron (sender)   → patronage (object)   → clients  = purpose
                              ↑             (receiver)
                              |                       = commitment
core group (helpers)  →  broker (subject) ←  rivals  = conflict
                                             (opponents)
```

In terms of the generalized symbolic media of social interaction (see Malina 1986a:77–97), the axis of purpose entails the generalized symbolic media of inducement and/or influence and the axis of commitment involves the generalized symbolic medium of commitment activation, while the axis of conflict involves the generalized symbolic medium of power.

6 Studies of the word *mesites* (for example, Oepke 1968) usually launch into cosmic and philosophical mediation rather than adhering to the mundane realities of social brokerage, although the word is in fact used that way. Consider how 1 Tim. 2:5f. sounds within the scenario of patronage: "For God is one and the broker between God and men is one too, the man Christ Jesus, who gave himself as a ransom for all, a duly witnessed event."

REFERENCES

Aalen, Sverre (1962) "'Reign' and 'House' in the Kingdom of God in the Gospels." *New Testament Studies* 8:215–40.

Barr, David L. (1987) *New Testament Story: An Introduction*. Belmont, CA: Wadsworth.

Black-Michaud, Jacob (1975) *Cohesive Force: Feud in the Mediterranean and the Middle East*. New York: St Martin's.

Boehm, Christopher (1984) *Blood Revenge: The Anthropology of Feuding in Montenegro and Other Tribal Societies*. Lawrence: University Press of Kansas.

Boissevain, Jeremy (1974) *Friends of Friends: Networks, Manipulators and Coalitions*. New York: St Martin's.

Carney, Thomas F. (1973) *The Economies of Antiquity: Controls, Gifts and Trade*. Lawrence: Coronado.

—— (1975) *The Shape of the Past: Models and Antiquity*. Lawrence: Coronado.

Danker, Frederick W. (1982) *Benefactor: Epigraphic Study of a Graeco-Roman and New Testament Semantic Field.* St Louis: Clayton.

Eisenstadt, Shlomo N. and Louis Roniger (1984) *Patrons, Clients and Friends: Interpersonal Relations and the Structure of Trust in Society.* Cambridge: Cambridge University Press.

Hall, Edward T. (1959) *The Silent Language.* Garden City: Doubleday.

Hollenbach, Paul W. (1982) "The Conversion of Jesus: From Jesus the Baptizer to Jesus the Healer." *Aufstieg und Niedergang der römischen Welt* II 25/1:196–219.

Horsley, G. H. R. (1981) *New Documents Illustrating Early Christianity,* Vol. I. North Ryde, NSW: Macquarie University Press.

Judge, Edwin A. (1960) *Social Patterns of Christian Groups in the First Century.* London: Tyndale.

Landé, Carl H. (1977) "Introduction: The Dyadic Basis of Clientelism." pp. xiii–xxxvii in Steffen W. Schmidt, James C. Scott, Carl Landé and Laura Guasti (eds) *Friends, Followers and Factions: A Reader in Political Clientelism.* Berkeley/Los Angeles: University of California Press.

Malina, Bruce J. (1985) *The Gospel of John in Sociolinguistic Perspective.* 48th Colloquy of the Center for Hermeneutical Studies, Herman (ed.) Waetje. Berkeley: Center for Hermeneutical Studies.

—— (1986a) *Christian Origins and Cultural Anthropology: Practical Models for Biblical Interpretation.* Atlanta: John Knox.

—— (1986b) "'Religion' in the World of Paul: A Preliminary Sketch." *Biblical Theology Bulletin* 16:92–101.

—— (1993) *The New Testament World: Insights from Cultural Anthropology.* Rev. ed. Louisville: Westminster/John Knox.

—— (1994) "Religion in the Imagined New Testament World: More Social Science Lenses." *Scriptura* 51:1–26.

Oepke, Albrecht (1968) "*mesites, mesiteuo.*" in G. Kittel (ed.) *Theological Dictionary of the New Testament* 4:598–624. Trans. Geoffrey W. Bromiley. Grand Rapids: Eerdmans.

Pitt-Rivers, Julian (1968) "Pseudo-Kinship." in David L. Sills (ed.) *International Encyclopedia of the Social Sciences* 8:408–13. New York: Macmillan/The Free Press.

Rouland, Norbert (1979) *Pouvoir politique et dépendance personnelle dans l'Antiquité romaine: génèse et rôle des relations de clientèle.* Brussels: Editions Latomus.

Saller, Richard P. (1982) *Personal Patronage Under the Early Empire.* Cambridge: Cambridge University Press.

Veyne, Paul (1976) *Le Pain et le Cirque: Sociologie Historique d'un Pluralisme politique.* Paris: Editions du Seuil.

White, L. Michael (1982) *Domus Ecclesiae – Domus Dei: Adaptation and Development in the Setting for Early Christian Assembly.* Ann Arbor: University Microfilms International; Yale University Dissertation.

Yoder, John Howard (1972) *The Politics of Jesus: Vicit Agnus Noster.* Grand Rapids: Eerdmans.

Part IV

THE QUESTION OF TIME AS FIRST-CENTURY MEDITERRANEAN VALUE

7

CHRIST AND TIME

Swiss or Mediterranean?

INTRODUCTION

It is some fifty years ago that Oscar Cullmann's book, *Christus und die Zeit*, appeared (1946). With the publication of an English version, the book was required reading for most of us, who found it compelling, theologically illuminating and very useful. A revised English version that chronicled the author's debate with his critics was published in 1964. Shortly before that, James Barr argued that the meanings given to the biblical words for "time" by Cullmann and others were not really to be found in the documents in question. Cullmann's methods were typically eisegesis rather than exegesis; and his *Christ and Time* revealed contemporary hope rather than past biblical belief (Barr 1962). Others pointed out the impossibility of Cullmann's insistence on the distinctiveness of Judaism and Christianity in the ancient world relative to their mode of historical understanding (see Momigliano 1966; Press 1977; Gabba 1981).

In this chapter, I wish to raise once again the question broached by Cullmann. While he and his contemporaries poorly understood the timeframe utilized by New Testament authors, he did offer good advice when he stated: "The frame within which the writers of the New Testament worked ought to be the same limits which New Testament scholars accept for their work. This means that we must at least attempt to avoid philosophical categories" (1964:11). To this I would only add that we must likewise avoid those cultural categories from which the inappropriate philosophical categories in question derive. As I hope to show, the ancients were quite different from us moderns in time perception. Furthermore, circum-Baltic peoples were and are fundamentally different from circum-Mediterraneans (Quigley 1961;1973). And it is the first-century Mediterranean appreciation of time that the New Testament interpreter must appropriate if only to be fair to the authors and their communities.

In this vein, the Second Vatican Council's *Dogmatic Constitution on Divine Revelation* (*Dei Verbum*) has urged biblical interpreters, professional and non-professional, to pay attention to, among other things, "the customary and characteristic styles of perceiving ... at the time of the sacred writer" (Abbott 1966:120). Among the basic modalities of perception required for interpretation, time perception is crucial for discovering the meaning of what people say and do. This is a significant point since "not even the simplest assertion about human conduct can be made without some underlying theory of temporality" (Maines 1987:303). And it was the first-century Mediterranean temporal orientation that undergirded New Testament assertions about human conduct. As Bourdieu has noted: "Awareness of time is not simply one of the dimensions of [one's] life experience, but rather the form in terms of which that experience is organized" (Bourdieu 1963:55–6). For people always have an image of time and space in the mental maps they use to make sense of their experiences. People need to know where they are. To locate themselves people employ an assessment of both extension in space and duration in time, an assessment of placement and of process. This assessment of placement and process sets the coordinates of that cognitive map upon which we situate ourselves and the persons, objects and transactions we need to understand and evaluate. Relative to time, Nuttin has noted that the "time perspective is the temporal zone to which one's mental view virtually extends itself when considering the objects and conscious determinants of behavior" (1985:21). Persons, things and events are situated on or located in the temporal zones of our mental maps by means of cognitive representations. What I wish to do is set out a way of understanding time as that dimension of human experience functioned on the mental maps of most people in the first-century eastern Mediterranean.

In the course of growing up in our society, we have all learned how to think and feel in terms of mental maps fully outfitted with their intellectual and emotional furniture. Societies as a whole and specific groups within societies share various value orientations, including a temporal orientation. Through enculturation we have learned our social group's favored range of preferred responses to questions of placement and process. In sum, we have also learned the temporal orientation favored by "American society" (Iutcovich *et al.* 1979:73). A patient observer can come to discern the various value orientations at work in a society or group by noting where people "at any one time focus their attention when standards for behavior and thinking are needed to guide them in solving problems as they arise in life" (Iutcovich *et al.* 1979:74).

Anyone studying US society soon finds out that mainstream, middle-class America is future-oriented. People live achievement-directed lives focused on relatively distant goals. They work and act in the present in order some way to realize some far-off purpose, whether it be a college degree, money for their children's education, retirement income or the like. The present always serves as a means to some more distant end. I teach an annual course on the values transmitted in US primetime TV story-lines. To help students understand the distinctiveness of US values, I generally compare these with the values mediated through New Testament story-lines. What led me to the investigation of time in the New Testament writings is the fact that typically American future orientation simply does not exist in any New Testament story. As a matter of fact, I hope to demonstrate that it could not exist there. So what happens when a future-oriented American reads something like the Synoptic gospel account of Jesus' description of the coming of the Son of Man? Of course, it turns out to be a description of some future end of the world, even though in the passage Jesus explicitly states: "Truly, I say to you, this generation will not pass away before all these things take place" (Mark 13:30; Matt. 24:34; Luke 21:32). According to the same gospel tradition, Jesus likewise said: "Truly I say to you there are some standing here who will not taste death before they see that the kingdom of God has come with power" (Mark 9:1; similarly Matt. 16:28; Luke 9:27). These Synoptic passages refer to events presented in the gospels as presumably having been realized during the lifetime of those within Jesus' earshot. Yet Americans read them as referring to something still to come. Obviously the lifetimes of the persons addressed in those passages have long ago come to a close; the events announced have not occurred. Why do people bother to read about them as though they still have to be realized? Why don't they consider such statements as "inoperative," and become selectively inattentive to them? Does US future orientation contribute to the way American readers read "eschatology" in the New Testament?

FUTURE ORIENTATION COMPARED WITH
PRESENT ORIENTATION

This question became even more salient for me when I began to use the model of value orientation preference developed by Kluckhohn and Strodtbeck (1961). This anthropological model is widely used by a number of people in disciplines as varied as nursing, medicine, business and education (see, for example, Papajohn and Spiegel 1975; Iutcovich *et al.* 1979; Spiegel 1982; Attneave 1982; Harris and Moral 1987). People in those areas are urged to use the model in order to understand their clients and the differing perspectives they bring to professional transactions. For our purposes, I should simply like to note that, among other items, the model lists time preference as one of its categories. Time preference looks to the following question: When people are faced with a vital problem, do they turn initially to the past, the present or the future to find a solution to the problem? And which of the three serves as backup should the first orientation not work? As they grow up, are children urged to keep their ancestors in mind and to live up to their accomplishments and status? Or are they to pay attention to their present experiences and the people presently around them? Or are they to set goals for themselves to be realized at some distant future date, as when they are urged to become a doctor, lawyer, teacher, pilot, etc.? Which is the primary orientation, which the secondary and tertiary?

The study of various groups of immigrants to the US as well as studies of societies around the world presented by people using the Kluckhohn and Strodtbeck model indicate that future orientation as primary or secondary preference was and is extremely rare on the planet. And it was surely not to be found in any peasant society. Peasant societies invariably have the present as first-order temporal preference; secondary preference is past; and the future comes in as third choice. Since Mediterranean societies of the first century were examples of classical peasant societies, by and large, the primary preference in temporal orientation at that period and place was the present, with past second and future third. The exception was Roman elites, with their ancestrism (see Fortes 1970:164–200; Todd 1985:33–44; Nisbet 1964:257–71; Harris 1986:81–95). Roman elites had the past as their primary preference, with the present second and the future an extremely remote third. For the Romans showed complete indifference to the future; they were simply not concerned with long-range planning in any field. Quigley, for example, has argued:

> These Roman ruling groups were not hampered by theories or ideologies, although quick with rationalizations. They never found logical obstacles to action, because they cared nothing for logic. In fact, they had no long-range idea of what they were doing – ever. It has often been said that the Romans had no plans of world conquest and that they became rulers of the world in fits of absent-mindedness, like England acquired its empire. This may be correct, but it means nothing. The Romans had no long-range plans for world conquest because they had no long-range ideas on anything.
>
> (1983:374)

To return to the general Mediterranean populace, proverbs such as the following underscored the present: "Tomorrow will be anxious for itself," "Let the day's own trouble be sufficient for the day" (Matt. 6:34); "Do not be concerned from morning until evening, and from evening until morning about what you will wear" (*GThom.* 36; POxy. 655.1). And whether one prayed: "Give us this day our daily bread" or "Give us today tomorrow's bread" (Q Matt. 6:11; Luke 11:3), emphasis was still on the present. Such preference is typical of non-elites in agrarian societies in general. Present orientation as first-order preference meant not only that there were no schedules or time tables, but also that "it is not for you to know times or seasons which the Father has fixed by his own authority" (Acts 1:7).

Secondary past preference might be seen in the *Magnificat*, where Mary is described as saying: "For behold, henceforth all generations will call me blessed" (Luke 1:48). Was the Lukan reader expected to believe that all people from that moment on would call Mary blessed? Or is the obvious meaning of the passage that all people from all past generations up to Mary's present were to do so? And what of a statement such as Heb. 13:8: "Jesus Christ is the same yesterday and today and forever?" Does it express the past, present and future, or simply an endless today, hence an abiding present? Likewise, do the thanksgivings at the opening of the Pauline letters (listed, for example, in Roetzel 1982:40) list descriptions of the past, present and future, or move from the past to an extended present? Further, are statements about those who "have their reward" contrasted with those who receive a "reward from your Father who is in heaven" in Matt. 6:2,5,16 intended to compare those who are rewarded at present with those who defer their reward for some indefinite future, albeit with God? Or are both about reward now, underscoring the fact that those who already have their own sort of reward are not to receive a reward from God at present? And why do Jesus' statements on the rewards of discipleship include "a hundredfold now in this time" or "manifold more in this time" (Mark 10:28–30; Matt. 19:27–9; Luke 18:28–30)? Why is there no mention of some next generation, or future generations, or future time periods in the New Testament? We read of this age and the age to come, but nothing of ages to come or of a new generation in the age to come! It seems quite clear, for example, that Matthew's "close of the age" (Matt. 28:20) was to have been witnessed by "some standing here," belonging to "this generation" (Matt. 16:20; 24:3), again with no other generation in sight. Does this happen because of a profound theological belief that all would come to an end with Jesus' generation? Or is it rooted in the cultural myopia deriving from the extreme present temporal orientation which Jesus shared with his society? There surely is no expressed concern for the future in the Synoptic story-line. And it would appear that the same holds for the entire New Testament since any time description consisting of this age and a rather proximate age to come has no room for a future of the sort we speak of. Even the quintessential "future-oriented" book of the New Testament, the book of Revelation, is about the present. In his sky journeys, John the seer considers the arrangement of the stars in the sky at creation to explain what is happening in his own world, hence from past to present; and the celestial Jerusalem is descending already now (see Malina 1993b; 1994b; 1995a). To what, then, would New Testament prophecies refer? Did they in fact refer to the future or to the present? Is the presumed future orientation seen to underpin such prophecies actually derived from the Bible or is it the product of rather recent experience?

James M. Jones has noted that for future orientation to work in a society two cultural elements are required: first, people must share a strong belief in the conditional probability that if some act is performed in the present, there is great probability of realization of a goal-state in the future; and second, people must have strong commitment to value goals whose attainment can only occur in the future (Jones 1988:23–4). These elements are realized in delayed gratification, in saving for the future, in planning for rather distant goals. Yet for these elements to be credible and realizable, there is a

184

necessary condition: the survival needs of the present such as food, clothing, safety and shelter, must be assured. Such present survival needs were never assured to anyone in antiquity apart from an elite handful. If only for this reason, there will surely be no evidence for future orientation as primary or secondary value preference in Mediterranean antiquity. And apart from the US there is not much evidence for its existence in much of our contemporary world either. Future orientation tends to cut down the present to but a quickly vanishing point, so that the present becomes ephemeral. As the point vanishes, we are left simply with a past and a future, or better, a future and a past. This is not the case with people who share a present-oriented temporal preference. As we shall see, their present covers a broad sweep marked off only by the horizons of the imaginary past on the one side and the imaginary future on the other. At this point, consider the differences between present and future orientations, culled from Jones (1988:21–36), shown in the Table on page 186.

Given contemporary theological positions that are future-oriented and presumably based on the Bible, one might inquire into the origins of these positions. To contemporary present-oriented people, future orientation is considered a waste of perfectly good present experiences, a cause of unwarranted tension, and the best way to frustrate what is actually happening. If in fact there was no one in the ancient world, neither Greek nor barbarian, who might have been future oriented, have all future-oriented theological positions been necessarily read into the Bible? Did anyone in the ancient world experience the alleged tension between the "already and the not yet" that they were supposed to have experienced? Were there any millenarists, as defined today (for example, Rayner 1982), even among members of the community that shared the hopes of the Revelation of John (see Malina 1993b; 1994b; 1995a)? I would argue that the only scholarly evidence for the existence of anxiety and concern about a perceived delay of a parousia, for interest in eschatology, or for some future-oriented apocalyptic was in the eyes of liberal, Enlightenment-oriented, nineteenth-century northern European biblical interpreters and their twentieth-century heirs (see Carmignac 1979:133–96). I would contend that the presumed future-oriented categories of the Bible are in fact not future-oriented at all, but present-oriented. And I would pose the following question: If all first-century Mediterranean persons had a present (or past – for Roman elites) temporal orientation as their primary focus and

185

Present orientation	*Future orientation*
• localizes objects and goals in the present	• localizes objects and goals in the extended or distant future
• activity occurs in the present, to achieve proximate goals	• activity occurs in the present, to achieve remote goals
• the extended present is a unit of personal expression	• time is a unit of impersonal value
• temporal integration makes the proximate forthcoming continuous with the present, yet with no personal control over the realization of outcomes	• temporal integration makes the distant future continuous with the present, with cause–effect cognition that enables personal control in achieving outcomes
• present behaviors are presumed to express feelings at that time	• present behaviors are presumed to work toward achieving some desired future goals
• affective, group-focused processes dominate present-oriented behaviour	• cognitive, individualistic-focused processes dominate future-oriented behavior
• the forthcoming derives from continued survival or existence; since survival is precarious, focus is on maintaining positive outcomes in the present in order thereby to assure what is forthcoming; hence the assessment of the forthcoming is the same as the assessment of the present	• future follows from the successful attainment of proximate goals relating to the future; survival in the present is taken for granted; hence the assessment of future goals directs present behavior
• thus the present drives and propels what is forthcoming	• thus the future drives and propels what is present
• feedback for present-oriented people comes from immediate social interaction and concerns present survival and positive affective support.	• feedback for the future-oriented people comes from the realization of proximate goals and concerns knowledge of status of contingencies impacting on future goals.

expressed this focus in their writings, would not the future-oriented categories of much contemporary theology be "appropriations" of biblical text-segments?

FIRST-CENTURY MEDITERRANEAN TIME PERCEPTIONS: BUILDING A MODEL

The purpose of this chapter is to facilitate a reading of the New Testament with the present as primary temporal orientation. What would the New Testament documents mean if read with a present orientation that was preclock, premonastic, pre-Newtonian, pre-Enlightenment, pre-Industrial Revolution and pre-Einsteinian? If these shells could be removed from our future-oriented, mathematically based, chronologically sensitive, rather abstract eyes, how would we situate ourselves in duration? What sort of forecasts or predictions could we make? How would one make and keep an appointment? What would we use to set a calendar? Where could we find a calendar? You may notice that nearly all the words I have just used are applied in our society to social inventions and skills that did not exist in the first-century Mediterranean: manipulable numerals, arithmetic using a zero, abstract and impersonal chronology, abstract and numerical calendars, or the abstract categories: past, present and future (for numerals, see Menninger 1969; for calendars Zerubavel 1981; for grammatical tenses, Serbat 1975; 1976; Pinkster 1983).

The lack of such items points to a social system that did not require them, if only because the social system was focused on what concretely existed. This feature points to present temporal orientation, based on attention to what is present. Because of what concretely is, people could to some extent utilize what concretely was since it went before and accounts for what is. For example, I could speak of my ancestors because they went before and account for me and my kin group today. Similarly, present-oriented people could perceive what concretely is going to be because it is rooted in what is. I might talk of the coming birth of a child because I know the actually pregnant mother. Likewise, as a first-century Judean, I might talk of the city or temple that is coming since I know that God presently has an available city or temple in the celestial regions that served to model the actual, impermanent city or temple (Heb. 13:14; Rev. 21:2; Exod. 25:40; Ezek. 40–2).

To construct a set of present-oriented lenses, I shall use the following layers: first, a distinction between modern abstract time perception and traditional experienced and imaginary time; second, a distinction between modern linear separable time and traditional cyclical and procedural time; and finally, a distinction between abstract historical and operational time and traditional historical and operational time. I hope to indicate what it might be like to read the New Testament with present-oriented, first-century Mediterranean lenses.

Modern abstract time and traditional experienced and imaginary time

Americans for the most part share a highly abstract notion of time. The fact that people can be paid for time, that time is measured rather precisely both in broadcasting and in phone use, that people can and must refer to a large array of dates on insurance applications so that they can fit into a statistically determined actuarial table, that people are expected to be aware of a large number of personally irrelevant dates – all these instances and more point to time in our industrial age as something abstract. With our time perception we can speak of duration numerically, just as with our statistics we can speak of illness, birth, wealth and the like numerically. The Industrial Revolution and the asceticism and discipline it entails (see Malina 1995b) have led to abstract quantity orientation as the usual way to speak about significant things in life, including duration (see McGrath and Kelly 1986; Zerubavel 1981).

For the present-oriented person of antiquity, reality meant only the experienced world and experienced time. There was, therefore, really no true past or true future of the sort typical of societies based on a nineteenth-century sense of history and a twentieth-century general education in abstraction, such as ours. Our society and its disembedded social institutions along with their roles and statuses are all the outcome of post-Enlightenment ideals realized for better or worse through twelve years of required schooling. At least by high school, the result is enculturation in abstraction, in "rational consciousness," as a normative cultural pattern. For us the future includes probable as well as possible outcomes of present events. It can be described statistically as an abstract series of non-contradictory possibilities. It is imagined without commitment to its actual realization, without commitment to the persons involved and what it might mean to them on the concrete level. What is future may not be attached to any reality at all. Rather the future arises from some statistically infinite number of possibilities equally able to occur or not. A projection of such an abstract, imaginary future usually depends upon consideration of a set of variables rather than on a full scenario of individual living persons. We know how many people will get cancer this year and from what causes, but we do not know if *I* shall get cancer and if I do, why me? Our abstract future is an impersonal future, forming a realm of abstract and indeterminate possibilities. Bourdieu has indicated that this northern European and American way of articulating duration is quite foreign to traditional Mediterranean peasants. In place of our abstractions, these peasants might be said to divide time into experienced time and imaginary time.

Experienced time

Experienced time is the perception of duration solely within the perceived horizon of the world of actual experience. This is the horizon of the present. It does not matter whether this duration is rooted in spiraling repeatable occurrences or in processual phenomena. What counts is that these fall within the horizon of actual experience in the actual present. What belongs to experienced time is the present. Bourdieu describes this present as

> the whole of an action seen in the unity of a perception including both the retained past and the anticipated future. The "present" of the action embraces, over and above the perceived present, an horizon of the past and of the future tied to the present because they both belong to the same context of meaning.
>
> (Bourdieu 1963:59–60)

The present, then, is a single context of meaning that often is of long duration, depending on the process or event involved. I wish to suggest that it was such a present that served the perception of people in the first-century Mediterranean. Because the present encompassed a rather long duration, "this generation," for example, was a sufficiently accurate reference to the present, indicating a "present tense" spanning some forty or more years.

While this way of referring to the present might seem odd to us who favor points in time to mark the actual "now," we do in fact have a number of experiences of such a long-lasting present in our own culture. Think of a long-lasting symbolic interpretation of a biological process, such as designating a given person "mother" or "father." Usually parents are considered "present-tense" parents during the entire lifetime of their child. Regardless of our respective ages, we continue to say: "This *is* my mother and father." Or recall some long-perduring feeling such as a profound fit of affection or raging hatred lasting a week, a month, a year or longer. Abused and codependent persons know the awesome presence of such feelings rooted in age 2 or 3 and enduring eighty-two or eighty-three years. Or consider child-bearing, a process that covers a nine-month long present of pregnancy and at least a ten-year-long present of childhood. Healing from a broken leg or a cut, raising crops, listening to a symphony with many movements, going on a vacation and the like are all instances of activities with a rather broad actual or experienced present. The immediate future bound up with the present as well as previous activity still resonating in the present are all part of that present, still experienced and all actually present.

Now imagine such an understanding of the present as the usual one, with the instantaneous, micro-second present as unreal and abnormal. Imagine "clocks" which regularly tell time by indicating nothing more accurate than rainy season and dry season, this generation and the next generation (cf. the gospels). For greater precision, imagine an invitation requesting that you arrive punctually, that is, in March or April of this year (cf. Paul's travel plans in Rom. 15:23–9). Since there is nothing of a chronographical nature worth paying attention to, the main focus of duration assessment becomes the qualitative time period, the *kairos*. Actually, in peasant society all time worth telling is "kairotic," including the time for milking the goats.

The result of such a cognitive focus is that what a person *was* aware of in the past relative to what one *is* aware of at present as well as what *one is on the point of being* aware of because of the past and present all form a single meaningful now, the actually present. The antecedent and the forthcoming blend in with the continuing. Things unfold not because of some external plan, or some schedule of events that has to be followed, but because the various outcomes of some given activity are simply forthcoming. Thus along with being a qualitative reality, duration is invariably seen as process. Even the much-approved Greek philosophical conception of the "Great Year," probably Babylonian in origin, is rooted in a process focused on the present. The Great Year consists of 36,000 solar years, and every Great Year event in the entire cosmos as well as on earth repeats itself down to the minutest detail. Needham (1981:133) notes that this is due to "resumption by the planets and constellations of their original places." It is likewise rooted in and serves to support the "image of limited good" quite prevalent in antiquity (Malina 1993a:90–116). The same might be said for the Israelite speculative notion of "a world week of six epochs of 1,000 years each" (Rordorf 1968:48). However, both the Great Year and the World Week were based on the sort of abstract speculation and mathematical demonstration which present-oriented, experienced time, traditional people found as unreal as a dream; those conceptions belonged to the imaginary realm of possibilities where adherence to actuality must be suspended and the rights of God usurped, as we shall see.

Processes can be aborted at times. Pregnancy ends with the expulsion of the fetus, and healing ceases with renewed injury. Such interruption involves severing the outcome of some process by cutting away the organic connection of that outcome to the present. But one's own experience or that of some experienced person has shown the invariable connection of outcome to process. This means that the forthcoming is experienced as already present (Bourdieu 1963: 66). Experienced time can only be based upon procedures rooted in the organic nature of things. Such experienced time, of course, is found along with duration experienced in repetitive, technological operations, such as grinding and milling, sowing and reaping and the like. Focus is not, however, on the repetitive technological aspect, but on persons: the grinder and the miller, the sower and the reaper, and the processes in which they find themselves *vis-à-vis* the processes of nature, for example, planting and harvesting, baking and cooking. As the proverb has it: "The builder of a house has more honor than the house" (Heb. 3:3). Yet in all activity, God is somehow present: "For every house is built by some one, but the builder of all things is God" (Heb. 3:4). Likewise, the celestial motion of the heavens, something we consider non-organic, was part of the organic processes of the cosmos because of the fact that heavenly bodies were controlled by an array of non-human "persons."

Compare this view with our contemporary abstract time. As a rule, our abstract time is rooted in calendars that simply count off periods and clocks with precise hour, minute and second designations. Similarly, abstract time requires an understanding of history as a chronologically based description of what really happened. It also deals with the future in terms of statistical procedures and a host of measuring devices having little to do with celestial motion. Modern production, whether in factory or farm, considers output apart from any connection with organic process. People are expected to eat at "mealtime," whether they are hungry or not. Abstract time, with its past, present and future, has dissolved "the organic unity which combines present and 'forthcoming' in the process of production. This is the unity of the product itself, lost in the transition from craftsmanship to industrial technological specialization" (Bourdieu 1963:66).

Imaginary time

For people in the ancient world, there was the reality of the concrete present with its concrete antecedents and its forthcoming concrete outcomes. However, there was also the sphere falling outside the horizon of the experienced world. This was the imaginary. The antecedents to the present and the forthcoming rooted in it were concrete and actual; the past and the future were abstract and imaginary. What stood beyond the horizon of the present was the region of imaginary time, the world of past and future. Imaginary time covers everything that does not exist in the present. It thus covers our past and future. In other words, imaginary time looks to all that happened earlier than any living witness in fact experienced as well as all the possibilities wrapped up in the modalities of what actually does not exist: what can/could, may/might, shall/should, will/would or ought to be. The statistical future of infinite possibility can be described by these modalities, as can the imaginary past deriving from what could have, might have, should have, must have, ought have and would have been.

The imaginary world is the world that cannot be directly and immediately linked with the universe of experience. This imaginary world, thus, cannot be validated by experience. What may appear absurd or impossible in the context of experience may be realized in remote times and places. In the imaginary world and its imaginary time (past and future), possibilities have the essential property of being equally able to come about or not to come about. As a domain that can actually impinge upon the world of experience, the imaginary world and imaginary time in an Israelite framework are the domain exclusive to God, for whom all things are possible (Gen. 18:14; Jer. 32:27; Matt. 19:26; Luke 1:37; Rom. 4:21). To say that all those things are possible for God means that all those things presently not possible for human beings will forever remain so. The past and the future as the possible, then, cannot belong and never will belong to human beings. To glimpse the world of the distant past or of the future, the world of the possible, is to assume divine prerogatives. In Israel such insolence was idolatry, while for Greeks it was hubris. The possible past and the possible future are simply closed to human beings.

Thus, on the one hand, the need for prophets in Israel to tell about distant origins, whether of the human family or of the people of Israel. Only God could know that imaginary period, and hence only God could reveal it through his prophets. And the same holds for the future that falls outside the purview of what comes forth from the present. This is why God alone knows what falls in imaginary time (see Mark 13:32; Matt. 24:36; Acts 1:7). On the other hand, statements such as "Behold, he is coming with the clouds and every eye will see him, every one who pierced him, and all tribes of the earth will wail on account of him" (Rev. 1:7) indicate experienced time. "Everyone who pierced him" was still available. The same holds for Paul's reference to "we who are alive, who are left until the coming of the Lord" (1 Thess. 4:15–16). The process set under way with the death and resurrection of Jesus is viewed as present and experienced.

So for members of Jesus movement groups, God's Kingdom was forthcoming, Jesus' emergence as Messiah with power was forthcoming, the transformation of social realities in favor of God's people was forthcoming. Yet for the audiences of Mark, Matthew and Luke, things obviously changed. The coming of Jesus is moved now into imaginary time. For the coming of the Son of Man with power in Mark and Matthew, for example, was now future, a piece of imaginary time known only to God: "But of that day or that hour no one knows, not even the angels in heaven, nor the Son, but only the Father" (Mark 13:32; Matt. 24:36). And the same with hopes for social transformation in Luke's group: "It is not for you to know times or seasons which the Father has fixed by his own authority" (Acts 1:7). In the New Testament writings, we can see how the forthcoming became future, how the experienced became imaginary.

Evaluating experienced time and imaginary time

With their sensitivity to the experienced world, first-century Mediterraneans applied rather different criteria of validation for events said to occur within the experienced world and those claimed to have happened outside the horizon of that world in the realm of the possible (Bourdieu 1963:60–1). In the case of the experienced world and all its trappings, the only accepted criteria arose from sensory experience – seeing, touching or hearing (see, for example, Mark 16:6–7; Matt. 28:6–7; Luke 24:24,36–9; 1 Cor 15:5–8). Should these be absent or not available, then the requisite judgment was formed on the basis of the credibility owed a person known to be worthy of belief. Beyond the horizon of experience and those who could vouch for it, one found a broad frontier marking the beginning of a universe where everything was naturally possible. Criteria for assertions of truth in this area were much less demanding and all affirmations that somehow fitted the major cultural story of the group were worthy of acceptance (Bourdieu 1963:61). But it would be foolhardy in the extreme to make decisions for the world of experience on the basis of the imaginary and its past and/or future. It was quite different with the experienced and its antecedent and forthcoming components.

More specifically, the forthcoming was the unfolding or developing horizon of the experienced present. Here a person apprehended the potentialities inherent in some continuing, actual event, potentialities envisioned in terms of actual realization among actual people. There was no reference to future possibility or probability, only to what was going to be and must be because it already is. Thus, "the kingdom of Heaven/God is at hand" (Mark 1:15; Matt. 4:17), or "The Son of man must suffer many things" (Mark 8:31; Matt. 16:21; Luke 9:22). And the discerning know that it already is because it can be clearly seen as deriving from what is. The remainder of the harvest is seen in the first fruits that enable the rest of the harvest to be put to use (Rom. 8:23; 1 Cor 15:20; Jas. 1:18; Rev. 14:4) just as a tree's branches were already in the roots and the whole lump of dough is in the dough of the first fruits (Rom. 11:16). The firstborn embraces all the rest of the offspring or of creation because the firstborn enables the rest to come forth (Rom. 8:29; Col. 1:15, 18). Similarly a mustard seed is grasped not only with its color, form and other directly perceived properties, but also with qualities potentially inherent in it, such as "nesting place for birds," etc. These potentialities are apprehended in the same way as persons know the names and functions of parts of a house into which they have never stepped before. They are known on the basis of experience, their own or another's. What is forthcoming is perceived in the same way as that

194

which is actually present and to which the forthcoming is linked by an organic unity. What is potential is already present in some actual reality. It does not arise from some statistically infinite number of possibilities equally able to come about or not. Rather, the potential cannot not come about, since as it is understood, it is just as much present as any other actually present, directly and immediately perceived object. Such perceptions of the forthcoming then derive from an experienced world full of challenges, tasks to be performed and threats to one's group, not from some imaginary world.

What is forthcoming stands at the concrete horizon of the present. It need not be imagined since it can be directly and immediately perceived. What distinguishes the forthcoming rooted in the potential and the future rooted in the possible is not greater or lesser remoteness from the directly perceived present. This in fact is the way we perceive our future. Rather what is distinctive of the forthcoming in comparison with the future is the degree of immediate and direct organic connection with some presently experienced person, event or process. When exactly that potentiality might be realized is not at issue as it would be for us. Rather the item at issue is the inevitability of outcomes rather than how many and when. The reason for this is that the person, event or process actually present often embrace a discernible set of outcomes, all present and held together within a single context of meaning, but more or less distant within objective time (Bourdieu 1963:61–2). Consider the set of children of a newly married couple, the harvests of a recently bought field, the work of a recently acquired set of oxen. The children, harvests and work are not future but forthcoming, standing at the horizon of the experienced world.

Forthcoming and antecedent features of the experienced world, however, can slip into the imaginary when experience undergoes alteration. The children of a marriage may cease to be forthcoming due to infertility or old age (as in the story of Abraham and Sarah, Gen. 18:11–14, and Zechariah and Elizabeth, Luke 1:36–7). The promise of recently acquired land may vanish with war, drought and erosion. The forthcoming thus becomes future; the experienced becomes imaginary. While this shift from experienced time to imaginary time may be quite painful, it would normally be accepted with a shrug of the shoulders and with a "Never mind!" typical of peasants and their "Nothing ventured, nothing gained" outlook. Luke's description of the shattered expectations of the disciples going to Emmaus would be typical (Luke 24:13–24).

Modern linear separable time and traditional cyclical and procedural time

Ours is a *linear separable time* conception. We are taught to consider time as linear, a unidirectional past, present and future that is separable into various discrete compartments. These slices of time form a schedule according to which people are expected to do one thing at a time. Such measurable, sliceable time is then comparable to other measurable and sliceable items, such as money or consumer goods. People invest now for future returns, hourly wages are paid, and time is given monetary value. Problems with time, when duly noted, are to be eliminated on time. Thus people with this perception have a sense of urgency to adopt behavior that would eliminate the problem. Cultural goods and roles are chosen in terms of how well they perform and fulfill their intended functions. As Graham has perceptively noted:

> People who share this perception think of time as a road or ribbon that stretches from the past into the future, and along which one progresses. The past is old in that it has already been experienced, and time spent in the past cannot be recovered. The future is new in that it represents a different set of situations for which one can prepare. Time spent in the past that did not contribute to the present state can be considered as wasted. It is also thought that time properly spent now will put one in a much better position in the future, and this better future state forms the basis of the idea of progress. Activities are not seen as ends in themselves, but rather means to ends, the attainment of which lies somewhere in the future.
>
> (1981:336)

Furthermore, Hall has characterized such people as having monochronic time (M-time) in which they can do only one thing at a time. He writes:

> For M-time people reared in the northern European tradition, time is linear and segmented like a road or a ribbon extending forward into the future and backward to the past. It is also tangible; they speak of it as being saved, spent, wasted, lost, made up, accelerated, slowed down, crawling, and running out. These metaphors should be taken very seriously because they express the basic manner in which time is conceived as an unconscious determinant or frame on which everything else is built.
>
> (Hall 1976:16)

Everything important is scheduled, and hence classified, sealing in two or more people off from the group for a period. Emphasis is on schedules, segmentation and promptness. Again, such a perspective on time requires a level of social discipline and intellectual abstraction among the general populace that did not emerge in the larger cities of northern Europe until well into the Industrial Revolution.

> In this sense, only in the sociocultural milieu where the status of the sciences, philosophy, psychology or biology is already greatly developed – and developed in a certain way – is any systematic conception of time possible; and only there and then does it emerge and diffuse. In this sense all elaborate conceptions of time in any field of thought are socioculturally conditioned and are sociocultural time in a broad sense.
>
> (Sorokin 1943:168)

The time-perspective initiated with the Industrial Revolution is expressed in *clock time*. Clock time is any objective, external, non-social referent for measuring the duration of the unfolding of behavior. Such clock time simply replicates linear separable time perception. While the calendars of antiquity might be said to be objective and external, they were hardly non-social since they either derived from divine injunction for a given society or marked off the periods of influence of celestial beings on a given society. In this sense there simply was no clock time in the ancient world.

In its place, traditional peoples have what Lauer calls "social time." *Social time* "refers to the patterns and orientations that relate to social processes and to the conceptualization of the ordering of social life" (Lauer 1981:21). Social time derives from social relations and social transactions; it is influenced by and expresses the story, feelings, beliefs and values of a people. Social time is present oriented, functional, non-directional and polychronic.

As for this last feature, it is significant to point out that Mediterraneans were and are polychronic time (P-time) people, usually doing several things at once. P-time emphasizes involvement with people and completion of transactions with people, not adherence to schedules. P-time is not easily measurable. It forms a set of unrelated frames of interaction rather than a ribbon or a road, and every given frame is meaningful (Hall 1976:14). Furthermore, Mediterranean non-elites surely held and hold a *mañana* attitude. For the first century, evidence would be the previously cited proverbs quoted by

Jesus in Matthew's gospel: "Tomorrow will be anxious for itself";
"Let the day's own trouble be sufficient for the day" (Matt. 6:34).
Now, what the *mañana* attitude actually involves is that the Mediter-
ranean person

> puts off for an indefinite mañana those things that can be put
> off, and does today those things that can only be done today.
> If what must be done today is work . . . the work is done. . . .
> If what must be done today is something else . . . then what
> must be done now or never is done and what can be postponed
> until another time – work perhaps – is postponed.
>
> (Saunders 1954:120)

From the viewpoint of realizing some sort of distant goals, putting
off until tomorrow does not materially affect the probability of
successful goal attainment. Hence there is little motive not to put
things off. Present orientation in the world of experienced time is
rooted in experienced disvalue of delayed gratification or anticipa-
tory goal behavior for present survival. Distant goals relate to the
imaginary world, not the present.

Hence, we can safely assert that the people of the ancient Mediterranean knew nothing of linear separable time. They could not
experience any urgency based on some scheduled time. And of course
they did not attach money value to time and had no interest in
some abstract, calendric future. Consequently, those periodizations
of biblical time based on a matrix of linear, separable time, time
presumably running like a ribbon from creation to consummation,
were simply impossible for the people who gave us the Bible. As
Zerubavel (1981:31–69) notes, with the rise of monasteries and their
schedules, irreversible linear, separable time emerges. Hence someone
like the twelfth-century Cistercian monk Joachim of Flora (d. 1202)
could propound a linear theory of "history" while the thirteenth-
century Franciscan Roger Bacon could hold that human knowledge
would increase progressively until the "end of the world" (Russell
1981:59–76). If the end was to be like the beginning, whether it
be in the Great Year of Greek philosophers or in the Week of Years
of Israelite seers, the resulting process would be cyclical rather than
linear.

At this point I should simply like to note that the distinction
often made by biblical theologians between linear time and cyclical
time is not very clear. It is rather difficult, for example, to speak of
linear, irreversible time when the time-line heads toward a future

marked by the appearance of a Messiah, paradise, or any other entity which exists at the beginning of the time line (at creation). This is not an irreversible time-line, but a return to the beginning or a trans-ference of the beginning to the end; the result is a completed cycle as the time-line attaches to the beginning. My point is that there is little basis for contrasting the presumed linear time of the Bible with the cyclical time of non-biblical peoples. For if the final stage is marked by the restoration of paradise (Israelite) or the return of a preexistent Messiah (Christian), we are in any case at the beginning. The fundamental question is not linear versus cyclical, but *whether the cycle occurs but once or continues indefinitely*. The answer seems to depend upon the social organization of a given society as well as upon its value orientation and the actual realization of those values (for non-biblical cases, see the compilation of Eliade 1963).

On the other hand, cyclical processes simply underscored present orientation. For example, Aristotle's theory or model of the return of political systems, a cyclical view of time, shows primary prefer-ence for the present; his model is essentially present oriented (see Koselleck 1982:41).

The social time of traditional peoples had two dimensions to it, a cyclical one and a procedural one. Observation of the personally caused non-biological cosmic motion of heavenly bodies served to develop an assessment of duration as recurring; this is cyclical time or spiraling time. On the other hand, those organic biological processes such as reproduction, life stages, sickening and healing enabled an understanding of duration as process; this is procedural time (Graham 1981:35–42).

Cyclical time

Cyclical or recurring time is rooted in the motion of divinely controlled heavenly bodies; such motion or change is presumed to be significant for assessing human behavior. Thus in Gen. 1:14–18 we read how

> God said, "Let there be lights in the firmament of the heavens to separate the day from the night; and let them be for signs and for seasons and for days and years, and let them be lights in the firmament of the heavens to give light upon the earth." And it was so. And God made the two great lights, the greater light to rule the day, and the lesser light to rule the night; he

made the stars also. And God set them in the firmament of the heavens to give light upon the earth, to rule over the day and over the night, and to separate the light from the darkness. And God saw that it was good. And there was evening and there was morning, a fourth day.

With change indicated by the motion of heavenly bodies, a person perceives the same activities as recurring according to some repeatable pattern. This perspective looks to those dimensions of a culture in which actions are punctuated by the movement of the moon, sun and stars, with life organized around agriculture, food gathering or hunting. Such activities are often related to those recurrent celestial movements. Similarly, any human experience considered from the viewpoint of its frequent and similar patterned occurrence among one's fellows is considered cyclical and most often irreversible. Having children, sowing and planting, menstruation and the like are repeated experiences in the human community. Thus cyclical time can serve as synonym for human experiences that happen more or less in the same way and rather frequently.

This celestial, non-biological mode of noting changes in human experience takes on the quality of continuing process because the movement of the heavenly spheres is under the control of non-human "persons," whether God or gods or other beings. Such recurring movement underscores the sameness of life, even in face of change. As a result, people expect a "heaven and earth," an outfitted cosmos, a tomorrow that is exactly like yesterday. "So long as the earth remains, seed time and harvest, cold and heat, summer and winter, day and night, shall not cease" (Gen. 8:22). When this mode of marking duration is applied to social realities, the result is an unchanging social system. Such an immutable social system is, of course, the preferred perception of elites who have firm faith in the enduring quality of their social preeminence. And, as a rule, it was these elites who took charge of "keeping time." The time they kept was recurring traditional time.

During the time of Christian origins, Jerusalem was the priestly administrative city that marked events for the Judean polity, and this by the will of God. As is well known, ancient modes of reckoning time developed in administrative cities to mark occurrences of meaningful political and elite events. Since religion was embedded in politics and kinship, such political and elite events appear as religious, sacred events to us (see Malina 1986a). Measure was derived from a cosmic phenomenon set in motion and continued in motion by God, and hence indicated by God in the celestial realm. Sorokin has observed:

> This illustrates specifically the thesis that almost all of the important characteristics of the time conception of either the natural sciences, of philosophy and metaphysics, of theology, or of psychology and biology are stamped by the needs, status and nature of the sociocultural milieu in which such conceptions are born and diffused. With the proper variation, this is applicable to any important characteristic of time conceptions. In this broad sense, the mathematical, physical, biological, psychological, and metaphysical time conceptions all are already socially organized time systems, conditioned by the sociocultural environment in which they are conceived and diffused.
>
> (1943:170)

From the viewpoint of cyclical traditional time, the temple city of Jerusalem was one big clock marking time solely and only for Judeans. Conceptions of time and their clock were purely local affairs until the Renaissance. Thus, Sorokin (1943:169) observes that the time of classical mechanics and its clock emerged with the internationalization of society in the later Middle Ages. He refers to the mechanical clocks of the 14th and 15th centuries and the new cosmogony, physics and mechanics which reached their full development in 16th and 17th centuries. None of these conceptions of time and its clock could or did emerge in the purely local societies that had no need of such timekeepers applicable to all societies as in previous periods. Obviously it was in the interest of Jerusalem elites to mark time, to be in control of the time-signaling system and thus to control time and the people who marked time by the Jerusalem Temple. Temple time simply concretized the recurrent and divinely controlled quality of recurrent time. The arrangement could only lead people to realize that they could not affect the future in any way. Current actions would not affect the future, only the experienced world of the present.

Procedural time

Procedural time is rooted in the processes of biological organisms. Such processes are presumed to be significant for assessing the quality and meaning of human behavior. With duration perceived in terms of organic processes a person will perceive the events of human experience as processual unities that have to be done right and carried to term. What counts is adequate completion of some activity, not the amount of time spent on it. Here the present covers the whole period of the process in question. Any human experience considered from the viewpoint of its singular and infrequent patterned occurrence among one's fellows is considered processual. Marriage, the birth of a firstborn son, menopause, old age and the like are events that happen but once to individuals as a rule. Thus procedural time can serve as a synonym for human experiences that happen rarely or only once to human beings; these are therefore infrequent, notable occurrences.

Such time is typical of those dimensions of a culture in which tradition is passed on by way of ritual activity. Things are done "when the time is right," a phrase that does not refer to time, but to the completion of some antecedent, necessary event. Thus: "When the fullness of time was come, God sent forth his Son" (Gal. 4:4; Eph. 1:10). Similarly, the various numbered schemes in apocalyptic writings as well as the sequence of events that have to occur in the unfolding of the scenario of the coming Son of Man (Mark 13:3–27 and parallels) point to procedural time. Graham notes: "Once the event begins, the stages in its completion have no time dimension to them, and any attempt to alter the procedure in order to save time would be considered ridiculous, like chopping off the 18th hole of a golf course in order to save time during a match" (1981:337). This perspective could never really be the main way of noting duration in a society where time is embedded in the economy, such as the US. For with procedural time, time is never money, never to be saved, never a consumer good. "People following a procedure without regard to time are consuming the procedure, not the time. The idea of basing a choice on the usage of time would be completely rejected" (Graham 1981:337).

If something has to be done, a problem faced, and the like, people feel constrained to follow standard operating procedures, with no thought to alternatives. Procedural time and cyclical time enmesh in the unfolding of such customary process. For example, in Palestine campaigns of all sorts were invariably carried out at the outset of the dry season if only because that is when it is fitting (see 2 Sam. 9:1). An announcement such as: "The Kingdom of Heaven is at hand" fits procedural time. So does the behavior of those disciples in the gospel story who leave what they are doing and follow Jesus. The tempo of life in the Mediterranean was set by the rhythm of rainfall and prolonged sunshine (Boissevain 1982/3). The activity of Jesus in the Synoptic story fits the right time for getting things done, for proclaiming the kingdom, at the onset of the dry season. The activity in Galilee is over before the next year's rainy season. There is no mention of traveling or activity in the rain. This is more than "an argument from silence," since in the Mediterranean, the winter, rainy season is a period of staying at home, of limited social activity. Plans for the Passover trip to Jerusalem would have taken place during the rainy season. Undoubtedly that Passover trip, coming at the beginning of another dry season, looked like quite the right time for proclaiming the kingdom in Judea. According to the Synoptics, the Jesus group lasted for a single dry season ending at the close of the rainy season with a Passover. The Christian movement described in Acts got under way at the right time soon after that, another dry season open to traveling and prolonged public interaction.

Again, people sharing a traditional, social time perception, with its cyclical and procedural aspects, are essentially present oriented. For them the experience of duration is the concrete feature of life that forms actual time. And yet people can imagine all sorts of things happening at variously imaginable times. This leads us to the next distinction.

Abstract historical and operational time versus traditional historical and operational time

Rayner distinguishes historical time from operational time. Historical time, he says, is "concerned with the ordering of events or periods in the life of an individual or a society, which are of contemporary significance. Historical time is non-repetitive, marked by epochs, and is learned or remembered" (Rayner 1982:256). On the basis of this description, *historical time* is an interpretation of times past and/or future formulated with a view to some present concern by those vitally interested in those present concerns. An example of this learned historical dimension is the ordering of historical periods in any textbook: ancient, medieval, modern, contemporary etc. Similarly, the genealogies in the New Testament carefully trace persons as far back as they affect the standing of Jesus in the story in question. Likewise, creation stories, ancient and modern, belong to the category of historical time since their main purpose is to give a warrant to present social norms and value orientations. On the other hand, visions of the future presented with a view to having impact on the present also belong to historical time as previously defined.

Traditional historical time

What, then, is the difference between historical time in traditional, ancient societies and in our own? It seems that both we and traditional peoples look to our past (and future) with a view to having impact on the present. In this we are quite the same. However, since the Renaissance, Europeans and Americans after them have had at their disposal a sense of history (Burke 1969). This sense of history entails the belief that people in the past were different from people in the present, and hence that human societies need not be the way they are. The ancient motto *historia magistra vitae* no longer means what it meant to the past-oriented Romans who coined it – that human nature being always the same, incidents from the past serve as sure guides to present behavior (Koselleck 1982:21–38).

Modern historical time, then, has to be distinguished from pre-Renaissance historical time. The latter is much like imaginary time previously described and clearly belongs within that dimension of traditional time perception. Imaginary time plus the new feature of relationship to the present produces historical time. For why do people bother imagining the past to have been the way they think it was? It seems that they do so essentially and fundamentally to have some effect on the present. And the same for the future. People picture the future to be the way it presumably will be essentially and fundamentally to have some effect on the present. This holds for science fiction scenarios as well as for descriptions of "the next life."

Modern historical time, on the other hand, serves the needs of the present largely in terms of an agenda charted by society's temporal orientation preference. Future-oriented societies such as the US will be concerned with history quite differently than the past-oriented societies of northern Europe. And both will differ from traditional societies since modern historical time will be much concerned about what really happened as well as intimating what it means for the present.

Traditional operational time

The counterweight to historical time in Rayner's model is operational time. *Operational time* is concerned with functionally marking some regular interval for the purpose of performing some present common practical task or reaching some common present practical goal. "Operational time is repetitive, marked by regular intervals concerned with the job in hand and/or repeated operations, and it is experienced rather than learned about" (Rayner 1982:257). Operational time more or less covers what Bourdieu called experienced time for traditional peoples, and the abstract, linear separable clock time of moderns. Thus operational time indications include contemporary calendar and clock indications, such as "I'll be there next Monday at 7.15 a.m. sharp" as well as first-century notices such as: "When it is evening you say: 'It will be fair weather; for the sky is red.' And in the morning, 'It will be stormy today, for the sky is red and threatening'" (Matt. 16:2–3). Rayner sees the distinctive quality of operational time as deriving from experienced ecological constraints rather than from imagination. The cold of winter, the heat of summer, the length of a pregnancy or a growing season and the like all affect the perception of duration. Yet any sort of time indication is the outcome of the social interpretations of the changes and processes that affect group members both socially and environmentally. For people invariably act within social and environmental contexts or settings, and are markedly influenced by those settings. They are therefore subject to the constraints imposed by those social and environmental realities. Yet the relation of people to environment is reciprocal rather than unidirectional, dynamic rather than static (see Stokols 1988:234–5). Hence operational time as time controlled by ecological constraints alone is not sufficiently defined to serve as a counterpart to historical time.

If historical time is characterized by patterns of interpretation overlaid on the past and future to serve present concerns, then *operational time* is duration modelled to fit present pragmatic activity, with its ecological and social constraints. To make the notion of operational time usable for the ancient world, we shall have to distinguish between traditional operational time, which is identical with Bourdieu's experienced time, and modern operational time, which is abstract, linear and separable. With this in mind we can profit from Rayner's differentiations between historical and operational time.

205

To begin with, environmental constraints are weaker on historical time than on operational time. For example, a traditional history can describe the sun standing still, water parting or a person walking on water – environmental constraints recede. On the other hand, historical time is subject to greater social constraints than is operational time; there are great social constraints on deviating from stories that give warrant to present privilege. Moreover, periods of historical time are usually of far different length than are cycles of nature. Periods judged important by storytellers, for example, are made to be longer than those they judge insignificant; these latter are often compressed or omitted. In the case of the gospels, we have the period of Jesus' infancy, given some space by Matthew and Luke and omitted in Mark, as compared with Jesus' witnessed activity, given the greater share of the story. Historical time may be collapsed, compressed or extended in ways impossible for operational time. Activities must run their course, even recurring ones. In this sense operational time is procedural, even in recurring activity such as sleeping, milling, sowing and reaping. The social significance of these activities, once defined in the culture, is not likely to vary so greatly from day to day if daily activities are involved. But when annual, festival events such as harvesting or pilgrimage are involved, then we find differences in the duration of successive days largely due to the procedures involved in the festivals. But such alteration in the duration of festive operational time is never observable between successive epochs of historical time. Operational time will always reveal the social constraints put upon it by the cultural interpretation of the ecology. So long as it is rooted in the experienced world and experienced time, operational time cannot be contracted or extended as historical time is (Rayner 1982:257). On the other hand, traditional historical time has all the earmarks of imaginary time. Like imaginary time, it deals with the past and the future, with the possible, with what is knowable to God alone. For this reason, traditional historical information about the possible past and the possible future will always require some divine warrant. Once a witnessing generation passes, such information is closed to human beings unless God discloses it.

I offer the following comparison between traditional historical time and traditional operation time to sum up the foregoing discussion:

Historical time	*Operational time*
• imaginary time based on the imagination of the "historian"	• experienced time based on social experience
• creates and orders past and future in imaginative ways significant to the present	• creates and orders the present in terms of cultural cues for meaningful existence
• based on imaginary retrojections and projections, celestial cycles and biological and social processes	• based on present experience of inorganic celestial cycles and organic biological and social processes
• since nature repeats itself, events in history can be known by present experiences	• present experience is norm of judging historical validity
• marked by epochs, qualitative periods	• marked by meaningful present processes and recurring activities
• concerned with present social meanings	• concerned with the present or the social meanings of repeated operations
• images of the past and future must be carefully inculcated, learned and subsequently remembered	• directly verifiable experienced rather than taught and learned; readily recoverable to memory from ambience
• interprets social processes and their constraints (for example, social roles) as rooted in the natural environment and its constraints	• interprets natural environmental processes and their constraints as rooted in social process and its constraints (for example, things have always been done this way)
• weaker environmental constraints (mountains can move, the sun stop, stars fall from the sky, etc.)	• weaker social constraints (ideal kinship norms unrealized, values compromised, etc.)
• periods of time can be compressed or extended since based on imagination; important periods longer than unimportant ones	• periods of time cannot be compressed or extended since controlled organic processes, except psychologically (events seem short or long)
• interprets the present period as enduring or shortly ending	• experiences present activity as past directed and/or present focused

207

I sum up the foregoing discussion with a sketch of Mediterranean time on the following page Figure 2.

CONCLUSION

I have argued that during the period of Christian origins there was a distinctive circum-Mediterranean conception of time that differed greatly from our own. It does not seem useful to compare the questionable uniqueness of popular ancient Israelite time with philosophical ancient Greek time, as Cullmann and others have done. Most comparisons of Israelite with Greek in the first-century Mediterranean are usually misplaced if only because the two clearly have more in common than not, especially when compared with a third mode of perception always implicitly presupposed in the comparison, namely the modern interpreter's own. Consequently, my intention has been to compare first-century Mediterranean time perception and our own US twentieth-century views and to develop some useful model for understanding first-century Mediterranean statements about time.

What remains is to apply that model of traditional time to those areas commonly and misleadingly labeled "eschatology," "apocalyptic" and the "parousia." All three areas have one feature in common: they refer in various ways to the process by which the forthcoming was transformed into the possible for early Christian generations. Jesus was once perceived by present-oriented people as the forthcoming Messiah with power. This perception of theirs was rooted in actual, experienced time situated in an operational realm abutting the horizon of the present. Given the press of events, however, this perception had subsequently proceeded beyond that horizon into the realm of the possible, of the future, rooted in imaginary time. Of course, the realm of imaginary time was accessible only to prophets, this time Christian prophets. And this shift from forthcoming to future occurred during the period of Christian origins. A social science approach to interpretation would focus on that group of early Christians who experienced the shift.

The model presented here suggests a range of questions for historians and exegetes. For example: How much credence or confidence did first-century Mediterranean Christians put in the newly reorganized, non-forthcoming aspects of their present? Given their present orientation, what did this generation of Christians think and feel about their hopes, now part of the imaginary future? What was it

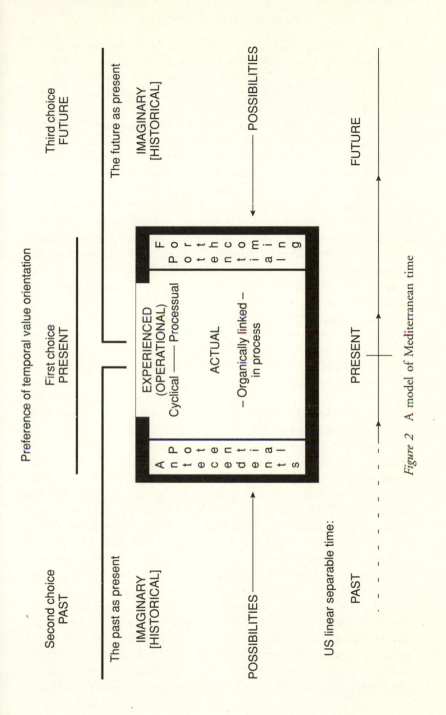

Figure 2 A model of Mediterranean time

that moved their assessment of Jesus beyond the boundaries of their experienced, operational world to the imaginary, historical realm of the future, of the possible? And how did these people assess the imaginary, historical as compared with their previous concrete assessment of the experienced, operational?

These are significant questions because we know that when present-oriented people are confronted with a problem, it is not the best solution that is sought but only one that works here and now, a "good enough" solution (Graham 1981:340). What were some of the "good enough" solutions adopted by early Christians, and kept or discarded by later elite leadership? Further, we also know that if there are alternatives, traditional present-oriented people make their choices in terms of present utility only. An inferior product available now is better than a superior product in the future since the future is generally discounted (Graham 1981:340). What, then, were some of the "inferior products" chosen by early Christian non-elites as expected hopes, revealed promises and Messianic empowerment failed to come forth in the present? And how did early Christian leaders deal with these choices, especially before Constantine?

The foregoing presentation allows for several clear conclusions:

First, in the New Testament period there was no tension between the "now" and the "not yet." When those writings were written and collected, there was only emphasis on a rather broad "now." On the other hand, the "not yet" is a continual concern of persons from future-oriented societies.

Second, the areas variously called "eschatology," "apocalyptic" and "the delay of the parousia" have to be rethought (see Malina 1995a). For if in fact the New Testament lacks the future orientation of the sort we experience, then the features of the future which modern commentators discover might well be an anachronistic and ethnocentric overlay (see Borg 1986; Malina 1986b; 1994a; Mack 1987). All the evidence indicates that New Testament authors were present oriented. They were fundamentally and directly concerned with the present, as were Jesus and the others described by those authors. The future as the realm of the possible was or is exclusively God's.

Third, the role of the prophet as a person in a present-oriented society has to be rethought. Ancient Israelite "historical" books such as the Pentateuch and the Former Prophets had to be written by prophets because they described events of the distant past. And the Later Prophets are prophetic because they describe events of both the distant past and the non-forthcoming future. What both realms have in common is that they are the imaginary and possibility-filled areas known only to God, who speaks through prophets. What did Christian prophets in fact say? To what end?

Of course, the list can go on. In sum, however, my point is that there surely are differences between pre-Einsteinian, pre-Industrial Revolution, pre-Enlightenment, pre-Newtonian, premonastic Mediterranean perceptions of time and the perceptions of time common to most contemporary American Bible readers, professional and non-professional. I hope that I have touched upon the more obvious and important ones. And I hope that I have adequately indicated that the theme of Christ and time is still a significant one.

REFERENCES

Abbott, Walter M. (ed.) (1966) *The Documents of Vatican II*. New York: America.

Arendt, Hanna (1958) "What Was Authority." pp. 81–112 in Carl J. Friedrich (ed.) *Nomos I: Authority*. Cambridge, MA: Harvard University Press.

Attneave, Carolyn (1982) "American Indians and Alaska Native Families: Emigrants in Their Own Homeland." pp. 55–83 in Monica McGoldrick, John K. Pearce and Joseph Giordano (eds) *Ethnicity and Family Therapy*. New York/London: Guilford.

Barr, James (1962) *Biblical Words for Time*. Studies in Biblical Theology 33. London: SCM.

Boissevain, Jeremy (1982/3) "Seasonal Variations on Some Mediterranean Themes." *Ethnologia Europaea* 13:6–12.

Boman, Thorlief (1960) *Hebrew Thought Compared with the Greek*. London: SCM.

Borg, Marcus J. (1986) "A Temperate Case for a Non-Eschatological Jesus." *Forum* 2/3:81–102.

Bourdieu, Pierre (1963) "The Attitude of the Algerian Peasant toward Time." pp. 55–72 in Julian Pitt-Rivers (ed.) *Mediterranean Countrymen: Essays in the Social Anthropology of the Mediterranean*. Paris/La Haye: Mouton.

Broshi, MaGen. (1986) "The Diet of Palestine in the Roman Period – Introductory Notes." *Israel Museum Journal* 5:41–56.

Brown, Peter (1982) "Town, Village and Holy Man: The Case of Syria." pp. 153–65 in his *Society and the Holy in Late Antiquity*. Berkeley/Los Angeles: University of California Press.

Burke, Peter (1969) *The Renaissance Sense of the Past*. New York: St. Martin's Press.

Carmignac, Jean (1979) *Le Mirage de l'eschatologie: royauté, règne et royaume de Dieu sans eschatologie*. Paris: Letouzey et Ané.

Cullman, Oscar (1946) *Christus und die Zeit*. Zollikon: Evangelischer Verlag.

—— (1964) *Christ and Time: The Primitive Christian Conception of Time and History*. Rev. ed. Trans. Floyd V. Filson: Philadelphia: Westminster.

Eliade, Mircea (1963) *Myth and Reality*. New York: Harper & Row.

Elliott, John H. (1990) *A Home for the Homeless: A Sociological Exegesis of 1 Peter, its Situation and Strategy*. Rev. ed. Minneapolis: Fortress.

Eviatar, Zerubavel (1981) *Hidden Rhythms: Schedules and Calendars in Social Life*. Chicago: University of Chicago Press.

Fortes, Meyer (1970) "Pietas in Ancestor Worship." pp. 164–200 in his *Time and Social Structure and Other Essays*. London School of Economics Monographs on Social Anthropology 40. New York: Humanities.

Gabba, Emilio (1981) "True History and False History in Classical Antiquity." *Journal of Roman Studies* 71:50–62.

Graham, Robert J. (1981) "The Role of Perception of Time in Consumer Research." *Journal of Consumer Research* 7:335–42.

Hall, Edward T. (1959) *The Silent Language*. Garden City: Doubleday.

—— (1976) *Beyond Culture*. Garden City: Doubleday.

Harrington, Daniel J. (1988) "Second Testament Exegesis and the Social Sciences: A Bibliography." *Biblical Theology Bulletin* 18:77–85.

Harris, Philip R. and Robert T. Moral (1987) *Managing Cultural Differences: High-Performance Strategies for Today's Global Manager*. 2nd ed. Houston: Gulf.

Harris, William V. (1986) "The Roman Father's Power of Life and Death." pp. 81–95 in Roger S. Bagnall and William V. Harris (eds) *Studies in Roman Law in Memory of A. Arthur Schiller* Leiden: Brill.

Hopkins, Keith (1978) *Conquerors and Slaves*. Sociological Studies in Roman History 1. Cambridge: Cambridge University Press.

Iutcovich, Mark, Charles E. Babbitt and Joyce Iutcovich (1979) "Time Perception: A Case Study of a Developing Nation." *Sociological Focus* 12:71–85.

Jones, James M. (1979) "Conceptual and Strategic Issues in the Relationship of Black Psychology to American Social Science." pp. 390–432 in A. W. Boykin, A. J. Franklin and J. F. Yates (eds) *Research Directions of Black Psychologists*. New York: Sage.

—— (1988) "Cultural Differences in Temporal Perspectives: Instrumental and Expressive." pp. 21–38 in Joseph E. McGrath (ed.) *The Social Psychology of Time: New Perspectives*. Newbury Park: Sage.

Keenan, James G. (1981) "On Village and Polis in Byzantine Egypt." pp. 479–85 in Roger S. Bagnall, Gerald M. Browne, Ann E. Hanson and Ludwig Koenan (eds) *Proceedings of the XVI International Congress of Papyrology*. American Studies in Papyrology 23. Chico: Scholars Press.

Kluckhohn, Florence Rockwood and Fred L. Strodtbeck (1961) *Variations in Value Orientations*. Evanston: Row, Peterson.

Koselleck, Reinhart (1982) *Futures Past: On the Semantics of Historical Time*. Trans. Keith Tribe. Cambridge. MA: MIT.

Kübler-Ross, Elisabeth (1969) *On Death and Dying*. New York: Macmillan.

Lauer, R. H. (1981) *Temporal Man: The Meaning and Uses of Social Time*. New York: Praeger.

Lerner, Robert (1972) *The Heresy of the Free Spirit in the Middle Ages*. Berkeley: University of California Press.

McGrath, Joseph E. and Janice R. Kelly (1986) *Time and Human Interaction: Toward a Social Psychology of Time*. New York: Guilford.

Mack, Burton L. (1987) "The Kingdom Sayings in Mark." *Forum* 3/1:3–47.
MacMullen, Ramsay (1974) *Roman Social Relations: 50 B.C. to A.D. 284.* New Haven: Yale University Press.
Maines, David R. (1987) "The Significance of Temporality for the Development of Sociological Theory." *Sociological Quarterly* 28:303–11.
Malina, Bruce J. (1986a) "The Received View and What it Cannot Do: III John and Hospitality." pp. 171–94 in John H. Elliott (ed.) *Semeia*, Vol. 35: *Social-scientific Criticism of the New Testament and Its Social World.* Decatur, GA: Scholars.
—— (1986b) "'Religion' in the World of Paul: A Preliminary Sketch." *Biblical Theology Bulletin* 16:92–101.
—— (1993a) *The New Testament World: Insights from Cultural Anthropology.* Rev. ed. Louisville: Westminster/John Knox.
—— (1993b) "Apocalyptic and Territoriality." pp. 369–80 in Frederic Manns and Eugenio Alliata (eds) *Early Christianity in Context: Monuments and Documents. Essays in Honour of Emmanuel Testa.* Jerusalem: Franciscan Printing Press.
—— (1994a) "Religion in the Imagined New Testament World: More Social Science Lenses." *Scriptura* 51:1–26.
—— (1994b) "The Book of Revelation and Religion: How Did the Book of Revelation Persuade?" *Scriptura* 51:27–50.
—— (1995a) *On the Genre and Message of Revelation: Star Visions and Sky Journeys.* Peabody: Hendrickson.
—— (1995b) "Power, Pain and Personhood: Asceticism in the Ancient Mediterranean World." pp. 162–77 in Vincent L. Wimbush and Richard Valantasis (eds) *Asceticism.* New York: Oxford University Press.
Menninger, Karl (1969) *Number Words and Number Symbols: A Cultural History of Numbers.* Cambridge, MA: MIT
Mizruchi, Ephraim H. (1982) "Abeyance Process and Time: An Exploratory Approach to Age and Social Structure." pp. 112–22 in Ephraim H. Mizruchi, Barry Glassner and Thomas Pastorello (eds) *Time and Aging: Conceptualization and Application in Sociological and Gerontological Research.* Bayside, NY: General Hall.
Momigliano, Arnaldo (1966) "Time in Ancient Historiography." *History and Theory* Beiheft 6:1–23.
Needham, Joseph (1981) "Time and Knowledge in China and the West." pp. 92–135 in J. T. Fraser (ed.), *The Voices of Time: A Cooperative Survey of Man's Views of Time as Expressed by the Sciences and the Humanities.* 2nd ed. Amherst: University of Massachusetts Press.
Nisbet, Robert A. (1964) "Kinship and Political Power in First-Century Rome." pp. 257–71 in Werner J. Cahnman and Alvin Boskoff (eds) *Sociology and History: Theory and Research.* New York: Free Press.
Noblit, George W. and R. Dwight Hare (1988) *Meta-Ethnography: Synthesizing Qualitative Studies.* Qualitative Research Methods Series 11. Newbury Park: Sage.
Nuttin, Joseph (1985) *Future Time Perspective and Motivation: Theory and Research Method.* Louvain: Louvain University Press/Lawrence Erlbaum.
Ong, Walter J. (1959) *American Catholic Crossroads: Religious – Secular Encounters in the Modern World.* New York: Macmillan.

Papajohn, John and John Spiegel (1975) *Transactions in Families*. San Francisco: Jossey Bass.

Pinkster, H. (1983) "Tempus, Aspect and Aktionsart in Latin (Recent Trends 1961–1981)." *Aufstieg und Niedergang der römischen Welt* II 29/1: 270–319.

Press, Gerald A. (1977) "History and the Development of the Idea of History in Antiquity." *History and Theory* 16:280–96.

Quigley, Carroll (1961) *The Evolution of Civilizations*. New York: Macmillan.

—— (1973) "Mexican National Character and Circum-Mediterranean Personality Structure." *American Anthropologist* 75:319–22.

—— (1983) *Weapons Systems and Political Stability*. Washington: University Press of America.

Rayner, Steve (1982) "The Perception of Time and Space in Egalitarian Sects: A Millenarian Cosmology." pp. 247–74 in Mary Douglas (ed.) *Essays in the Sociology of Perception*. London: Routledge & Kegan Paul.

Roetzel, Calvin J. (1982) *The Letters of Paul: Conversations in Context*. 2nd ed. Atlanta: John Knox.

Rordorf, Willi (1968) *Sunday: The History of the Day of Rest and Worship in the Earliest Centuries of the Christian Church*. Philadelphia: Westminster.

Russell, J. L. (1981) "Time in Christian Thought." pp. 59–76 in J. T. Fraser (ed.) *The Voices of Time: A Cooperative Survey of Man's Views of Time as Expressed by the Sciences and the Humanities*. 2nd ed. Amherst: University of Massachusetts Press.

Sauer, Val J., Jr. (1981) *The Eschatology Handbook*. Atlanta: John Knox.

Saunders, Lyle (1954) *Cultural Differences and Medical Care: The Case of Spanish-Speaking People of the Southwest*. New York: Russell Sage.

Serbat, G. (1975; 1976) "Le Temps du verbe en Latin." *Revue des Etudes Latines* 53:367–90; 54:308–52.

Shils, Edward (1975) *Center and Periphery: Essays in Macrosociology*. Chicago: University of Chicago Press.

Sorokin, Pitirim A. (1943) *Sociocultural Causality, Space, Time: A Study of Referential Principles of Sociology and Social Science*. Durham, NC: Duke University Press.

Sparkes, B. A. (1962) "The Greek Kitchen." *Journal of Hellenic Studies* 82:121–37.

Spiegel, John (1982) "An Ecological Model of Ethnic Families." pp. 31–51 in Monica McGoldrick, John K. Pearce and Joseph Giordano (eds) *Ethnicity and Family Therapy*. New York: Guilford.

Stokols, Daniel (1988) "Transformational Processes in People–Environment Relations." pp. 233–54 in Joseph E. McGrath (ed.) *The Social Psychology of Time: New Perspectives*. Newbury Park: Sage.

Todd, Emmanuel (1985) *The Explanation of Ideology: Family Structures and Social Systems*. Trans. David Garrioch. Oxford: Blackwell.

Zerubavel, Eviatar (1981) *Hidden Rhythms: Schedules and Calendars in Social Life*. Chicago: University of Chicago Press.

Part V

THE QUESTION OF THE RECEIVED VIEW

8

THE RECEIVED VIEW AND WHAT IT CANNOT DO

INTRODUCTION

The "Received View" is a label used in the philosophy of science to characterize the prescribed way of asking and answering questions in a given academic discipline. It is the way of understanding things currently in vogue among a large number of practitioners and in the popular mind (Webster, Jacox and Baldwin 1981:23). The Received View is a very powerful and dogmatic orthodoxy, controlling academic departments, and key journals as well as grant- and/or fellowship-bestowing agencies. The Received View dictates the criteria that are to control "convincing" and "unconvincing" contributions to the field. As a label, the term "Received View" is a sarcastic and unfriendly one in the hands of its critics, and it is in this sense that it has been adopted here.

THE RECEIVED VIEW IN BIBLICAL STUDIES

The Received View is under attack in a number of disciplines ranging from nursing (Webster, Jacox and Baldwin 1981), through sociology (Verdon 1980, 1981, 1982), to economics (McCloskey 1983). There are those of us in biblical studies who are dissatisfied with the Received View in our discipline as well, largely because it is not adequate to its aims and claims, i.e. to interpret biblical documents historically. Meanings, past and present, that are realized in language are in fact ultimately rooted in a social system (see Halliday 1978). If this be the case, then to interpret a text and set forth its historical meaning(s) requires some significant appreciation of the social system(s) in which the texts were produced (see Malina 1982; 1983; 1991; 1996). Supporters of the Received View, however, are generally

217

unaware of or unconcerned with social systems. As a result, scholars currently adopting the Received View continue to produce some of the best nineteenth-century commentaries ever written (see Collins 1983, for example, for a Received View introduction to the New Testament, including structuralism and social history).

Some characteristic features of the Received View include: a passion for full bibliography (under pain of acute embarrassment at missing even a single item, thus throwing heavy doubt on an author's scholarly ability); for non-statistical word counts; for definitions and excursus of supposedly "theological" words; the confusion of theology (doctrine of God) with ideology; the identification of meanings in ancient texts that turn out to be suspiciously the same as those held by the Received View on other grounds; the endless reference to other biblical passages in such a way as to imply, for example, that New Testament authors knew each other's works well. All these features make the Received View questionable, at least in the US cultural context.

Furthermore, gatekeepers of the Received View find terms such as culture, social structure, politics, economics, social interaction, social ambivalence and the like unacceptable, or use them indiscriminately and without sensitivity to their specialized meanings. Yet they find no problem in defining and imposing words such as theologoumenon, demythologize, deeschatologize, parousiac, Christ-event, paschal mystery and the like on whatever publics they choose. The jargon words, of course, more often than not derive from Germany, as does the Received View itself. There is little I care to say about the Germanic bias; *de gustibus* and all that. But it is important to note that the Received View in biblical scholarship does in fact derive from German scholarship (see, for example, Oden 1980; Hynes 1981:87–114). As a set of implicit theories, the Received View was imaginatively designed to meet a set of culturally specific problems, notably those spawned by the belated impact of the Enlightenment, industrialization and nationalism in Germany (see Iggers 1968; Anchor 1972; Lowie 1954).[1]

In theology, of course, the Received View looked (and looks?) to German religious values and the religious institutions that realized it. Accordingly, it may be no wonder that many US students are left unsatisfied with the methods and outcomes of the Received View. Too much study time yielding too little pastoral pay-off is frustrating; too much native ability with not enough culturally relevant challenge is boring. After all, listing who said what about what (the scholarly hand count) is a useful first step only if it leads to more than just another vote. For any scholarly first step should feed into the basic question: What meanings did the biblical author(s) impart to his/their audience, and what meanings might those dimensions take in the various Christian movement groups of today? The rejection of the Received View, however, is not a rejection of the fine, historical contributions to the Western scholarly tradition made by nineteenth-century German scholars from Karl Marx down. The problem is that we find ourselves at the turn of the twentieth-century, and in a culture that has gone through some significant step-level changes since the 1800s. Are things still all that much the same in the "Western" scholarly tradition today as they were a century and a half ago? See Barraclough (1978:6ff.) for historians who believe so!

On the other hand, another group of biblical scholars, also dissatisfied with the Received View, has returned to old Athenian education – artistic rather than intellectual (for example, literary aspects of the Bible, literary structuralism, reader-reception models, psycholinguistics in general). This reaction focuses on how an author said what he said. It can be distinguished from the Received View's focus on what an author said and meant to say. What the literary view and the Received View have in common is that they are both heavily psychological. They differ in that the literary view strives for ahistoricity, while the Received View is eminently historical. To protect the Received View from the ahistorical encroachments of the literary perspective, as well as to deal with the difficulties generated by the Received View in the world of contemporary scholarship, some of its proponents have settled upon a compromise. This compromise often takes the name of "social history."

THE RECEIVED VIEW AND "SOCIAL HISTORY"

Social history is a relatively recent approach to interpreting the past. Historical research of the nineteenth-century saw its task as the description of "what really happened" in the past. This was realized by the historian's discovery of "new facts" and the elimination of error by the exercise of "historical criticism." Historical criticism meant (and means) the marshaling and interpretation of data in terms of the historian's imaginative faculties and individual genius. Since about 1950 a number of historians have formally taken up the questions and procedures of social scientists to produce "social history" – the study of human beings as group members immersed in given societies in the past (Hobsbawm 1971; see also Hecht 1968). Social scientists approach their sources with specific questions in mind, with a view to locating the information generated by those questions within some theoretical framework of concepts and hypotheses to produce intelligibility and interpretations. Social historians proceed in the same way,

> but in practice there are two main differences. The first is that the historian's conceptualization tends to be implicit, arbitrary, and unsystematic, whereas the social scientist's is explicit and systematic. The second is the (social) historian's tendency, because his sources usually provide him with some sort of loose narrative pattern to which the facts can be related, to evade so far as possible the theoretical issues, and also to deal for preference less with the underlying structure than with events and personalities, which are usually far more sharply delineated in historical records than in the materials anthropologists and sociologists commonly use.
>
> (Barraclough 1978:49–50)

Table 3 offers a listing that compares the Received View with a feasible alternative, which might be called the "Social Science View" (see Malina 1982; 1983; 1991; 1996). Perhaps the latter will become the Received View of tomorrow.

AN EXAMPLE OF THE RECEIVED VIEW

The main trouble with a number of scholars who study social history with a view to interpreting the Bible is that they are often neither social enough nor historical enough, except in terms of the Received View's assessment of history as described above.[2] To move this discussion to a more concrete level, I shall choose a manageable New Testament text recently treated by a scholar in terms of social history. I hope to indicate how such treatment admirably follows the canons of the Received View and even adds to our fund of knowledge. Yet in the end, such studies still leave the question of interpretation and meaning unresolved.

Furthermore, since I am committed to the sociolinguistic view that a text is a meaningful configuration of language intended to communicate, only actual or theoretical whole documents from texts. In the Received View, "text" means "preaching text" and can be any

Table 3 Comparing the Received View with the Social Science View

The Received View	The Social Science View
Full bibliography; no items missing	Adequate bibliography; librarians provide full bibliography
Mathematical word counts	Statistical tests, for example, X square
"Theological" words and "concepts" are focused on	"Theology" is called ideology, unless it is in fact describing a "theos" model
Words and ideas chosen for treatment are those relevant to the world of the Received View	Words and ideas chosen for treatment are those relevant to the time of the document under scrutiny
Culture described in the document looks amazingly like the culture of the adherents of the Received View	Culture described in the document has little or nothing in common with that of the interpreter(s)
Bible is always a necessary intertextual referent	Bible as intertextual referent requires proof or testing
Dogmatic in presentation	Open and questioning in presentation
Offers assertions for interpretation, i.e. untestable generalizations	Offers a wider frame of reference or model for interpretation
Its history is intuitive history, based on the insights and genius of the individual historian	Its history is an explicit social science enterprise, based on some articulate hypothesis testable by others
Current view or leading opinion depends on a hand count of intuitive authorities	Current view or leading opinion depends on probability of fit with increasingly refined models

bit of language, from word to extended passage. But words, sentences and passages are not *texts* but *text-segments*. What text-segments have in common, as a rule, is that they are understandable but not interpretable, for example, "She did so!" (see Halliday 1978 *passim*). Words suggest thoughts, and sentences express complete thoughts, but only texts communicate meaning(s). It would seem the better part of wisdom, then, to refuse to deal with text-segments apart from their texts. While words and sentences do, in fact, need to be understood, interpretation requires fitting the whole text into some larger frame of reference. If we are after historical meaning, and meaning derives from and constitutes the social system, then this larger frame for New Testament texts is first-century Mediterranean society in general, and a given, concrete audience in particular.

For a text which can be read quickly and which has received ample, recent Received View consideration, I propose 3 John. This text is interesting in many ways for social science analysis. Large quantities of information from the prevailing social system are required to provide the interpreter with the meaning it yielded its original receiver(s). This information simply cannot be generated without some social science models. To see this point, consider how an advocate of the updated Received View treats it. I choose as my "straw man" Abraham J. Malherbe's treatment of "Hospitality and Inhospitality in the Church," a reprint of his 1977 article (Malherbe 1977), now in his revised and expanded *Social Aspects of Early Christianity* (Malherbe 1983). Malherbe offers all the hallmarks of the *au courant* advocates of the updated Received View: a disdain for theory; a remarkable unconcern for defining the terms under discussion (here: hospitality); a passion for up-to-date historical bibliography, the more esoteric the better; a sort of hand-count assessment of previously published work, generally beginning with the historical "stars" of the past, who most often turn out to be German in training and/or primary enculturation.

Alternatively, my own emphasis derives from the social sciences and focuses upon the process of getting back to the original audience of a given writing by means of the social system scenarios within which the original communication took place. To do this with some verifiable credibility, one needs social science theories and models that are quite explicit, if only to keep the interpreter and his or her social system from intruding and distorting the original range of communications encoded in the texts (see Malina 1983). Consider 3 John now.

Thanks to recent comparative literature studies (Funk 1967; Kim 1972), we know that 3 John is a Hellenistic letter, specifically a letter of recommendation for a person going to a situation where the letter writer has an inhospitable foe, namely Diotrephes. Thus comments relative to the letter are sure to speak of the rank of the sender, the addressee and the persons mentioned in the letter (were they church officials or not?). Brown, for example, describes 3 John as follows:

A letter from the Presbyter to Gaius urging his continued hospitality to missionaries (and to Demetrius in particular) – a hospitality now all the more important because Diotrephes has refused it in the church in which he ranks first.

(1982:699)

He offers the following literary outline of the letter: opening formula (sender, addressee, health wish): vv. 1–2; body of the letter: vv. 3–14; concluding formula: v. 15 (1982:701–2).

Recent commentators will note the question of inhospitality, and use it to make several significant historical points: the period of the letter is characterized by mobility, the rise of a network of inns, the need for and practice of private hospitality. Malherbe notes, for example, that:

> The mobility which characterized the period brought with it a system of inns which sought to meet the needs and desires of travelers. The inns, however, did not enjoy a good reputation among the upper classes, being considered centers of all sorts of nefarious activities and offering poor service. Whenever possible, therefore, discriminating travelers availed themselves of the hospitality of business associates and other acquaintances. The early church reflects the mobility of Roman society as well as the practice of private hospitality.
>
> (1983:95)

> In addition to the material support of travelers, Christian hospitality was further manifested in the phenomenon of the house church. In its earliest period the churches had no buildings designed for their religious services and seem to have met primarily in hospitable homes.
>
> (1983:96)

Malherbe would have us believe that his essay is "sociology" (1983:122, and below). Yet his social description lacks the theoretical modeling and explicit use of generalizations that the sociological approach utilizes to remove ambiguity. On the contrary, the foregoing observations are replete with ambiguity. To begin with, the interpretative model being applied is left at the implicit and impressionistic level, and without further qualifications, the resulting observations are simply ethnocentric. For example, Malherbe does not define what he means by "mobility," nor does he specify the quality of the mobility to which he refers. Presumably he means physical mobility. But physical mobility bears a whole range of social meanings, not the least of which is the solidarity or lack of it symboled by the horizontal plane.[3]

In any analysis of the social organization of the first-century Mediterranean, four "mobility" dimensions, both singly and in combination, have to be considered. The *vertical dimension* (high/low, up/down), the natural symbol of power (Schwartz 1981), is but one aspect, perhaps of little direct concern to Rome's subjects because the center of the empire preempted the symbol (see Brunt 1982). Other aspects include the dimension of *size or mass* (bigger/smaller relating to landholdings, slaveholdings, income or some other measurable quantity deemed socially significant); the dimension of *depth assessment* (surface to deep, relating to influence, perspicuity and the like); and finally, the dimension of *horizontal classification* (first/last, relating to commitment, loyalty, precedence, prestige). Physical mobility on a horizontal plane is quite often a natural symbol of this last dimension, the dimension that counted in the first-century Mediterranean (see Malina 1993:28–62). Furthermore, physical mobility takes on culturally specific meanings (and functions, for functionalists), depending on whether it is pilgrimage, business travel, mass exile, teamstering army movements, and the like.

Moreover, Malherbe speaks of hospitality as though the meaning of the term were quite apparent to contemporary US persons, who use the term largely to refer to the entertaining of relatives and friends. He presumes that Christians met for "religious" services, again presuming that his readers know what he means. I suggest that terms such as mobility, hospitality and religion in a first-century Mediterranean letter have little if anything to do with contemporary US experience, and hence are precisely and specifically the terms needing clarification. But this is only the beginning.

Throughout his brief essay, the author is much concerned with the question of "office." For example:

> From events in Thessalonica (Acts 17:5–9) we know that such patrons (i.e. hosts who extended hospitality) assumed legal responsibility for the groups meeting in their houses. Exactly what status in the congregations which met in their houses this service conferred on them is not totally clear. An answer to that question involves one's understanding of the meaning of *proistemi* in its various contexts in the New Testament, a matter that cannot be gone into in detail here. It would appear

certain that in the Pauline letters the term does not denote an office. . . . Be that as it may, the Pastorals do not provide evidence that bishops derived authority from providing hospitality to the church. What authority they may have had they derived elsewhere.

(Malherbe 1983:97–9)

Of course, the problem here is who was/is concerned about "office," and the link between hospitality and "office," etc.: the first-century Christian or the twentieth-century churchman? I find the question simply irrelevant and misleading relative to the real issues at stake in the first-century Mediterranean world. For what is at stake is not "office," but the moral brokerage ability and honor of the Elder/Presbyter (see Boissevain 1974:147–63; Malina 1988 on brokerage).

When Malherbe moves on to giving reasons for compliance or non-compliance with the request for hospitality by the Elder, he has recourse to the usual superficial psychology we have come to expect from the Received View. Thus, for example: "One reason given for fulfilling the request is that the recommended person may testify (*martureo*) to the writer of the good reception with which he had met" (1983:103). But the question is why such "testimony" would matter at all. This point is left unanswered. Or again:

Third John is, then, at once a commendation of Gaius for his earlier hospitality, and a recommendation of Demetrius. It should further be noted that, although it is a personal letter, v. 15 would indicate that it has a wider reference than Gaius alone.

(1983: 105 and n. 47: "Cf. also Philemon,
which is more than a purely personal letter.")

Again, why would these letters have the more than personal quality which Malherbe feels they do? No attempt to explain the point is made. Hospitality, moreover, remains undefined and undescribed.

As he concludes his essay, Malherbe focuses on an explanation for behavior as follows:

What is at issue is Diotrephes' refusal to receive the letter of recommendation that has been written: "but Diotrephes who likes to put himself first (*philoproteuon*) among them, does not welcome (*epidechetai*) us." The Elder seems to think that

225

> Diotrephes had seen in the letter a threat to his own preeminence in the church, and that he had therefore rejected the letter as well as the bearers. In letters of recommendation, such as the letter referred to in v. 9, the request on behalf of the persons recommended was that they be received for the sake of the writer.
>
> (1983:106)

Why this practice? How does it refer to the narrower context of hospitality and the wider context of Mediterranean social structure and cultural values? Malherbe does not answer such questions. His psychologistic explanation proceeds as follows:

> The reception of the letter and its bearer proved the good will of the recipient toward the writer. It is such an understanding of *epidechomai* that is present in vv. 9 and 10. Diotrephes had shown his ill will toward the Elder by refusing his letter and his emissaries. In addition, he slandered the Elder, and adding insult to injury, imposed his will on the brethren who would act contrary to his wishes. We must be content with the fact that we do not know what Diotrephes' reasons were for his conduct. We are limited to the Elder's view of the matter and he sees it as a purely personal issue.
>
> (1983:107)

Why a purely personal issue in a letter meant to be more than personal? Is it in fact the case that we do not know the reasons for Diotrephes' conduct, or rather that Malherbe does not know them because he does not take Mediterranean society seriously enough as an interpretative framework? To be sure, he does not seem to know or care about the rules of hospitality typical of the culture, and hence raises a series of non-questions, again, a procedure common in the Received View. Part of the reason for such non-questions lies in the categories used by the interpreter. For example, he states in a note:

> It is probably significant that III John, which is itself a letter of recommendation, does not request that hospitality be extended to the traveling brethren for the sake of the Elder. Instead, Diotrephes is threatened with (v. 10) and Gaius is promised (vv. 13 ff.) a personal visit. It is noteworthy that even in recommending the brethren to Gaius, he offers theological rather than personal reasons for doing so.
>
> (1983:107, n. 50)

Of course, the categories called "theological" and "personal" in this description are Malherbe's. The extent to which they explain anything at all, or how they might be significant for the author of 3 John and his recipients, is undemonstrable except in terms of Malherbe's insistence. Again, to state one's position directly and clearly without any wider frame of reference to warrant the position is typical of the dogmatic approach of the Received View. It is the collection of dogmatic views of "authorities" that constitutes the range of authoritative opinions available to scholars and laymen alike. It is important to underscore the fact that such opinions are for the most part rooted in implicit assumptions and impressionistic models. For this reason the positions generated by the Received View are simply untestable. Furthermore, it often appears that its adherents adopt its results more out of loyalty than argument, more through networking and group feelings than intellectual articulation. However, as Brannigan has pointed out (1981), this is not all that unusual among scholarly scientists.

These are some of the difficulties I find with Malherbe's explanation of 3 John. There are more, and he is by no means the only representative of the Received View. However, his chutzpah makes him a good illustration. Consider the final paragraph of the book, newly written for its reedition:

> I have been criticized quite properly for my indiscriminate use of "social" and "sociological." I have difficulty accepting, however, the suggestion that "social description" be used for the type of investigation that I have attempted, and that "sociological" be reserved for analysis or interpretation that makes use of the methods and models of the discipline of sociology. Such a limitation of the latter seems to me to be arbitrary.
>
> (1983:122)

What is curious about this statement is that Malherbe is not concerned about standard usage, is perfectly at home with Germanisms and would have us rewrite the dictionary on his behalf. Since language and labeling with language are in fact quite arbitrary, why does he not call his work *The Socioreligiological Sociopolitology of Early Christianity*? After all, both "religiology" and "politology" are good Germanisms, and a prefixed "socio-" before words already referring to essentially social behaviors is *de rigueur*. And since the Received View is rooted in German scholarship, and since in German usage there is no difference between *sozial* and *soziologisch*, why should

there be a difference in English? For what is in fact the first exegetical language if not German?

Be that as it may, let us turn to the meanings communicated by
means of the text called 3 John. On any reading, it does in fact deal
with hospitality, recommendations for hospitality, the refusal of
hospitality and the threat of a personal visit instead of a letter to
deal with the refusal of hospitality. What, then, is hospitality in the
Mediterranean world?

HOSPITALITY IN THE MEDITERRANEAN WORLD

Hospitality might be defined as the process for changing an outsider's
status from that of stranger to guest (for the definition and what
follows see Pitt-Rivers 1977:94–112). The outsider is "received" and
socially transformed from stranger to guest (on "stranger," see Schütz
1964; Elliott 1990 *passim*). Hospitality, then, differs from entertaining family and friends. The hospitality process is quite crucial
in societies with great emphasis on the distinction between ingroup
and outgroup (see Malina and Neyrey 1996). Such societies have
the tendency to treat outsiders as simply non-human (the social basis
for torture, war, unconcern for distributive justice, racism, genocide,
etc.). If strangers are not to be eliminated, either physically or socially
(see Matt. 10:14–23), they have to be "received," or shown hospitality. The process will have three stages to it: (1) evaluating the
stranger (usually with some test about whether guest status is
possible); (2) the stranger as guest – the liminal phase; (3) from
guest to transformed stranger (at times with another test). Consider
each phase in turn. (I shall make reference to instances of the hospitality process in the Bible in general, if only because most readers
of this chapter will recognize them. For more examples from biblical
times presented in the Received View fashion, see Sisti 1967; Stählin
1967).

Evaluating the stranger

The first step in the hospitality process is evaluating the stranger. The
stranger is potentially anything and certainly a threat to the way things
are. He or she must be tested as to whether he or she will subscribe
to the norms of the community into which he or she comes. The
testing, a sort of measuring or stock-taking, is undoubtedly to know
where the stranger fits into the purity arrangements of the world.

The person deemed capable of receiving hospitality has an inter-mediary social position between the hostile and mysterious outside world and the interior structure of the community (Pitt-Rivers 1977:113). The problem then is how to admit a representative of the outside into the purity lines of the community for a while and then allow the outsider to return to his or her proper place without altering the social fabric (on purity lines, see Malina 1993:149–83). Hospitality necessarily puts the guest in a liminal or marginal posi-tion since the guest is an outsider now on the inside, yet not an insider since the guest must return to the outside. Another way of dealing with strangers and the threat that they entail is to do away with them (physically: killing, beating, molesting, robbing, bodily removal, i.e. with force; socially: ignoring them so that they must move on, i.e. showing signs of aversion; or challenging them for their honor, i.e. insult, mockery etc., so that they are humiliated and move on). Three main points are to be noted here: the role of stranger, the stranger as guest and the stranger as challenger.

The stranger role

In the ancient (and Mediterranean) world a stranger possessed no standing in law or custom within the visited group; hence it is neces-sary for the stranger to have a patron in order to gain the protection of the local laws and gods (see Landé 1977a on patron–client as a supplement to failing social institutions; and for a summary overview of research, see Eisenstadt and Roniger 1980; for New Testament applications, see Malina 1988). To offend the protégé or client is to offend the protector/patron. The protégé/client is embedded in the social space of the patron. Thus the stranger is incorporated only through a personal bond with an established community member. The stranger has only the status of being statusless. There is no presupposition of the universality of humankind. There is only the particularity and specificity of the total or partial stranger. The partial stranger is a person received on the basis of kinship or fictive kinship (relative from a distant place, fellow believer, fellow guildsman, fellow worker at a common job), but not on the basis of place of origin, which served in Mediterranean antiquity as a principle of species differentiation (see Bodson 1982; Malina 1992; Malina and Neyrey 1996).

However, in relation to his patron, the stranger has social standing, i.e. that of guest or client/protégé. The status of guest, thus, stands midway between that of hostile stranger and community member. Becoming a guest derives from a practical, *ad hoc* rather than moral, transformative incorporation into the community.

Since the stranger is potentially anything, he must be tested as to whether he can subscribe to the rules of the new culture. Officials (Josh 2:2) or concerned citizenry (Gen. 19:5) might conduct such tests. On the other hand, invasion from the outside might simply be repelled (see Mark 5:17, where the Gerasenes ask the stranger, Jesus, to leave, or Luke 9:53, where the Samaritans "would not receive him," perhaps because he would not be a proper guest "because his face was set toward Jerusalem"). An invitation to speak can be a test (Acts 13:14–15), while letters of recommendation can excuse from a test, although sometimes not (see, for example, 2 and 3 John; Rom. 16:3–16; 1 Thess. 5:12–13). Frequently the ritual of foot-washing marks the movement from stranger to guest (see Gen. 18:4; 19:2; 24:32; notably lacking in Luke 7:36–50). At bottom each village (and neighborhood or quarter in larger cities) attempts to be autonomous, with its own standards/customs. Standing achieved in one community, therefore, is not directly transferable to another, nor is status ascribed by one society necessarily recognized in another. The possibility of finding an equivalent standing (even for mutual understanding) may be missing, for example, to be a Roman Catholic priest in a Buddhist country, a South American general in a small town in the US, a Hindu Brahman in the Texas hill country, a Galilean craftsman/healer among the Jerusalem urban elite. The test, when given, attempts to assign an acceptable but temporary social location to the stranger.

The stranger as guest

To fulfill the role of guest, strangers must at least understand and follow the conventions which relate to hospitality and which define the behavior expected of them. They must know how to play the role of guest. Thus the Greek distinction between *xenoi* = strangers who know how to behave as Greek guests; *barbaroi* = strangers who know nothing at all, not even the language, and hence who are totally uncivilized (see Gauthier 1973, correcting the valuable observations of Benveniste 1973:71–83).

The stranger as challenger

The appearance of a stranger in a community where he had neither kin nor friends would itself be a challenge to the community, the invasion of the outside into the social space of the inside (on challenge, see Malina 1993:34–44). Thus some local riposter (a self-appointed or group-appointed champion) will take up the challenge in the name of the group. If the stranger defeats the champion in the contest, he proves himself better than the whole community, and hence is entitled to be honored by the community (not so for barbarians, who do not challenge but combat and seek to annihilate). In the Synoptic tradition, when Jesus sends the Twelve he expects his core disciples to be "received" by honorable persons (Mark 6:11, par.). Should no hospitality be offered, they are to perform the symbolic (and insulting) action of "shaking off the dust on your feet." After all, honor is gained by all in the community through the visit of an honorable person. On the other hand, a shameful community is not worthy of the presence of honorable visitors.

Three types of strangers thus emerge from this initial step of assessment:

(a) One who is recognized as better than the best challenger in the community: there is no problem with his precedence in the community;

(b) One who is vanquished by the local riposter and thus owes his life/continued presence to his local patron; he is thus attached to the community by the intermediary of his victor;

(c) One who has no friends/kin within the community, who is simply ignored (given barbarian status), and hence treated as an outlaw who could be despoiled or destroyed with impunity, simply because of his potential hostility.

The stranger as guest – the liminal phase

Since transient strangers lacked customary or legal standing within the visited community, it was imperative that they find a patron, a host. Hosts would be established community members, and through a personal bond with them (something inns cannot offer), the stranger was incorporated as guest or client/protégé. To offend the guest is to offend the host, who is protector and patron of the guest (poignantly underscored in the case of Lot, Gen. 19:1–10). Yet such patronage can yield more trouble than honor (for example, Prov. 6:1).

Considering the various ways in which people of various cultures speak of the infringement of hospitality by host and guest, it seems that "a certain general sense informs them all, entitling us to talk about the law of hospitality in the abstract in contrast to the specific codes of hospitality exemplified in different cultures" (Pitt-Rivers 1977:109). This sort of general law of hospitality derives from social necessity. "For the same reason that the criminal is said to define the law the essentials of the law of hospitality can best be seen in the actions which constitute its infringement" (109).

Rules for guests

A guest may infringe on the requirements of hospitality in different ways:

(a) By insulting the host or by any show of hostility or rivalry; a guest must honor the host (Jesus eating with sinners neither accuses them of being sinners nor asks them to change: Matt. 9:10; Luke 5:29);

(b) By usurping the role of the host, for example, making oneself at home when not yet invited to (in the home of another, Jesus heals when asked: Mark 1:30); taking precedence (see Luke 14:8); giving orders to the dependents of the host (Jesus refuses to command Mary: Luke 10:40); making claims or demands on the host or demanding or taking what is not offered (see Luke 7:36–50, where Jesus is the perfect guest; and the rules for traveling disciples: Mark 6:10, par.);

(c) By refusing what is offered. The guest is above all bound to accept food (see Luke 10:18; the directives to disciples for their travels would force them to accept patronage: Mark 6:8, par.; see also 1 Cor. 9:4).

Rules for the host

A host may also infringe on the requirements of hospitality:

(a) By insulting guests or by any show of hostility or rivalry;

(b) By neglecting to protect guests and their honor. For guests individually are embedded in the host. Thus while fellow guests have no explicit relationship, they are bound to forego hostilities, since they offend their host in the act of offending one another. The host must defend each against the other since both are his guests (thus Paul's problem with the Lord's supper in 1 Cor. 11:17–34);

(c) By failing to attend to guests, to grant them the precedence which is their due, to show concern for their needs and wishes or, in general, to earn the good will which guests should demonstrate. Note how in Luke 7:36–50 Simon the Pharisee fails on all counts with his guest, Jesus: no footwashing; no kiss; no anointing; no keeping away the sinful woman; the parable in Luke 7:40–1 represents Jesus' defense of his honor as guest. Finally, failure to offer the best is to denigrate the guest (John 2:10).

While element (a) is the same for both guest and host, elements (b) and (c) are complementaries. This assures that a stranger will rarely, if ever, reciprocate hospitality, hence its necessity and value (see Matt. 25:38,43, among the traditional Israelite works of mercy).

Hospitality does not entail mutual reciprocity between individuals. Yet it can nevertheless be viewed as a reciprocal relationship between groups. Such hospitality to traveling Christians is both urged (see Rom. 12:13; 1 Pet. 4:9) and much practiced (for example, Acts 17:7; 21:17; 28:7; Rom. 16:23). A society such as the first-century Mediterranean valued the free circulation of persons between its communities. People traveled, for example, on pilgrimage, to seek out healing, to collect and distribute money, to attend meetings at central locations, to bring information, news or instruction to others, and the like. Such a society required a law of hospitality: Do as you would be done by; receive the stranger so that you will be well received.[4]

From guest to transformed stranger

The stranger-guest will leave the host either as friend or enemy. If as friend, the guest will spread the praises of the host (see, for example, 1 Thess. 1:9; Phil. 5:16), notably to those sending the stranger (see, for example, Mark 9:37). If as enemy, the one aggrieved will have to get satisfaction (for example, 3 John: see below).

Perhaps it is in the context of hospitality infractions that the meaning of John 1:10, "his own received him not," might best be understood. Any infringement of the code of hospitality destroys the structure of roles, since it implies an incorporation which has not in fact taken place or hostility readily resumed. Failure to return honor or avoid disrespect entitles the person slighted in this way to relinquish his role and revert to the hostility which it suppressed. The sacred quality in the relationship is not removed, but polluted. Once they are no longer host and guest, they are enemies, not strangers. Hence in the social context of the rules of hospitality, the Johannine "his own received him not" clues in the reader for the continuing conflict and hostility that is to follow. On the other hand, the situation in 3 John is different.

THE HELLENISTIC LETTER OF RECOMMENDATION

From the foregoing, the function of the letter of recommendation should be apparent. The purpose of the letter is to help divest strangers of their strangeness, to make them at least only partial strangers, if not immediate guests. The person writing a recommendation attests to the strangers bearing it on the basis of the word of honor of the attestor. To reject the recommended strangers is, of course, a challenge to the honor of the recommender. It spurns his honor, and requires an attempt at satisfaction on his part, under pain of being shamed.

Now, 3 John is a letter of recommendation sent in a world whose paramount values were honor and shame. Honor cannot be achieved or lost without an audience, a public that ascribes or withholds it (see Malina 1993:28–62). This is why those "private" letters of recommendation in the New Testament (Philemon and 3 John, for example) are not exactly private. They would not serve their intended purpose if they were private. In 3 John the Elder puts his honor on the line again to recommend Demetrius and any others he might send to Gaius. In the process he seeks satisfaction for the dishonor he suffered at the hands of Diotrephes; 3 John is the Elder's culturally required attempt at satisfaction. If he kept quiet about Diotrephes' rejection of his previous recommendation, he would lose his honor. By attempting satisfaction, he retains his honor, but at some cost. The cost in question is the publicity and consequent honor Diotrephes gains by being a discriminating host and patron with power. He becomes a person to be reckoned with.

With 3 John, we have evidence of unreceptive reaction to Johannine Christianity. Elsewhere I have argued that Johannine Christianity used antilanguage in order to maintain its antisociety (Malina 1984b; 1994). Such an antisociety is a metaphorical variant of the real world, of real society. In this view, Diotrephes' challenge to the Elder will have been one of many reactions to Johannine Christianity, leading to its ultimate demise as unworkable and unrealistic in the first- and second-century Mediterranean world (see Neyrey 1988; Montanists may have formed an antisociety similar to the Johannine, with a similar fate: see Aune 1983:313–16).

In sum, as far as the process called "hospitality" is concerned, while nearly all human groups offer "hospitable treatment, reception or disposition" to guests (definition of "hospitality" in *Webster's Seventh New Collegiate Dictionary*), the quality and type of the reception as well as the social definition of "guest" evidence specific differences. For example, in the US hospitality normally refers to entertaining relatives, friends and acquaintances, frequently with the presumption of individual reciprocity in the future. First-century Mediterranean hospitality normally refers to hosting a stranger, with the presumption of community reciprocity in the future. These specific differences derive from differences in cultural arrangements and social structure: living one's personal life indoors (US) versus outdoors (Mediterranean); human encounters as competitive (US) versus agonistic or filled with potential conflict (Mediterranean); type of personality involved, individualistic (US) versus dyadic (Mediterranean); assessment of the general status of strangers, members of the same nation with the same rights and obligations (US), or members of "them," of the outside, with no enforceable rights in our community (traditional Mediterranean); the purifying functions of money (US) versus honor (Mediterranean); and the like. In other words, a full, comparative description of hospitality in the US and the first-century Mediterranean world entails a description of the salient features of each social system. One reason for this is that hospitality, just as any other discrete piece of socially meaningful behavior, will replicate the core values and value objects of the society in question. Such a description is, of course, out of the question at this point. Instead, and by way of conclusion, Table 4 presents a comparative summary of the burden of this chapter and of the evident insufficiency of the Received View in biblical studies.

Table 4   Comparing 3 John in the Received View and in the Social
Science View

The Received View	The Social Science View
Models and methods are "objective," psychologizing and based on an unreflective sampling of a single culture, that of the interpreter	Models and methods are "social," culturally derivative from the social science, i.e. a wider, comparative sampling
What needs explanation in 3 John is:	What needs explanation in 3 John is:
1 church role and rank of persons mentioned;	1 meaning of social interaction of persons mentioned;
2 "realia," such as physical basis for mobility, inns, travel;	2 meaning of "realia," described in some comparative, cross-cultural way;
3 presuppositions: meaning of "religious," hospitality, recommendation, personal, etc.	3 requisites: definitions of "religious," hospitality, recommendation, personal, etc. in a cross-cultural way
Problem: office in earliest Christianity (a problem retrojected from the contemporary church)	Problem: quality of social interaction on the basis of what is "usual" and "normal" in the culture
Method of explanation: multiple paraphrase, i.e. frequently repeated restatement, in slightly different terminology, of what the document purportedly states	Method of explanation: presentation of a larger framework in which to insert the "domains of reference" referred to in the document
The approach is that/how knowledge	The approach is how/why knowledge
Significant questions seen to be posed by the document are often questions deriving from the interpreter's culture, hence ethnocentric non-questions	Significant questions seen to be posed by the document are those relevant to the larger cultural frame within which the document originated

NOTES

1   There simply seem to be no usable, general social histories of Germany, much less anything approximating a sociological analysis in the manner of Williams (1970) for the US. Of value for the question of nineteenth-century social history and academics is Jarausch (1982), with a fine sampling of useful bibliography. Lowie's (1954) anthropological study is of value for assessing so-called "groundbreaking" or "new" German studies, such as Schüssler Fiorenza's (1983) gynecocentric approach, hardly a challenge to the Received View, which it espouses. Gregory (1984) offers a balancing corrective to the main set of gynecocentric premises. In a more androcentric vein, I have noted, citing a number of other critics, that even Weber's charisma – now current coin in sociological analysis – is a German-based construct rather than a universally verifiable, human phenomenon (Malina 1984a).

2   Gary Nash (1972:79) has noted relative to American history: "Although American historians have amassed a vast literature on the Indian, they seldom have seen the necessity of employing anthropological or sociological categories in studying Anglo-Indian contacts, and they have rarely viewed the interaction as a dynamic process in which both groups acted and were acted upon." Of course, the same holds for biblical studies, *mutatis mutandis*.

3   This lack of precision or simple confusion about mobility in the ancient world is well illustrated by the following observation of Melko and Weigel in their useful book: "The mention of trade suggests that there was a considerable degree of horizontal mobility in the Ancient World. One could travel to trade, or one could travel for a new footing, leaving dissatisfactions behind, taking hope along. There were other places to go and means to get there. Even for punishment the city states used banishment, forcing dissidents to travel for the good of themselves and the state, and at the same time often leaving land and property to be distributed to others. In the sense that the same classes prevailed in most societies, and most people in any class remained what their parents had been, the social structure of the peaceful societies of the Ancient World was relatively rigid. In the sense that there was always scope for the most restless or ambitious to move horizontally or vertically, the social structure of these societies was quite flexible" (1981:157).

4   This, of course, is a functional explanation. A non-functional explanation would hold that: "the sacredness of hospitality and the honor which it confers derive not from any functional consequence of the belief but from the fact that the meeting with the stranger is a confrontation between the known world and the realms of mystery. ... The stranger derives his danger, like his sacredness, from his membership in the 'extra-ordinary' world. If his danger is to be avoided he must either be denied admittance, chased or enticed away like evil spirits, or vampires, or if granted admittance, he must be socialized, that is to say, secularized, a process which necessarily involves inversion. His transformation into the guest means therefore that, from being shunned and treated with hostility, he must be succored; from being last, he must be first;

from being a person who can be freely insulted he becomes one who under no conditions can be disparaged. The inversion implies a transformation from hostile stranger, *hostis*, into guest, *hospes* (or *hostis*) from one whose hostile intentions are assumed to one whose hostility is laid in abeyance. The word *hostis* claims therefore as its radical sense, not the obligation to reciprocal violence, but the notion of 'strangeness' which underlies this transition. The further extension to host is perfectly congruent, since strangeness is logically reciprocal, whether it enjoins distrust or hospitality. Both senses of the word *l'hôte* are conserved in French, which must find other ways to distinguish between host and guest. While the behavior enjoined by the relationship is essentially reciprocal, just as gifts are, there is a difference between reciprocal hostility and reciprocal hospitality: the first is simultaneous, the second can never be. Host and guest can at no point within the context of a single occasion be allowed to be equal, since equality invites rivalry. Therefore their reciprocity resides not in an identity, but in an alternation of roles" (Pitt-Rivers 1977:101–2).

REFERENCES

Anchor, Robert (1972) *Germany Confronts Modernization: German Culture and Society, 1790–1890*. Lexington, MA: D. C. Heath.

Aune, David E. (1983) *Prophecy in Early Christianity and the Ancient Mediterranean World*. Grand Rapids: Eerdmans.

Barraclough, Geoffrey (1978) *Main Trends in History*. New York: Holmes & Meier.

Benveniste, Emile (1973) *Indo-European Language and Society*. Trans. E. Palmer. Miami Linguistics Series 12. Coral Gables: University of Miami Press.

Bodson, Liliane (1982) "La Notion de race animale chez les zoologistes et les agronomes de l'antiquité." *Bulletin de la société l'ethnozootechnie* 29:7–14.

Boissevain, Jeremy (1974) *Friends of Friends: Networks, Manipulators and Coalitions*. New York: St Martin's.

—— (1982/3) "Seasonal Variations on Some Mediterranean Themes." *Ethnologia Europaea* 13:6–12.

Brannigan, Augustine (1981) *The Social Basis of Scientific Discovery*. Cambridge: Cambridge University Press.

Brown, Raymond E. (1982) *The Epistles of John*. Anchor Bible Vol. 30. Garden City: Doubleday.

Brunt, P. A. (1982) "A Marxist View of Roman History." *Journal of Roman Studies* 72:156–63.

Collins, Raymond F. (1983) *Introduction to the New Testament*. Garden City: Doubleday.

Eisenstadt, S. N. and Roniger, L. (1980) "Patron–Client Relations as a Model of Structuring Social Exchange." *Comparative Studies in Society and History* 22:42–77.

Elliott, John H. (1990) *A Home for the Homeless: A Sociological Exegesis of 1 Peter, its Situation and Strategy*. Rev. ed. Minneapolis: Fortress.

Funk, Robert W. (1967) "The Form and Structure of II and III John." *Journal of Biblical Literature* 86:424–30.

Gauthier, Philippe (1973) "Notes sur l'étranger et l'hospitalité en Grèce et à Rome." *Ancient Society* 4:1–21.

Gregory, James R. (1984) "The Myth of the Male Ethnographer and the Woman's World." *American Anthropologist* 86:316–27.

Halliday, Michael A. K. (1978) *Language as Social Semiotic: The Social Interpretation of Language and Meaning.* Baltimore: University Park.

Hecht, J. Jean (1968) "History: V. Social History." In David. L. Sills (ed) *International Encyclopedia of the Social Sciences* 6:455–62. New York: Macmillan/Free Press.

Hobbs, T. Raymond (1993) "Man, Woman and Hospitality (2 Kings 4:8–36)." *Biblical Theology Bulletin* 23:91–100.

Hobsbawm, E. J. (1971) "From Social History to the History of Society." *Daedalus* 100:20–45.

Hynes, William J. (1981) *Shirley Jackson Case and the Chicago School: The Socio-Historical Method.* SBL Biblical Scholarship in North America 5. Chico: Scholars Press.

Iggers, Georg G. (1968) *The German Conception of History: The National Tradition of Historical Thought from Herder to the Present.* Middletown, CT: Wesleyan University Press.

Jarausch, Konrad H. (1982) *Students, Society and Politics in Imperial Germany: The Rise of Academic Illiberalism.* Princeton: Princeton University Press.

Kim, Chan-Hie (1972) *The Form and Function of the Familiar Greek Letter of Recommendation.* SBL Dissertation Series 4. Missoula: Scholars Press.

Landé, Carl H. (1977a) "Introduction: The Dyadic Basis of Clientelism." pp. xiii–xxxvii in Steffen W. Schmidt, James C. Scott, Carl Landé and Laura Guasti (eds) *Friends, Followers, and Factions: A Reader in Political Clientelism.* Berkeley: University of California Press.

—— (1977b) "Networks and Groups in Southeast Asia: Some Observations on the Group Theory of Politics." pp. 75–99 in Steffen W. Schmidt, James C. Scott, Carl Landé and Laura Guasti (eds) *Friends, Followers, and Factions: A Reader in Political Clientelism.* Berkeley: University of California Press.

Lowie, Robert H. (1954) *Toward Understanding Germany.* Chicago: University of Chicago Press (repr. 1978).

McCloskey, Donald N. (1983) "The Rhetoric of Economics." *Journal of Economic Literature* 21:481–517.

Malherbe, Abraham J. (1977) "The Inhospitality of Diotrephes." pp. 222–32 in Jacob Jervell and Wayne A. Meeks (eds) *God's Christ and His People: Studies in Honour of Nils Alstrup Dahl.* Oslo: Universitetsforlaget.

—— (1983) *Social Aspects of Early Christianity.* 2nd ed., enlarged. Philadelphia: Fortress.

Malina, Bruce J. (1982) "The Social Sciences and Biblical Interpretation." *Interpretation* 37:229–42; reprinted in slightly expanded form, pp. 11–25 in Norman K. Gottwald (ed) *The Bible and Liberation: Political and Social Hermeneutics.* Maryknoll, NY: Orbis, 1983.

—— (1983) "Why Interpret the Bible with the Social Sciences?" *American Baptist Quarterly* 2:119–33.

—— (1984a) "Jesus as Charismatic Leader?" *Biblical Theology Bulletin* 14:55–62.

—— (1984b) *The Gospel of John in Sociolinguistic Perspective.* 48th Colloquy of the Center for Hermeneutical Studies. Ed. Herman Waetjen. Berkeley: Center for Hermeneutical Studies.

—— (1986) *Christian Origins and Cultural Anthropology: Practical Models for Biblical Interpretation.* Atlanta: John Knox.

—— (1988) "Patron and Client: The Analogy Behind Synoptic Theology." *Forum* 4/1:2–32.

—— (1991) "Scienze sociali e interpretazione storia: la questione della retrodizione." *Rivista Biblica* 39:305–23.

—— (1992) "Is There a Circum-Mediterranean Person: Looking for Stereotypes." *Biblical Theology Bulletin* 22:66–87.

—— (1993) *The New Testament World: Insights from Cultural Anthropology.* Louisville: Westminster/John Knox.

—— (1994) "John's: The Maverick Christian Group: The Evidence of Sociolinguistics." *Biblical Theology Bulletin* 24:167–82.

—— (1996) "La antropología cultural mediterránea y el Nuevo Testamento." In *Congres La Biblia i El Mediterrani.* Barcelona September 18–22, 1995. (forthcoming).

Malina, Bruce J. and Jerome H. Neyrey (1996) *Portraits of Paul: An Archaeology of Ancient Personality.* Louisville: Westminster/John Knox.

Melko, Matthew, Richard D. Weigel *et al.* (1981) *Peace in the Ancient World.* Jefferson, NC: McFarland.

Moore, Wilbert E. (1974) *Social Change.* 2nd ed. Englewood Cliffs: Prentice-Hall.

Nash, Gary B. (1972) "The Image of the Indian in the Southern Colonial Mind." pp. 55–86 in Edward Dudley and Maximilian E. Noval (eds) *The Wild Man Within: An Image in Western Thought from the Renaissance to Romanticism.* Pittsburgh: University of Pittsburgh Press.

Neyrey, Jerome H. (1988) *An Ideology of Revolt: John's Christology in Social Science Perspective.* Philadelphia: Fortress.

Oden, Robert A., Jr. (1980) "Hermeneutics and Historiography: Germany and America." pp. 135–57 in Paul J. Achtemeier (ed) *Society of Biblical Literature 1980 Seminar Papers.* Chico: Scholars.

Pitt-Rivers, Julian (1977) *The Fate of Shechem or the Politics of Sex: Essays in the Anthropology of the Mediterranean.* Cambridge: Cambridge University Press.

Schüssler Fiorenza, Elisabeth (1983) *In Memory of Her: A Feminist Theological Reconstruction of Christian Origins.* New York: Crossroad.

Schütz, Alfred (1964) "The Stranger: An Essay in Social Psychology." pp. 91–105 in *Collected Papers*, Vol. 2: *Studies in Social Theory.* Ed. A. Brodersen. The Hague: Martinus Nijhoff.

Schwartz, Barry (1981) *Vertical Classification: A Study in Structuralism and the Sociology of Knowledge.* Chicago: University of Chicago Press.

Sisti, Adalberto (1967) "L'Ospitalità nella prassi e nell'insegnamento della Bibbia." *Studi Biblici Franciscani Liber Annuus* 17:303–34.

Stählin, Gustav (1967) *"xenos, ktl."* in G. Kittel (ed) *Theological Dictionary of the New Testament* 5:1–36. Trans. Geoffrey W. Bromiley. Grand Rapids: Eerdmans.

Verdon, Michel (1980) "Shaking off the Domestic Yoke, or the Sociological Significance of Residence." *Comparative Studies in Society and History* 22:109–32.

—— (1981) "Kinship, Marriage, and the Family: An Operational Approach." *American Journal of Sociology* 86:796–818.

—— (1982) "Durkheim and Aristotle: Of Some Incongruous Congruences." *Studies in History and Philosophy of Science* 13:333–52.

Webster, Glenn, Ada Jacox and Beverley Baldwin (1981) "Nursing Theory and the Ghost of the Received View." pp. 26–35 in Joanne Comi McCloskey and Helen K. Grace (eds) *Current Issues in Nursing*. Boston, MA: Blackwell Scientific Publications.

Williams, Robin M., Jr. (1970) *American Society: A Sociological Interpretation*. 3rd ed. New York: Knopf.

SCRIPTURAL INDEX

Acts
1 – 9   136
1:7   183, 193
2:17   99
6:7   160
8   5
8:32–33   5
12:17   161
13:14–15   230
14:1   39
15:13   161
17:5–9   224
17:7   233
18:4   39
19:10, 17   39
20:21   39
20:37   60
21:17   233
21:18   161
21:8–9   53
28:7   233

Rom.
1:11   171
1:14   39
1:16   39
4:21   192
5:12ff.   138
5:12–17   91
5:15, 16   171
7   138
7:1–25   91
7:2–3   87
8:23   194
8:29   194
11:16   194
11:29   171
12:6   171
12:13   233
15:23–29   190
16:3–16   230
16:16   60
16:23   233

1 Cor.
1:7   172
1:13ff.   167
1:24   39
5:3   44

6:9–10   43
7:7   172
7:17   91
9:4   232
11:2–16   53, 106
11:17–34   233
12:4, 9, 28, 30, 31, 172
15:5–8   194
15:20   194

2 Cor.
1:11   172

Gal.
1:15–16   100
3:28   39
4:4   100, 202
5:19–21   43

Eph.
1:10   202
4:32   60

Phil.
1:8   60
2:1   60
3:5   49
5:16   233

Col.
1:15, 18   194
3:11   39

1 Thes.
1:9   233
4:15–16   193
5:12–13   230

1 Tim.
2:5f.   174
4:14   172
5:9–16   106

2 Tim.
1:6   172

Titus
1:12   39
2:11–13   173

GENERAL INDEX

Aalen, S. 147–8, 174
Abbott, W. 180, 211
abstract time 188–9
abuse 76, 82, 114, 138
Achtemeier, P. 240
agonism 50, 145, 164, 235
agriculture 78, 200
Alliata, E. 213
ambiguity 223
anachronism 8, 29, 35, 104, 172
Anchor, R. 218, 238
anxiety 185
Augustine 106–7, 172
Aune, D. 235, 238
authority: defined 127; types of
    127–31, 134, 137, 141, 183,
    193, 211, 225

Babbitt, C. 212
Bagnall, R. 212
balanced reciprocity 76, 146, 172,
    173
Baldwin, B. 217, 241
Barr, D. 30, 174
Barr, J. 30, 211
Barraclough, G. 219–20, 238
Basso, K. 65
belief 7, 58, 74–5, 79–80, 89,
    108, 149, 179, 184, 194, 204,
    237
Bell, D. 78, 95
benefaction 143–8
benefactor 175
Benveniste, E. 230, 238

Berman, R. 26, 30, 35, 64
Betz, O. 133, 141
biblical studies: methods in 27,
    28, 97, 217, 235, 237
biography 5, 38, 39, 99
birth: meaning of 51, 53, 62, 79,
    97–9, 102, 105, 110, 113, 118,
    128, 187–8, 202
Black-Michaud, J. 160, 174
Black, D. 204
blasphemy 11
blood: as honor symbol 51, 64,
    93, 104, 174
Bloome, D. 15, 22, 27, 30
Bodson, L. 229, 238
Boehm, C. 43, 64, 160, 174
Bohannan, P. 127, 141
Boissevain, J. 150, 153, 158–9,
    161, 164–5, 167, 171, 174,
    203, 211, 225, 238
Bonaventure 67–8, 95
Borg, M. 210–11
Boskoff, A. 213
boundaries: social 77, 114, 210
Bourdieu, P. 180, 189, 191–2,
    194–95, 205, 211
Boykin, A. 212
Brannigan, A. 227, 238
broker 148–58, 163, 166, 171,
    174; Jesus as broker 149–58.
brokerage 151–7, 167–74,
    225
Broshi, M. 211
Brown, L. 64

247